SPECIAL OPERATIONS EXECUTIVE

This book presents a unique assessment of the Special Operations Executive (SOE) and brings together leading authors to examine the organization from a range of key angles.

Since the contributors presented their papers at the Imperial War Museum in 1998 at the first international conference on SOE, the release of many records has allowed them to develop the first authoritative analyses of the organization's activities. Their original papers are here amended and enriched to take account of the full range of SOE documents that have been released to the National Archives. The fascinating stories they tell range from overviews of work in a single country to particular operations and the impact of key personalities.

SOE was a remarkably innovative organization; it played a significant part in the Allied victory while its theories of clandestine warfare and specialized equipment had a major impact upon the post-war world. As SOE proved that war need not be fought only by conventional methods and by soldiers in uniform, the organization laid much of the groundwork for the development of irregular warfare that characterized the second half of the twentieth century and that is still here, more potent than ever, at the beginning of the twenty-first.

This book will be of great interest to students of Second World War history, intelligence studies and special operations, as well as general readers with an interest in SOE and the Second World War.

Mark Seaman spent more than 20 years as an historian with the Imperial War Museum. During that time he contributed to several exhibitions concerning SOE and was the organizer of the 1998 international conference upon which this book is based. He has written extensively on special operations and intelligence during the Second World War and acted as an historical consultant to television programmes and feature films. He is now an historian with the Cabinet Office.

STUDIES IN INTELLIGENCE SERIES
General Editors: Richard J. Aldrich and Christopher Andrew
ISSN: 1368–9916

BRITISH MILITARY INTELLIGENCE IN THE PALESTINE
CAMPAIGN 1914–1918
Yigal Sheffy

BRITISH MILITARY INTELLIGENCE IN THE CRIMEAN
WAR, 1854–1856
Stephen M. Harris

SIGNALS INTELLIGENCE IN WORLD WAR II
Edited by David Alvarez

KNOWING YOUR FRIENDS
Intelligence inside alliances and coalitions from 1914 to the Cold War
Edited by Martin S. Alexander

ETERNAL VIGILANCE: 50 YEARS OF THE CIA
Edited by Rhodri Jeffreys-Jones and Christopher Andrew

NOTHING SACRED
Nazi espionage against the Vatican, 1939–1945
David Alvarez and Revd. Robert A. Graham

INTELLIGENCE INVESTIGATIONS
How ultra changed history
Ralph Bennett

INTELLIGENCE ANALYSIS AND ASSESSMENT
Edited by David Charters, A. Stuart Farson and Glenn P. Hastedt

TET 1968: UNDERSTANDING THE SURPRISE
Ronnie E. Ford

INTELLIGENCE AND IMPERIAL DEFENCE
British intelligence and the defence of the Indian Empire 1904–1924
Richard J. Popplewell

ESPIONAGE: PAST, PRESENT, FUTURE?
Edited by Wesley K. Wark

THE AUSTRALIAN SECURITY INTELLIGENCE ORGANIZATION
An unofficial history
Frank Cain

POLICING POLITICS
Security intelligence and the Liberal Democratic state
Peter Gill

FROM INFORMATION TO INTRIGUE
Studies in secret service based on the Swedish experience 1939–45
C. G. McKay

DIEPPE REVISITED
A documentary investigation
John Campbell

MORE INSTRUCTIONS FROM THE CENTRE
Andrew Gordievsky

CONTROLLING INTELLIGENCE
Edited by Glenn P. Hastedt

SPY FICTION, SPY FILMS AND REAL INTELLIGENCE
Edited by Wesley K. Wark

SECURITY AND INTELLIGENCE IN A CHANGING WORLD
New perspectives for the 1990s
Edited by A. Stuart Farson, David Stafford and Wesley K. Wark

A DON AT WAR
Sir David Hunt K.C.M.G., O.B.E. (reprint)

INTELLIGENCE AND MILITARY OPERATIONS
Edited by Michael I. Handel

LEADERS AND INTELLIGENCE
Edited by Michael I. Handel

WAR, STRATEGY AND INTELLIGENCE
Michael I. Handel

STRATEGIC AND OPERATIONAL DECEPTION IN THE
SECOND WORLD WAR
Edited by Michael I. Handel

CODEBREAKER IN THE FAR EAST
Alan Stripp

INTELLIGENCE FOR PEACE
Edited by Hesi Carmel

INTELLIGENCE SERVICES IN THE INFORMATION AGE
Michael Herman

ESPIONAGE AND THE ROOTS OF THE COLD WAR
The conspiratorial heritage
David McKnight

SWEDISH SIGNAL INTELLIGENCE 1900–1945
C. G. McKay and Bengt Beckman

THE NORWEGIAN INTELLIGENCE SERVICE 1945–1970
Olav Riste

SPECIAL OPERATIONS EXECUTIVE

A new instrument of war

Edited by Mark Seaman

Routledge
Taylor & Francis Group

LONDON AND NEW YORK

First published 2006
by Routledge
2 Park Square, Milton Park, Abingdon, Oxon OX14 4RN

Simultaneously published in the USA and Canada
by Routledge
270 Madison Ave, New York, NY 10016

Routledge is an imprint of the Taylor & Francis Group

© 2006 Imperial War Museum

Typeset in Times by
HWA Text and Data Management, Tunbridge Wells
Printed and bound in Great Britain by
The Cromwell Press, Trowbridge, Wiltshire

British Library Cataloguing in Publication Data
A catalogue record for this book is available from the British Library

Library of Congress Cataloging in Publication Data
A catalog record for this book has been requested

ISBN10: 0–415–38455–9 (pbk)
ISBN10: 0–415–38398–6 (hbk)

ISBN13: 9–78–0–415–38398–1 (hbk)
ISBN13: 9–78–0–415–38455–1 (pbk)

CONTENTS

CONTENTS

PLATES

CONTRIBUTORS

Roderick Bailey is a researcher at the Imperial War Museum and the author of a history of SOE's Albanian Section.

Terry Charman is an historian with the Research and Information Department of the Imperial War Museum and the author of *The German Home Front 1939–1945* (1989).

Richard Clogg is the official historian of SOE in Greece and the author of *Greece 1940–1949. Occupation, Resistance, Civil War: A Documentary History* (2002).

Paul Cornish is a senior curator with the Exhibits and Firearms Department of the Imperial War Museum and co-editor of the series *The Materiality of Conflict* (2005).

M. R. D. Foot was Professor of Modern History at Manchester University and is the author of the official histories *SOE in France* (1966) and *SOE in the Low Countries* (2001).

Ivar Kraglund is Deputy Director of the Norges Hjemmefrontmuseum, Oslo, and the co-author of *Hjemmefront* (1987).

Knud V. Jespersen is Professor of History at the University of Southern Denmark, Danish Historiographer Royal and the author of *No Small Achievement: Special Operations Executive and the Danish Resistance 1940–1945* (2002).

Eunan O'Halpin is Professor of Contemporary Irish History, Trinity College, Dublin, and the author of *Defending Ireland: The Irish State and Its Enemies since 1922* (1999).

Maurice Pearton is the author of *British Policy towards Romania, 1939–1941* (1986).

Sir Brooks Richards was the head of SOE's AMF Section and the author of the official history *Secret Flotillas: Clandestine Sea Lines to France and French North Africa 1940–1944* (1996).

Mark Seaman is an historian with the Cabinet Office and the author of *Bravest of the Brave* (1997).

Bradley F. Smith was Professor of History at Cabrillo College, California, and is the author of *Sharing Secrets with Stalin: How the Allies Traded Intelligence, 1941–1945* (1996).

David Stafford is the author of *Churchill and Secret Service* (1997) and an official historian of SOE in Italy.

Duncan Stuart was SOE Adviser at the Foreign and Commonwealth Office 1996–2002.

Mark Wheeler was an official historian of SOE in Yugoslavia and is the author of *Britain and the war for Yugoslavia, 1940–1943* (1980).

Christopher Woods was an SOE British Liaison Officer in Italy 1944–45 and SOE Adviser (1983–88). He is an official historian of SOE in Italy.

Neville Wylie is a senior lecturer at Nottingham University and the author of *Britain, Switzerland and the Second World War* (2001).

ABBREVIATIONS

AAI	Allied Armies in Italy
Abwehr	German Military Intelligence
ACF	African Coastal Flotilla
AFHQ	Allied Force/s Headquarters (Mediterranean)
AMG	Allied Military Government
AMF	SOE Section operating into France from North Africa
ANCC	Anglo-Norwegian Collaboration Committee
Baker Street	London location of many of SOE's offices, euphemism for SOE London
BBC	British Broadcasting Corporation
Broadway	Location of SIS headquarters in London, short hand for SIS
BSC	British Security Coordination
BCRA	Bureau Centrale de Renseignements et d'Action
Beaulieu	Centre of SOE training 'finishing schools'
BK	Balli Kombëtar
BLO	British Liaison Officer
BP	Bletchley Park, wartime location of Government Code and Cypher School (GC&CS)
C	Chief of SIS, short hand for SIS
C2	US plastic explosive
CD	SOE Executive Head
CIGS	Chief of the Imperial General Staff
COS	Chiefs of Staff
CS	Foreign Office propaganda department
D	Section IX SIS, head of Section IX SIS
DCO	Directorate of Combined Operations
DDMI	Deputy Director Military Intelligence
DDOD(I)	Deputy Director, Operations Division (Irregular)
DF	SOE clandestine escape Section
D/F	Direction Finding (wireless)
DMI	Director of Military Intelligence
DMO	Director of Military Operations

DNI	Director of Naval Intelligence
DR/LC	SOE symbol for officer responsible for the Low Countries
DSO	Distinguished Service Order
DZ	Dropping Zone
EAM	ethnikon apeleftherotikon metopon (National Liberation Front)
E-boat	German motor torpedo boat
EH	Electra House
ELAS	ethnikos laikos apeleftherotikos stratos (Greek People's Liberation Army)
EU/P	SOE Polish/French Section
F	SOE French (Independent) Section
FANY	First Aid Nursing Yeomanry
Felucca	Mediterranean fishing vessel
FFI	Forces Françaises de l'Intérieur
Fingerprinting	Identification of the Morse signature of a wireless operator
FO	Foreign Office
FO	Forsvarets Overkommando (Norwegian High Command)
Force 133	SOE Greece, Romania and Bulgaria
Force 136	SOE South-East Asia
Force 266	See Force 399
Force 399	SOE Yugoslavia, Albania and Hungary (later Czechoslovakia and Poland)
GC&CS	Government Code and Cypher School
Gestapo	Geheime Staatspolizei
GHQ	General Headquarters
GSO1	General Staff Officer
GS(R)	General Staff (Research)
HMS	His Majesty's Ship
Home Station	SOE base wireless station
IS9	MI9
ISLD	Inter-Services Liaison Department (SIS)
ISRB	Inter-Services Research Bureau – SOE cover name
ISSB	Inter-Service Security Board
J	Italian Section/head
Jedburgh	Special Force units
JIC	Joint Intelligence Committee
LFP	Levant Fishery Patrol
LNC	Levicija Nacional Clirimtarë
Lysander	Light aircraft used for RAF clandestine operations
MAAF	Mediterranean Allied Air Forces
Maquis	French guerrilla units
MC	Military Cross
MD1	Ministry of Defence Research and Development Department

MEHQ	Middle East Headquarters
MEW	Ministry of Economic Warfare
MGB	Motor Gun Boat
MI5	Security Service
MI6	Secret Intelligence Service
MI9	Military Intelligence Section 9 – Escape and Evasion
MI(R)	Military Intelligence (Research)
MI(R)c	Military Intelligence (Research) technical development
Milice	Vichy counter resistance units
Milorg	Norwegian secret army
ML	Motor Launch
MO1(SP)	Cover name for SOE
MP	Member of Parliament
MTB	Motor Torpedo Boat
MT S/m	Mobile Transport Submarine
MFV	Motor Fishing Vessel
N	SOE Netherlands Section/head
NCO	Non-commissioned officer
NID	Naval Intelligence Department/Division
NKVD	Narodnyi Kommissariat Vnutrennikh Del (People's Commissariat for Internal Affairs) Soviet security/intelligence organization
No 1 SF	SOE Italy
NORIC	Norwegian Independent Company
1 SF	No. 1 Special Force
OG	Operational Group (OSS)
OGPU	Obyedinennoye Gosudarstvennoye Politicheskoye Upravleniye (Unified State Political Directorate) Soviet Security and Intelligence Service
One-time-pad	Cypher system
Orpo	Ordnungspolitzei
OSS	Office of Strategic Services
OVRA	Organizzazione de vigilanza e repressione dell'antifascismo
PE	Plastic Explosive
PF	Personal File
PIAT	Projectile Infantry Anti-Tank
POW	Prisoner of War
PPA	Popski's Private Army
PRO	Public Record Office
PWE	Political Warfare Executive
RAF	Royal Air Force
RE	Royal Engineer(s)
RF	SOE Gaullist/Free French Section
RN	Royal Navy

RNVR	Royal Naval Volunteer Reserve
RSAF	Royal Small Arms Factory
S	SOE Scandinavia Section/head
SAS	Special Air Service
SBS	Special Boat Section/Squadron
SD	Sicherheitsdienst
SD	Special Duty
Section D	See D
Section IX	See D
SF	Special Force(s)
SFHQ	Special Force Headquarters
Sicherheitsdienst	Nazi Party Intelligence Service
SIM	Servizio Informazione Militare
Sipo	Sicherheitspolizei
SIS	Secret Intelligence Service
SO	Special Operations
SO	SOE symbol for Minister of Economic Warfare
SO1	Special Operations 1 (propaganda)
SO2	Special Operations 2 (operational)
SO3	Special Operations 3 (planning)
SOE	Special Operations Executive
SOM	Special Operations Mediterranean
SOSO(A)	Staff Officer Special Operations (Adriatic)
SS	Schutzstaffel
SSRF	Small Scale Raiding Force
STS	Special Training School
T	SOE Belgian Section/head
TAC HQ	Tactical Headquarters
Ultra	Intelligence derived from Enigma encrypted German signal traffic
USNR	United States Naval Reserve
VCIGS	Vice-Chief Imperial General Staff
W/T	Wireless telegraphy/telegrapher
X	SOE German Section/head

INTRODUCTION

Mark Seaman

The Special Operations Executive (SOE) was only in existence for less than six years from July 1940 to January 1946 but its frequently controversial contribution to the Allied victory in the Second World War has continued to exact enduring attention amongst British and foreign scholars and the general public. A great deal has been written about the organization ranging from official histories and memoirs to biographies and journalistic investigations into its major *causes célèbres*. However, the quality of many of these works has, to say the least, been highly inconsistent. Much of the reason for these shortcomings has been the fact that, even though arguably the least secret of the United Kingdom's Second World War secret services, a great deal of SOE's history remained classified for decades after its demise. As a secret service, SOE's files stayed closed long after other mainstream official papers from the Second World War had been released to the Public Record Office (now The National Archives).

The shackles of secrecy, embodied in the terms of the Official Secrets Act that most SOE personnel had been obliged to sign, at first restricted its members from offering candid accounts of their wartime deeds. They were discouraged from writing or even talking about their activities while those who chose to describe their experiences in SOE adopted either a bland or a semi-fictional approach. A few other veterans with knowledge of scandals and cover-ups fell prey to the depredations of sensational journalism that did much to ensure that the controversy surrounding SOE persisted. However, by the end of the century and some 60 years after SOE's demise, the veil of secrecy had in large part been lifted. The writing of memoirs no longer caused the same palpitations in Whitehall as it formerly had done. Meanwhile, a substantial number of veterans (with official sanction) agreed to record personal testimonies of their wartime activities in interviews with the Imperial War Museum's Sound Archive or as contributors to a growing list of documentaries produced by the broadcast media.

Soon after SOE's disbandment, an SOE Adviser was appointed by the Foreign and Commonwealth Office to act as the official spokesperson on matters relating to SOE. The Adviser, Lieutenant-Colonel E. G. Boxshall, certainly provided guidance to veterans and prospective writers about SOE but his work was character-ized by a marked reluctance to release too much information that soon translated into an active policy of discouraging research. Fortunately, subsequent Advisers elected to pursue a more enlightened and cooperative attitude. Informed briefings and detailed correspondence based upon consultation of the closed SOE archive were provided for a wide range of enquirers. As a result of these sea changes, the serious study of the subject moved on apace. Meanwhile, the Waldegrave Initiative, promoting the release of hitherto classified government documents, resulted in a decision by Whitehall to begin the systematic release into the Public Record Office of those SOE files that had survived the frequent culling of the remaining archive. Duncan Stuart, the last SOE Adviser and the author of Chapter 17 of this volume '"Of historical interest only": the origins and vicissitudes of the SOE archive', has provided the first, fully-informed exposition of the history of SOE's documentation from the organization's wind down in the last months of the war to the papers' eventual arrival in the public domain. The release of the major files, beginning in 1993 with the Far East papers and concluding in 2003 with the Personal Files, elevated the study of the subject to an entirely new level. At last, the files (with, thankfully, relatively few redactions) were there for all to see. What had formerly been the exclusive purview of official historians was now open to a growing band of research students and to the media who found much to sate their voracious appetite for the juiciest of controversial issues.

In 1998 the Imperial War Museum, in association with the Gerry Holdsworth Special Forces Charitable Trust, recognized that the study of SOE's history had reached a watershed. The availability of many of SOE's papers and the willingness of several of SOE's luminaries to engage in an appraisal of the organization's history offered a unique opportunity. The decision was therefore taken to mark this landmark with the first ever major academic conference solely devoted to SOE. It was, however, decided that the event would be one to which veterans, students and the general public would have full access. The intention was to create a forum in which historians would offer interpretations gleaned from their work with the newly released files while SOE veterans would enrich the proceedings with their own recollections of events.

The conference took place at the Imperial War Museum on 27–29 October 1998. The programme, lecturers and veterans were selected to reflect as many of the major themes of SOE as possible. A comprehensive coverage of every aspect of SOE's existence was unattainable but a broad spectrum was achieved. Regrettably, it has not been possible to translate several features of the conference to the pages of this volume. A series of platform discussions followed the delivery of papers by historians or, on a few occasions, a panel of experts and veterans substituted for a paper. It was decided that France, one of SOE's most important geographical areas and the one that has attracted the most public attention, would be best treated solely as a discussion forum. A similar decision was made over how to address the question of SOE's legacy. The need to compress a very full, three-day conference into this single volume has resulted in the excision of the transcriptions of the panel discussions from these pages. However, the Imperial War Museum plans to post these important texts on its website. The other, most prominent redaction concerns the conference's examination of SOE's role in the war against Japan. A most successful session included two papers by historians and a lively panel discussion involving historians, SOE officers who operated behind Japanese lines and members of the RAF's special duties squadrons who provided the vital supply and transportation links. The 'forgotten army' tag used to describe the relative obscurity of Slim's 14th Army might with some justification be invoked regarding the efforts of SOE's Force 136 in South-East Asia. However, even if this part of the conference is not represented in this volume, readers should be reassured that the conference organizers did not fail to mark the importance of SOE's role in this theatre of operations.

If this volume concerns itself almost exclusively with SOE's endeavours in Europe, it is not inappropriate that the first chapter should seek to describe SOE's origins. These lay in the troubled international situation of the late 1930s and the realization by the Secret Intelligence Service (SIS) and the War Office that preparations needed to be made for an unorthodox, irregular type of warfare to meet the demands of an impending European war. To this end, in 1938, SIS created its Section D and the War Office formed a similar body, GS(R) – soon to be renamed MI(R). The men and women who served in Section D and MI(R) were innovators: conceiving, developing and implementing new methods and doctrines. Although they drew upon lessons learned from history and recent world events, they created something unique and, by the standards of the time, very modern. While France and Germany made a huge investment in military leviathans such as the fortificat-ions of the Maginot and Siegfried Lines, Britain, in contrast, was seeking to explore the radical potential of clandestine warfare. Much had been put in place by the outbreak of war in September 1939 and Section D and MI(R) then continued to mature throughout the following months. But the disasters that befell the Allies in the spring and summer of 1940 led to a demand for the reconfiguration of these original bodies. The amorphous relationship between Section D and MI(R) was finally concluded by the creation of a new organization to meet the fresh demands of war and, in July 1940, SOE was formed. Chapter 1 '"A new instrument of war": the origins of the Special Operations Executive' describes the genesis of British theories on clandestine warfare and the circumstances surrounding the creation of SOE.

Although tailored to meet the pressing demands of a war changed out of all recognition by the German victories of 1940, from the outset SOE's aims and objectives did not sit comfortably with the armed forces and the established machinery of government in Whitehall. In spite of having Churchill as its sponsor and being blessed by a gifted and intelligent leadership, SOE encountered frequent opposition from its peers. David Stafford's chapter 'Churchill and SOE' examines the pivotal role played by the Prime Minister in the organization's history. The other politician most associated with the birth of SOE was Dr. Hugh Dalton, the Minister of Economic Warfare. Terry Charman's paper, 'Hugh Dalton, Poland and SOE, 1940–42', throws light on Dalton's personality, his desire to secure control of SOE and his particular preoccupation with the fate of Poland. If SOE might be described as the progeny of Churchill and Dalton, sadly, the relationship between the co-creators was far from good. This antipathy sounded an early note of rancour in Whitehall that was to characterize much of SOE's existence. The new organization's ambition, novelty and unconventionality engendered friction with other government departments that manifested itself on both an institutional and personal level. The extent of this rivalry has been the subject of much debate, including accusations of internecine conflict that transcended mere peevishness and frostiness to reach a state of acute antagonism. The fratricidal relations went beyond professional competitiveness and have even encouraged allegations that SOE operations were deliberately sabotaged by its fellow secret services. However, one feature to emerge from the debate amongst the historians at the conference was a questioning of the true extent of this rivalry. It was posited that perhaps the historian's penchant for savouring the more pithy and acerbic comments to be found on contemporary documents had led to a failure to appreciate less spiteful minuting that recorded more harmonious expressions of approbation and gratitude. While there undoubtedly were rivalries and these were perhaps the overriding characteristic, historians and veterans recognized that there was also evidence of cooperation. SOE had its enemies but also its friends. Some influential figures such as Portal and Harris were not slow to express their scepticism of the efficacy of SOE's stratagems but there were others who became loyal allies. Several senior Allied commanders such as Eisenhower, Alexander and Slim were to express their gratitude for SOE's contribution to the campaigns in North-West Europe, the Mediterranean and South-East Asia.

One of SOE's greatest achievements was the development of a complex but highly efficient support system to facilitate its activities. Without this asset, SOE would have been consigned to theory and intent rather than possessing the ability to realize its objectives. Air support, maritime links and the development of specialist equipment were each discussed in the proceedings. Brooks Richards in his chapter 'SOE and sea communications' drew upon extensive knowledge of the archives from his position as an official historian but this was supplemented by his personal experience as an officer engaged in SOE's naval operations in the English Channel and Mediterranean. A paper on the role of the RAF in support of SOE was presented at the conference but is not featured in this volume. 'Weapons and equipment of the Special Operations Executive' by Paul Cornish was written from his unique perspective as a curator of the Imperial War Museum's firearms collection and as someone with ready access to its extensive holdings of SOE equipment. Although the relevant SOE files at that time had not yet been released to the Public Record Office (or had not survived), the conference benefited immensely from the contribution of SOE veterans who provided insights not only of their first-hand experience of the equipment but also the rigorous training programmes provided for agents.

But the examination of SOE's origins and an analysis of the support elements of SOE did not long delay the examination of what SOE did. It was not practicable for the conference programme to encompass a detailed exposition of the history of SOE's activities in every country but contributions describing a variety of case studies offered rich and diverse perspectives. Some of the authors chose an overview and others focused upon a salient feature. Ivar Kraglund 'SOE and Milorg: "Thieves on the same market" ') and Knud Jespersen 'SOE and Denmark' examined SOE's contribution to Norwegian and Danish resistance from national perspectives. They were also, of course, able to furnish important insights into Scandinavian documents and published sources otherwise inaccessible to most British scholars. Romania had been identified as an early strategic and economic target for Section D and Maurice Pearton in 'SOE in Romania' chronicled British attempts to realize its ambitions in this vital but volatile region. Four official historians gave the conference the benefit of their profound knowledge of the SOE archive. Michael Foot, Christopher Woods, Mark Wheeler and Richard Clogg each adopted a very different but highly illuminating approach. Foot achieved the near impossible in 'SOE in the Low Countries', giving a succinct outline not merely of SOE in the Netherlands but also its activities in Belgium and Luxembourg. Woods also offered an overview in his 'SOE in Italy', describing the phases of operational activity that constitutes the framework for his forthcoming history. Wheeler sensibly eschewed the minefield of the Tito–Mihailović controversy and elected to investigate the theme 'Resistance from abroad: Anglo–Soviet efforts to coordinate Yugoslav resistance, 1941–42'. Lastly, Clogg decided on a vignette, ' "Negotiations of a complicated character": Don Stott's "Adventures" in Athens, October–November 1943' that highlighted the impact of the individual in SOE's history and the often difficult interface between the officer in the field and his superiors hundreds of miles away at headquarters. It was important that young historians should be represented at the conference and Roderick Bailey's 'SOE in Albania: The "conspiracy theory" reassessed', an examination of covert communist influences on SOE endeavours in Albania, revealed an impressive familiarity with both public and private sources.

SOE was much concerned with the neutral states and the three papers on this subject offer a set of intriguing contrasts. Neville Wylie in 'SOE and the neutrals' examines the diplomatic and practical difficulties of carrying out activities in the neutral states of Western Europe. Bradley Smith in 'SOE in Afghanistan' has concentrated on a far-flung region of the war and related the complex story of the agent, Bhagat Ram, an all too rare example of successful collaboration between SOE and its sister agencies. Finally, Eunan O'Halpin's ' "Hitler's Irish hideout": a case study of SOE's black propaganda battles' showcases the sometimes comic endeavours of SOE's representatives in Ireland, Britain's closest neutral.

There was widespread regret at the conference that it had proved impossible to furnish papers on the German, Italian and Japanese responses to SOE. This absence of a perspective from 'the other side of the hill' – a view of SOE as seen by its Axis adversaries – was one of the few disappointments of the event. The missed opportunity to discover the quality and whereabouts of relevant documents on this facet of SOE's history was particularly unfortunate.

Many historians of SOE have examined the organization's demise, interpreting its end as the final triumph of its adversaries made manifest by an ignominious dissolution. Although there was not a paper presented on this subject, not least because this was a topic where the documents had not been released, a concluding panel discussion left no doubt that SOE's legacy was far more substantial than many historians had previously represented. A selection of SOE veterans and distinguished members of the post-war armed forces reported that SOE's legacy was most evident in the continuity of special operations doctrines, techniques and even equipment.

The papers in this volume indicate the high quality of scholarship now devoted to the study of SOE. The conference at the Imperial War Museum provided a marvellous forum for the development of the study of SOE's history and it is to be hoped that this book will help progress that programme and at last give SOE the kind of history that the organization and its veterans deserve.

1

'A NEW INSTRUMENT OF WAR'

The origins of the Special Operations Executive

Mark Seaman

An examination of the origins of the Special Operations Executive (SOE) has, understandably, been a feature of most published sources on the organization. Official historians have charted the course of Whitehall meetings and exchanges of memoranda while the memoirs of participants have helped provide a lively picture of events and personalities.[1] But in most of these accounts, the events of the last year of peace and the first year of war have only one conclusion: SOE. This chapter will not seek to describe the various clandestine operations that preceded the formation of SOE but will endeavour to chronicle the friendships and rivalries of this period and suggest that the path to Baker Street was far from immutable. Furthermore, it is hoped that a detailed examination of the origins of SOE will offer a helpful insight into the beginning of that organization's subsequent, troubled relations with Whitehall, the armed forces and the Secret Intelligence Service (SIS).

The First World War had witnessed only a limited utilization of irregular warfare. The prominence of T. E. Lawrence's exploits in Arabia perhaps bestowed a disproportionate level of attention that was reflected in some areas of post-war military thinking:

> He [Lawrence] is seen to be more than a guerrilla genius – rather does he appear a strategist of genius who had the vision to anticipate the guerrilla trend of civilized warfare that arises from the growing dependence of nations on industrial resources.[2]

This is not to say that the British Army had not acquired a broad experience of this type of warfare during the Allied intervention in Russia and, in particular, during the 'Troubles' in Ireland. However, British units had largely been on the 'receiving end' of such tactics and this experience of irregular warfare had resulted in a preoccupation with developing appropriate defensive responses. In contrast to the army, the nascent British secret service had engaged in 'offensive' activities during the conflict such as those recorded by George Hill, who operated in Russia at the end of the war:

> Under my direction for months the men in my organisation had been systematically harrying the Germans on Russian territory. This was done by engineering uprisings; by destruction of stores; by the wrecking of the railway lines over which their trains passed; in fact, by using violence wherever possible.[3]

In spite of accounts such as Hill's that reported the efficacy of clandestine warfare, post-war British defence planning perceived little need of it. However, by the mid-1930s the new threat posed by Nazi Germany resulted in a change of mind. Germany's nomination as the 'ultimate potential enemy' by the Defence Requirements Committee in its report of 28 February 1934 marked the recognition of a new and potent threat.[4] While the Secret Intelligence Service sought to provide adequate intelligence on Germany and its rearmament, in the summer of 1935 it also began to examine the need to confront this potential enemy by clandestine means.

SIS staff officers reported to Admiral Sir Hugh Sinclair, the Chief of the Secret Service ('C'), suggesting a wide variety of sabotage options against 'Germany, our most likely enemy'. However, it was clear that there was no existing framework to develop such activity and it was reported 'Probably the reason that sabotage has never been organised is that it is nobody's particular job.'[5]

But even within the secret, inner sancta of Whitehall, the concept of planning for sabotage, let alone carrying it out against countries with whom Britain was not at war, caused some misgivings. Consequently, SIS sought to cloak its intentions for offensive action by examining defensive considerations. It was therefore proposed that SIS planning for offensive sabotage operations be seen to evolve out of a review of Britain's own susceptibility to a similar form of external attack. A sub-committee of the Committee of Imperial Defence was established in the summer of 1935 to look into this with SIS's own agenda 'that the only effective reply to this form of attack is retaliation' firmly in place.[6]

In the absence of an opportunity to study SIS documents for this period, it would appear that something of a hiatus descended over the scheme until in January 1938 the question of sabotage was revived. Both Section VI (Industrial) and Section III (Naval) of SIS endorsed a recommendation that the potential of sabotage operations be readdressed and it was proposed that a Royal Engineer officer be recruited to prepare a detailed assessment.

The man chosen was Major Laurence Grand, a 39-year-old sapper who had been commissioned in 1917 and had subsequently served in France, Russia, India, Iraq, Kurdistan and the United Kingdom.[7] In 1934 he had been appointed Deputy Assistant Director of Mechanization in the War Office and it was at the conclusion of this posting (when he was looking forward to a summer's cricket at Chatham and a new appointment in Egypt) that he was approached for secondment to SIS.

He accepted on condition that this would not adversely affect his next army posting. Shortly afterwards he had a meeting with Colonel Stewart Menzies, the head of SIS's Military Section, and was then taken to meet 'C' himself, whom he later recalled resembled an 'American gangster'. Grand started work on 1 April 1938 in a sparsely furnished office in the basement of SIS headquarters in Broadway Buildings. His next-door neighbour was another new arrival who had been brought in to work on clandestine communications.[8] Neither of the newcomers was aware of what lay ahead and, as Grand later reflected:

> We were both very vague as to what we had to do – in fact we soon realised that we had come to fill a complete vacuum. There were no real secret communications and there was no organization for anything except the collection of information. We were starting from scratch with a vengeance.[9]

If Grand at first felt ill-equipped for secret service, he soon adapted and, in the opinion of several of his contemporaries, even came to be the very embodiment of the stereotypical spymaster, 'He was tall and thin, with a heavy black moustache. He never wore uniform, always had a long cigarette holder in his mouth, and was never without a red carnation in his buttonhole.'[10] Kim Philby, who began his British secret service career by working for Grand, commented upon the imaginative and ambitious nature of the latter's thinking, 'his mind was certainly not clipped. It ranged free and handsome over the whole field of his awesome responsibilities, never shrinking from an idea, however big or wild'.[11] Even Gladwyn Jebb of the Foreign Office and Ministry of Economic Warfare, who was to be closely associated with Grand's subsequent downfall and who criticized him as 'rather theatrical and James-Bondish', was nevertheless willing to concede that 'he was an able man who inspired loyalty'.[12]

Grand did not stay in his subterranean existence for long and moved to the 6th floor of a neighbouring office block at No. 2 Caxton Street. As the work and the size of his staff increased, more offices were taken over linked, in the best traditions of spy thrillers, by confusing passageways (including one into the St. Ermin's Hotel) and an especially constructed internal staircase to another floor in the building. He set about his task with what was to become a characteristic hallmark of enthusiasm:

> his imagination flaring ahead of our schemes, each one of which seemed to him a war-stopper. If, as so often happened, one of his schemes or ours came to nothing, he showed no disappointment, called for more and never let his enthusiasm descend to the level of a cautious 'Wait and see'.[13]

On 31 May 1938 he submitted his 'Preliminary survey of possibilities of sabotage' that identified likely areas and methods of sabotage. The response from within SIS was mixed with comments 'that it was ambitious, it merely scratched the surface, that it went too far and too fast, that it was too wide or that too much of it was of doubtful practicality'.[14] Whatever the reservations, Grand pressed on, identifying the need to draw up a list of potential sabotage targets, develop special devices and clandestine communications and locate likely saboteur recruits. In a supplement to his report he predicted that setting up the organization would demand an expenditure of £20,000. This does not seem to have totally dismayed his superiors and he was appointed head of a new department of SIS, Section IX or, as it was more popularly known, Section D, with Grand taking the symbol 'D' for himself.

Typically, Grand was keen to develop foreign links and in the summer and autumn of 1938 he visited Czechoslovakia to engage in meetings with members of the Czechoslovak General Staff and to survey the Skoda Armaments works with a view towards preparing it for sabotage in the event of further German aggression. He also set about recruiting an engineer to work on the development of scrambling telephone conversation and commissioned research into innovative sabotage devices. Grand was also desirous of exploiting propaganda potential. He made plans for aggressive propaganda against Germany using neutral countries as the notional point of origin in order to mask the material's connection with Britain. He was similarly interested in the potential of 'black' wireless broadcasting and funded the Joint Broadcasting Committee out of his own secret vote.[15] This was an area already under consideration elsewhere in Whitehall and during the Munich Crisis Sir Campbell Stuart had been asked to head a small branch of the Foreign Office to examine its potential. Based at Electra House, the department was subsequently named EH or, after its chief, CS and was to constitute yet one further complication in the numerous permutations of Whitehall's clandestine activities.

Meanwhile, at the War Office, another Royal Engineer was pursuing a parallel, if less secret, course to Grand's. Major J. C. F. Holland's career was already impressive. During the First World War he had been transferred to the Royal Flying Corps and was awarded the Distinguished Flying Cross. His service also included a period in Ireland during the 'Troubles'. In the spring of 1938 he was appointed to the War Office's GS(R) Section, a department deemed not secret enough to remain in obscurity, for its creation was announced in *Hansard* on 9 March 1938:

> When so much instruction is to be gained from present events the absence
> of any branch exclusively concerned with purely military research is
> noticeable, and a small section to study the practice and lessons of actual
> warfare will be established.

Furthermore, the Deputy Chief of the Imperial General Staff minuted 'I have introduced a research section directly under me. This section must be small, almost anonymous, go where they like, talk to whom they like, but be kept from files, correspondence and telephone calls.' Holland was, in large measure, left to his own devices and in January 1939 presented his preliminary report. His superiors were sufficiently impressed to authorize the secondment of two further officers.

The first was a fellow sapper, Major M. R. Jefferis, the second, Major C. McV. Gubbins, was a gunner with a wide range of experience to rival Holland's.

It was clear that such similar enterprises undertaken separately by SIS and the War Office ran the risk of duplication of endeavour and, therefore, waste. On 20 March 1939 Grand submitted his 'Scheme D' report to Sinclair. It strongly emphasized the lessons to be learnt from the Irish Republican Army's methods during the 'Troubles' along with similar conclusions drawn from experiences in Russia and policing the Empire. A wide range of activity was discussed including the elimination of Gestapo agents in Romania, the supply of guerrilla bands in Poland and the fostering of a national revolt in Italian Libya. He requested the appointment of Holland as GSO1 for the project and estimated that it would need 25 other officers and a war chest of £500,000. A copy of the report was sent to Major-General F. G. Beaumont-Nesbitt, the Deputy Director of Military Intelligence (DDMI), and two days later, a briefing was given to the Chief of the Imperial General Staff, Viscount Gort. The next day (23 March) another meeting was held at the Foreign Office at which the Foreign Secretary, Lord Halifax, his Permanent Under-Secretary, Sir Alexander Cadogan, Gort, Menzies and Grand were present. Halifax expressed concern at the funding of a sabotage organization and, not unnaturally, sought reassurance that His Majesty's Government would be suitably distanced from the plan. Grand was able to put his mind at rest and Halifax concluded the meeting by agreeing 'in principle with the scheme, which he now intended to forget'. But before his amnesia set in, Halifax agreed to discuss the matter with the Prime Minister and the Chancellor. In the words of SOE's most eminent historian, 'By this decision SOE was begotten; but the child was long in the womb.'[16] Such a diagnosis is understandable but does not fully reflect the ebb and flow of the next 18 months when it often looked as if no such organization as SOE would ever emerge.

Section D and GS(R) were now so closely entwined that the latter moved into the former's offices in Caxton Street, Westminster, close to SIS's headquarters in Broadway. Furthermore, GS(R)'s expansion was funded from SIS's secret vote. But far from inhibiting Holland's fertile mind, the new arrangement gave him scope for expansion. There is something of a conflict of opinion regarding the relationship between Grand and Holland. A close associate of Holland stated 'he and Grand got on well together' while others have suggested that their radically different outlooks and temperaments engendered hostility.[17] However, the two men seemed, at the very least, to have achieved a *modus vivendi* and, when Hitler invaded Czechoslovakia in March 1939, Grand's contingency plans and Holland's thoughtful development of the theory and practice of guerrilla warfare seemed set to be a useful addition to Britain's arsenal during the drift towards war.

On 3 April 1939, Holland submitted a report in which he asserted his intention 'To study guerrilla methods and produce a guerrilla "F[ield] S[ervice] R[egulations]" '. Moreover, he advocated the stepping up of links with the general staffs of countries under threat of German expansionism and proposed the enlistment into the project of British military attachés in these countries. In order to achieve this, Gubbins undertook a tour of the Baltic countries and Poland in May and visited the Balkans in July. It was also decided to begin to 'talent spot' likely candidates from within the armed forces, especially officers with languages and experience of foreign countries. One such recruit was Peter Wilkinson, an officer of the Royal Fusiliers who had been in Prague at the time of the German invasion. He was invited to lunch by Gubbins:

> He said that it now seemed highly probable that, if war broke out, large areas of eastern Europe would be overrun by the Germans and that, in that event, there would be scope for guerrilla activity behind the German lines. He went on to say that he was a member of the secret branch of the War Office which was making preparations for this eventuality and that he was selecting serving officers and civilians for training in guerrilla warfare for possible employment of this sort.[18]

Wilkinson's admission that 'any job which involved cold luncheons washed down with Chevalier Montrachet and finishing up with fraises de bois merited careful consideration' lends an offhand motivation to one of the most distinguished careers in special operations during the Second World War but it also conveys something of the leisurely and closed evolution of the programme. Wilkinson went on to attend one of the training courses held at Caxton Hall around the corner from Gubbins's office. He was less than impressed by the lectures, feeling that 'we might have been more profitably employed spending a weekend re-reading T. E. Lawrence's *Seven Pillars of Wisdom*'.

Perhaps Wilkinson may have been a little more positive had he had the chance to read GS(R)'s 'Investigation of the possibility of Guerrilla Activities' prepared for the DCIGS. There was much worth reading including a most perspicacious report by Gubbins on the potential of irregular warfare in Poland:

> The importance to Poland of preparations for guerrilla warfare is much heightened by the veritable withdrawals her armies will be compelled to carry out in the early stages of a war in face of the more numerous and powerfully equipped forces of the Reich. Until such time as the pressure of her Western allies can become effective, it must be accepted that considerable portions of her territory will fall into German hands.

With the international situation rapidly deteriorating, there was still time for another redefinition and change of title before war broke out. On 27 June 1939 GS(R) was placed under the control of the DDMI and was re-christened MI1(R).[19] Its charter was conveniently brief and clearly expressed: 'The planning of para-military activities, under the direction of the DDMI. Liaison with MO branches as regards co-ordination with War Plans. Preparatory action in peace in conjunction with other organisations.' This new type of warfare had become sufficiently part of the fabric of Britain's war plans for an MI(R) component, led by Gubbins, to form part of the British Military Mission to Poland. Its brief was to seek to implement some of the schemes that he had laid out in his paper some three months earlier.

At last all the planning and the targeting of Germany seemed vindicated with the outbreak of war. In a memorandum dated the day Britain declared war, MI(R) specified its role and the state of the relationship with Section D

> Clearly there must be the very closest liaison between MI(R) and Section D. They will equally be studying possibilities and preparing for action where it is more appropriately in their sphere. Research must therefore be carried on together. As to the resultant action, broadly it is for Section D when action must be sub-terranean, i.e., in countries which are in effective occupation, and it is for us, when the action is a matter of military missions, whether regular or irregular. It should be remembered that the Arab Revolt was fostered and directed by what was really a military mission.

However, further administrative changes soon appeared to accentuate the differences between the two bodies. MI(R) was reclaimed by the War Office and moved out of Section D's premises. 'With the declaration of war Colonel Holland took action. Within days we were swept through the streets into a room on the third floor of the War Office ... Our branch lost the 'D' and became once more MI(R).'[20]

Section D was also on the move, evacuating to its war headquarters at the Frythe, a residential hotel near Welwyn in Hertfordshire. The conditions there have been described as 'adequate, if somewhat crowded' and apart from meetings in London, the Section conducted most of its business from there, only returning to the capital in March the following year. Two other establishments were also acquired shortly after the outbreak of war with the propaganda section taking over the Old Rectory, Hertingfordbury in mid-September and the special devices section under Lieutenant-Commander A. J. G. Langley moving to Aston House in October.

It is difficult to be precise about the relations between Section D and MI(R) at this time. The split between the two bodies is not entirely borne out by the recollections of Peter Wilkinson who recalled that in the opening eight months of the war 'as much of my time was spent at the headquarters of Section D in Caxton Street as in MI(R). I was given a desk in their Balkan section and allotted the secret symbol DH/M.'[21]

It is similarly problematic to assign the precise origins of the numerous innovations in irregular warfare made during this period. Most studies of the subject, supported by the recollections of participants, ascribe Holland (with his MI(R) team) as the 'visionary', devising the Commandos (Independent Companies), deception planning (Inter-Services Security Board) and even advocating the use of helicopters. However, Grand, perhaps claiming the credit for MI(R) work over which he saw himself as the controller, wrote that he had come up with the idea of 'stay behind' parties (Auxiliary Units) and an escape and evasion section (MI9). Both these concepts have also been attributed to MI(R). In spite of what must by now have grown into an impressive file of inter-departmental memoranda, the demarcation line between the two bodies remained blurred. It was laid down that MI(R) was more avowable, and that its officers would not undertake the type of subversive activity in neutral countries and the manipulation of diplomatic rules that Section D contemplated. But in contradiction of this, early in 1940 Wilkinson was sent to the Balkans to investigate problems on courier lines centred on Belgrade, Budapest and Bucharest. Travelling on a courier's passport he was the custodian of a dozen bags of diplomatic mail for the various legations he was to visit but amongst his personal luggage he carried .45 revolvers and time fuses destined for Polish and Czechoslovak patriots. His trip reflected the difficulties attendant upon such 'illegal' activities causing problems to conventional diplomatic procedures compounded when he reached Bucharest by the Section D Polish contact who pointed out the revolvers 'were too heavy and bulky and, moreover, fired rimmed ammunition which was unobtainable in Poland. He said that he proposed to drop them in the Danube at the first opportunity.'[22]

It is open to question how long the Section D/MI(R) collaboration/duplication would have continued had not the 'Phoney War' ended so dramatically in the spring of 1940. The German onslaught caught Section D and MI(R) almost as much by surprise as it had their masters in Broadway and the War Office. The MI(R) party attached to the British Military Mission to Poland had arrived on the scene too late to develop the schemes that they had been nurturing for so long. An earlier effort made by an MI(R) party sent to Finland in December 1939 had also been frustrated by the course of events. Last minute missions despatched to Norway following the German invasion were also unable to make a significant contribution to the campaign. Section D did not fare any better. The denial to Germany of Swedish war material had been a long-term and important element of Section D's planning but, as the Germans fought to establish their bridgeheads in Norway, Grand's chief agent in Stockholm was arrested. When the Germans attacked in the west, Britain's clandestine preparation once again disappointed. Perhaps too much attention had been paid to the Balkans, but then few had imagined the scale of the Allies' collapse. A few brave and a few foolhardy operations took place as the Low Countries and France were overrun. Section D officers were instrumental in spiriting away a consignment of industrial diamonds from Amsterdam and, it has been claimed, a substantial amount of gold bullion from Bordeaux. They were less successful in their attempts to rescue Madame de Gaulle and the Section suffered what is cited as its only fatality when Captain Norman Hope was amongst the casualties of an RAAF Walrus sent to Brittany to investigate her whereabouts. MI(R)'s endeavours were, in keeping with their military associations, more concerned with scorched earth actions such as the burning of oil stocks and installations at Gonfreville.

It was now, as Section D and MI(R) personnel were either evacuating or concluding their business on the continent, that Beaumont-Nesbitt perceived that the time was ripe for a reorganization and on 5 June 1940 submitted to the VCIGS papers prepared by MI(R) proposing a 'directorate of the War Office to plan and carry out all operations and activities of an irregular nature'. In spite of what, at the time, might be assumed to have been rather more pressing matters, the question was reviewed both by Anthony Eden, the Secretary of State for War, and Churchill. Signifying the new prevailing conditions, on 13 June a meeting was convened to 'discuss certain questions arising out of a possible collapse of France'. In spite of the calibre of those attending (Hankey, Menzies, Grand and Holland) and the critical timing of the meeting, nothing of any great moment regarding clandestine warfare was decided. The primary consideration appears to have been the need (and difficulty) of securing information from territory occupied by the enemy. But in spite of, or because of, the crisis, Whitehall decided to take a closer look at the two clandestine organizations. Cadogan made an appreciation of the state of affairs and on 28 June 1940 he circulated a paper on subversive activity. In an accompanying letter to Beaumont-Nesbitt he wrote, 'One of the tasks the Prime Minister has given me is to keep in touch on his behalf with secret offensive action against the enemy, i.e. sabotage, underground propaganda, the organisation of civil resistance, etc.'

Cadogan's report began with the assertion that 'The direction of sabotage in enemy and neutral countries, and subversive activities in enemy and enemy-controlled countries, seems to call for review.' He did not stop at review but actually proposed:

9. They [sabotage and subversion] should be concentrated under one control. They should probably be divorced from SIS, which is more concerned with intelligence, and has enough to do in that sphere, and placed under military authority as an operation of war.
10. If this is accepted, it might seem wise to amalgamate 'D' organisation with MI(R), the whole thus coming under control of the DMI. If possible, the staff should be housed in the War Office.
11. If that were accepted, the DMI would take over the whole 'D' organisation, and be responsible for (1) sabotage, (2) subversive propaganda, and (3) to some extent, propaganda in all countries.

The concentration of these activities under military control seemed neater than the present arrangement but even Cadogan was obliged to concede that the DMI as chief executive would still need to be responsible to the War Office, Foreign Office and Ministry of Information for his operations. This split responsibility did not mean that there would be any change in the financing of the activities and Cadogan concluded:

15. The funds required would have to come from the SIS vote and could be paid through the Director of the SIS, who might be able, from his experiences to give advice as to their application

This did not sit well with Hugh Dalton, the Minister of Economic Warfare, who, as a man possessed of strong personal ambitions regarding the control of subversive warfare, confided in his diary, 'It [Cadogan's paper] proposes to give too much to DMI. I concert counter-measures and invoke the aid of Atlee [Deputy Prime Minister]. I think it should be under him, with me doing a good deal of it.'[23] Dalton clearly did more than make an approach to Atlee and Cadogan testily recorded in his own diary 'Dalton ringing up hourly to get a large finger in the Sabotage pie'.[24]

On 1 July the matter was discussed at a meeting at the Foreign Office with most of the interested parties in attendance.[25] In spite of general assent to Cadogan's proposals, Dalton emerged as the most vociferous opponent of the former's recommendations. He espoused the belief that that there was a clear distinction between 'war from without' and 'war from within'. He held that 'the latter was more likely to be better conducted by civilians than by soldiers' and that sabotage and subversion were decidedly 'war from within'. The meeting concluded with Halifax asking those present to consider the names of suitable nominees as controller of the new organization. Having pushed the claims of the Ministry of Economic Warfare at the meeting, the next day Dalton followed this with a letter to Halifax proposing Atlee, supported by himself:

> So far as I myself am concerned, I shall be very glad to render such help as I can towards an intensive 'war from within' the enemy territories and indeed, I feel that, in this connection, Economic Warfare has perhaps been defined somewhat too narrowly in the past.

He also wrote a more lengthy paper on the type of organization he envisaged, not surprisingly emphasizing the paramountcy of civilian participation in it.[26] In large part this urgency resulted from Dalton's concern that his claims stood a good chance of being overlooked and in his diary entry for 10 July he recorded, 'there has been a great to-do today. Beaumont-Nesbitt has been pulling every string. Chiefs of Staff Committee – always apt to be girlish – and Ismay threatening to resign.' More importantly, he feared that his less than convivial relationship with Churchill might see the Prime Minister favour one of the other candidates such as Lord Hankey, Admiral Keyes, Admiral Cork and Orrery, Lord Cranborne, Lord Lloyd and Lord Swinton. Dalton's diaries vividly convey his unease coupled with his feverish agitation that Atlee and other Labour members of the Cabinet strenuously represent his best interests.

He seems therefore to have been singularly unaware of the actual strength of his position for, on 8 July 1940, Halifax wrote a note to Churchill clarifying their agreement the previous evening that Dalton would take over Section D and MI(R). On 11 July another meeting was held between Halifax, Chamberlain, Atlee and Cadogan. Had he but known, Dalton surely would have derived some reassurance from the fact that he now also had the support of Cadogan although less pleasant would have been the news that the latter confided in his diary about the affair,

'P.M. (put up to it by Morton) is against Dalton taking over and wants to lump the whole thing under Swinton'.[27] But at last, on 16 July Dalton was summoned to Downing Street and Churchill informed him of his decision to entrust resistance and irregular warfare to him.[28] That same day, Halifax wrote to Dalton formally asking him to take over 'these various activities and I therefore request that you will take over the "D" organisation which has hitherto been under my control'. Rather sheepishly a second note stated 'I should have included at the same time a request that you would do the same in regard to the EH organisation, insofar as it has hitherto been under my control'.

It might have seemed as if Dalton had won the day but there were still a few skirmishes to fight and a lot of tidying up of Section D and MI(R)'s affairs. The fate of MI(R) was to a great extent placed in the hands of a newcomer, Brigadier H. Wyndham, who was given the position of Deputy Director MI(R). He was described by Holland as 'a nice man doing an unpleasant job in an extremely nice way',[29] a reflection perhaps of the latter's recognition that the writing was on the wall for his creation. The recommendations were not long in being reached and on 2 October 1940 MI(R) was dismantled. In the light of the development of many of the schemes conceived by MI(R), its break up was a natural move and allowed these concepts to achieve real fruition in important bodies such as MI9 and the Inter-Services Security Board. Meanwhile, on 19 August Dalton had written a paper entitled 'The Fourth Arm' that encapsulated his ambitions for the new body under his control and he stressed his desire to acquire some of MI(R)'s most talented personnel for his own undertaking, 'If certain of the particularly gifted junior officers of M.I.R. could gravitate towards the latter, nobody would be more pleased than I.' Perhaps his greatest capture was Gubbins who, in spite of Dalton's prediction of civilian predominance in the organization, became the driving force behind SOE.

Almost inevitably, Section D's demise was to be rather more troubled. Grand's ego almost rivalled that of Dalton and even the most optimistic of souls would have doubted their ability to work together. On 28 August 1940 Dalton brought in Sir Frank Nelson, a former Conservative MP with connections with SIS to take over the 'sabotage' component of SOE, relegating Grand to a role as second-in-command. This did not sit well with the erstwhile head of Section D who clearly resented having his creation taken from him just as it seemed to be embarking on an even more challenging period. After all, Section D was by now a substantial entity, having grown to absorb a large proportion of SIS's resources and, it has been claimed, boasted more officers on its strength than the number serving in the Service's main body.[30] Regardless of Grand's proprietorial feelings, Nelson did not like what he found at Section D. He wrote to Jebb that there was 'no project anywhere near completion' and that the section needed a 'radical overhaul' and 'drastic reorganising on economic grounds alone'. Considering these fundamental criticisms, Nelson still expressed himself impressed by Grand but nevertheless recommended he be put 'outside the organisation'. In the absence of access to the files it is difficult to judge the full extent of Grand's machinations to be reinstated.

Certainly Dalton expressed in his diaries a recognition of the opposition to the decision and Sir Robert Bruce Lockhart on 17 August 1940 recorded in his diary that 'MI6 officers had preferred to resign rather than be under Dalton'.

Philby, who had some inside knowledge of these matters, wrote:

> Nelson's purge had been thorough-going. He had been gleefully assisted by some senior officers on the intelligence side of SIS, notably Claude Dansey and David Boyle, of whom more will be heard later. They were determined not only to 'get Grand', but to get all his henchmen as well.[31]

Philby was correct about Dansey's antagonism. As early as November 1938 Grand and Dansey had locked antlers over the former's request that the latter provide names of contacts in foreign industry with a view towards recruiting them for Section D activity. It will surprise no-one with any knowledge of Dansey's personality that he strenuously resisted this perceived attempt to poach his contacts. This was not to be the only clash and on 6 March 1940 Dansey had written to Menzies complaining that Section D was out of control, 'The question is, I think, whether Section IX is to conform and co-operate or to go on galloping about the world at his own gait.' Furthermore, Dansey harboured the gravest doubts about the worth of Grand's organization:

> Proof of results will probably always be lacking until after the end of the war, and then nobody wants to bother about it, least of all to trace back on the possible or probable results of propaganda or to check up on statements made by agents that such and such an explosion actually took place and was the work of the agents who claimed it as theirs.

Menzies, who had taken over as 'C' in November 1939 and who had been fully involved in Section D's development appears to have been rather less acerbi in his opinion of the organization. However, in a letter to Jebb on 4 September 1940 he confined himself to bemoaning the delay in notifying him of the decision to remove Section D from his control and pointed out his fears for the consequences of the new arrangements summarized as 'the grave disadvantages of running two sections of the Secret Service, with ultimately interlocking interest, under two masters'. He wrote that he welcomed a body that would guide sabotage and subversive activities and confirmed that he had no wish to retain responsibility for these types of operations, however he lamented the anticipated difficulty in future liaison with SOE agents who would need to make use of SIS 'machinery'.

By now, the die was cast for Section D's demise. As Dalton recorded in his diary on 18 September 1940 'Decided to dismiss King Bomba [Grand], who has been completely disloyal to his new chief [Nelson].'[32] He noted that the allegation had come from 'two officers in uniform, unwilling to put anything on paper' but who had made a statement to himself, Jebb and Vansittart. He eschewed a meeting with Grand, fearing that he would 'only falsify the interview, as happened before'. Instead he would send 'a brief and unargumentative letter'. The epistle was sent that very day and its severity merits its reproduction in full:

> I have given further thought to the arrangements concerning the D organisation and have reached the conclusion, with regret, that, under the re-organisation on which I have now decided, there will be no further opportunity for the use of your services. I must, therefore, ask you to take such leave as is due to you as from September 20th, and to consider yourself, as from that date, no longer a member of the D organisation. I am sending copies of this letter to Sir Alexander Cadogan, General Beaumont-Nesbitt, CD and C.

An anonymous member of the Ministry of Economic Warfare was moved the next day to append a heart felt minute, 'a pretty drastic letter of dismissal! I should have thought a word of thanks would not have come amiss'. Cadogan, making play of Dalton's nickname of 'Dr Dynamo' merely wrote the one word, 'Dynamic!'

Dalton's biographer claims a major campaign by Grand to restore himself to power in which he hoped to call upon the support of Eden and Desmond Morton and have the matter raised at Cabinet level. This politicking is perhaps the 'disloyalty' alleged by Dalton for in his diaries he also stated that Grand had written a letter to the War Cabinet and may have found allies with members of Churchill's inner circle such as Professor Lindemann and Brendan Bracken. But the threat from Grand proved to be of no great moment and Dalton wrote that he had heard that Churchill 'said that he "won't have a quarrel with Dalton over this".'[33] Furthermore, in Jebb, Dalton had acquired not only a 'Foreign Policy Adviser' but a seasoned Whitehall in-fighter who was able to watch Dalton's back in any Whitehall skirmishing. If Grand's letter of dismissal was offhand, there is something malevolent in Dalton's savouring of the former's defeat. Dalton dismisses 'a rather crawling and friendly letter'[34] from Grand and tells Jebb to find him a far off posting, preferring 'Hong Kong to Ireland'.[35] In the event, Grand went to neither place but his posting to the North West Frontier of India suggests the possibility of Ministry of Economic Warfare vengeance. But, once back in harness with the Royal Engineers, his career showed no ill effects of his digression into the secret world and he retired after the war as a major-general. His obituary in the Corps journal is suitably enigmatic but might also be an appropriate epitaph for the clandestine bodies from which SOE was created, 'It was a privilege to know him, none of us really understood him but we appreciated him.'

The unseemly removal of Grand and Holland's less acrimonious departure from the scene should not obscure the remarkable contribution made by Section D and MI(R) to SOE's eventual success. These organizations laid the foundations for SOE in doctrine, training, equipment and experience of clandestine warfare. If the balance sheet of Section D and MI(R)'s operational achievements is open to question, there can be no doubting that without their groundbreaking endeavours, SOE would have struggled to make its contribution the Allied victory in the Second World War.

Notes

1 All of the official histories of SOE have, to date, touched upon the organization's origins, M. R. D. Foot, *SOE in France*, London: HMSO, 1966; Charles Cruickshank, *SOE in the Far East*, Oxford: OUP, 1983; Charles Cruickshank, *SOE in Scandinavia*, Oxford: OUP, 1986 and M. R. D. Foot, *SOE in the Low Countries*, London: St Ermin's Press, 2001. David Stafford, *Britain and European Resistance 1940–1945, A Survey of the Special Operations Executive, with Documents*, London: Macmillan, 1980 offers some useful insights into the early days of the organization while Bickham Sweet-Escott, *Baker Street Irregular*, London: Methuen, 1965 gives an insider's view.

2 [B.H.] Liddell Hart, *T.E. Lawrence – In Arabia and After*, London: Jonathan Cape, 1935, p. 438.

3 George A. Hill, *Dreaded Hour*, London: Cassell, 1936, pp. 4–5.

4 Wesley K. Wark, *The Ultimate Enemy*, Oxford: Oxford University Press, 1986, p. 9.

5 Information supplied by SOE Adviser. Section D and MI(R) papers are now liberally sprinkled throughout the SOE papers at The National Archives, especially the Headquarters papers at HS 7.

6 Ibid.

7 Memoir by 'CEFT' in *The Royal Engineers Journal*, Vol. 90, No. 1, March 1976, pp. 68–9.

8 This was Richard Gambier-Parry who was destined to revolutionize SIS communications just in time for the pressing demands of world war. See Ellic Howe, *The Black Game*, London: Michael Joseph, 1982.

9 Information supplied by SOE Adviser.

10 Bickham Sweet-Escott, *Baker Street Irregular*, London: Methuen, 1965, p. 20.

11 Kim Philby, *My Silent War*, London: Panther Books, 1976, pp. 26–7.

12 Lord Gladwyn, *The Memoirs of Lord Gladwyn*, London: Weidenfeld and Nicolson, 1972, p. 101.

13 Joan Bright Astley, *The Inner Circle*, London: Hutchinson, p. 37.

14 Information from SOE Adviser.

15 See W. J. West, *Truth Betrayed*, London: Duckworth, 1987.

16 Foot, *SOE in France*, p. 3.

17 Bright Astley, *The Inner Circle*, p. 33. Peter Wilkinson and Joan Bright Astley, *Gubbins and SOE*, London: Leo Cooper, 1993, p. 35.

18 Peter Wilkinson, *Foreign Fields*, London: I B Tauris, 1997, p. 62.

19 More commonly, and for the purposes of this paper, known as MI(R).

20 Bright Astley, *The Inner Circle*, p. 40.

21 Wilkinson, *Foreign Fields*, p. 87.

22 Ibid., p. 89.

23 Ben Pimlott (ed.) *The Second World War Diary of Hugh Dalton 1940–1945*, London: Jonathan Cape, 1986 pp. 50–1.

24 David Dilks (ed.) *The Diaries of Sir Alexander Cadogan*, London: Cassell, 1971, p. 308.

25 Halifax, Lord Lloyd, Lord Hankey, Dalton, Cadogan, Beaumont-Nesbitt, Menzies, Desmond Morton and Gladwyn Jebb.

26 Foot, *SOE in France*, p. 8.

27 Dilks, *The Diaries of Sir Alexander Cadogan*, p. 313.

28 It is perhaps of interest to reflect that in spite of the oft-quoted invocation 'To set Europe ablaze', and his later interest in and even protection of SOE, Churchill's involvement in its

creation does not attract any mention in his memoirs nor barely a reference in his official biography.

29 Bright Astley, *The Inner Circle*, p. 51.
30 Christopher Andrew, *Secret Service*, London: Heinemann, 1985, p. 472.
31 Philby, *My Silent War*, p. 34.
32 Pimlott (ed.), *The Second World War Diary of Hugh Dalton*, p. 83.
33 Ibid., p. 84.
34 Ibid., p. 85.
35 Ibid., p. 85.

2

WEAPONS AND EQUIPMENT OF THE SPECIAL OPERATIONS EXECUTIVE

Paul Cornish

Few aspects of the history of the Special Operations Executive (SOE) have attracted so much attention, or spawned as many myths, as the arms and equipment used by that organization. In particular, the interest of publishers, programme makers and public alike has been seized by the plethora of specialized devices invented by SOE for use in clandestine warfare. I refer here to such exotica as silenced or concealed firearms and knives, concealed compasses, and elaborately camouflaged explosive devices. While these fascinating items were novel and unique, they were by no means the only equipment employed by SOE, nor indeed are they representative of the great bulk of it, which was of a more prosaic and practical nature. Due to the secret nature of SOE and the loss of many of its papers, sources of information on this subject are somewhat limited and fragmentary. Nevertheless, enough is available to provide an accurate picture of what was issued, how it was procured and how it was used to further SOE's mission of subversion and sabotage.[1]

I intend in this chapter to concentrate on the equipment used at the point of action; that is to say the weapons, explosives, and related sabotage devices. Naturally this leaves untouched important areas such as communication equipment (which would justify a study of its own), clothing, parachutes and a number of smaller gadgets. The importance of such equipment in facilitating the use of the weapons and explosives should not be forgotten. However, for reasons of conciseness and coherence, they will not be dealt with here. Conversely, discussion of the munitions themselves will necessarily be tempered by reference to the training and techniques which were essential to the employment of these weapons. I will also be taking into consideration their effectiveness compared to other means of sabotage and subversion.

Organization

Even before the outbreak of war, the minds of certain men within the intelligence services were being concentrated on the development of the weaponry of irregular warfare and sabotage. Two small departments were chiefly concerned in this: MI(R) of the War Office, specifically its MI(R)c sub-section; and Section D of the Secret Intelligence Service. Consequently, by the time the Special Operations Executive was established, in the summer of 1940, many of the personnel who were to conduct the development of its weapons were already at work, and production of some devices had actually commenced. SOE subsumed both MI(R) and Section D. However MI(R)c, under the leadership of Millis Jefferis, and with the powerful patronage of Churchill and Lord Cherwell, managed to maintain an independent existence. Originally based at Portland Place, it established a well-equipped research and design facility at 'The Firs', a house at Whitchurch in Buckinghamshire. Taking the title MD1, as the first department of the (newly created and somewhat notional) Ministry of Defence, it continued throughout the war to develop explosive devices and their ancillaries for both SOE and the armed forces.[2] SOE was by no means entirely reliant upon the inventiveness of the personnel of 'The Firs', for it possessed its own Directorate of Scientific Research. Initially SOE's weapons research and development took place at Station XII, based at Aston House, near Stevenage. In the summer of 1941, the new Director of Scientific Research, Professor D. M. Newitt, turned Station XII over to production only; moving its experimental element to Station IX. This establishment, which was to be responsible for a dazzling array of novel weapons and devices, was based at 'The Frythe', a small Welwyn Garden City hotel which had been requisitioned by Section D at the outbreak of war. Its location accounts for the prefix 'Wel' which was appended to many of Station IX's inventions: Welrod, Welbike, Welgun, etc. Station IX maintained a sub-section at Barnet, known as Section XV, which was responsible for developing the elaborately disguised explosives referred to above.

Less well known, but of inestimable value, was the work of the Arms Section. This was set up before the creation of SOE, and operated from Section D's Caxton Street headquarters. Its object was to procure and supply firearms, specifically non-standard issue pistols, for use by agents in the field. As the war progressed the Arms Section, as part of the SOE Supplies Directorate, took on responsibility for the procurement of standard issue weapons for use by resistance and partisan groups, although they were relieved of this task in 1943, by which time it had become too vast an undertaking for them to handle. Between October 1940 and July 1941 the Arms Section was based at 'The Frythe'. Due to pressure on accommodation (doubtless due to the arrival of the experimental team from Section XII), they then moved to nearby Bride Hall, known as Station VI. The importance of their work with regard to arming SOE and its secret armies will, I hope, become apparent at a later point in this chapter.

Sabotage

The sabotage of enemy equipment, installations and means of production, which was one of SOE's primary functions, necessitated the development of a host of specialized devices. However, perhaps the single most useful tool of sabotage, Plastic Explosive (PE), was already in production when SOE was formed. It had been developed in the late 1930s in the Royal Arsenal at Woolwich, and had swiftly attracted the attention of Section D. Its advantages were that it could be cut, shaped to cause maximum damage, and was stable enough to be stored and transported in safety. Sadly, for most of the war, PE was not in sufficient quantity and had to be supplemented by ammonal, gelignite, dynamite and, later, American-made C2.

For clandestine use it was obviously necessary, for the safety of the saboteur, to delay the detonation of explosive charges. MI(R)c were quick to provide a suitable means, in the form of the 'L' Delay (officially known as Switch No. 9).[3] This relied upon a lead element under spring tension which, at a predetermined time, would break, allowing a striker to fire the detonator to which the delay was attached. Station IX had already developed its own delay switch, generally known as the Time Pencil (Switch No. 10). This relied on the action of corrosive liquid upon a piece of wire retaining the striker. As with the 'L' Delay, Time Pencils were issued ready-timed to provide delays from a few minutes to many hours. It would appear that the Time Pencil was more commonly used than the 'L' Delay; over 12 million were produced. Extremely useful as these switches were, both types were affected by temperature. Users had to take high or low ambient temperatures into account, as they would either speed or retard detonation. It is also instructive to reflect upon the experience of Ben Cowburn and members of his 'Tinker' circuit during their exemplary sabotage of 12 railway engines at Troyes, on the night of 3/4 July 1943.[4] Time Pencils with a two-hour delay were used, but the first detonation occurred after only 30 minutes, with others following at 10 to 15-minute intervals.

The men at 'The Firs' produced some other useful switches such as the Pull Switch – used in conjunction with trip wires, the Pressure Switch and the Release Switch, which reacted to pressure being removed from it. The final refinement was the Universal Switch, which could be used in pull, pressure or release modes. Curiously, its inventor, Colonel Stuart Macrae, was later to bemoan this sophisticated device's lack of popularity in comparison with the simpler switches. While the Pull Switch and Release Switch were ideal for setting booby traps, the Pressure Switch was primarily intended for derailing trains. Placed beneath a rail, it was activated by a train passing over it. SOE employed another device for initiating the detonation of explosives in railways. This was clipped to the top of the rail and resembled a normal railway fog signal. Pressure from locomotive wheels detonated, via three percussion caps, a charge of black powder, which in turn fired a detonator which could be connected to a buried charge.

Further use was made of PE in pre-prepared explosive devices. Once again, MD1 led the way in developing them. First to appear was the Limpet, which used magnets to attach a PE charge to the hulls of ships. It was this weapon which was used by Special Operations Australia (SOA) personnel during the successful raid on Singapore harbour in September 1943, codenamed Operation 'Jaywick'. A smaller version of the Limpet was developed for use on dry land. Called the Clam, this neat device 5 $^5/_8$ inches by 2 $^1/_8$ inches) contained half a pound of PE and was designed for use with the 'L' Delay. Over 2 $^1/_2$ million were produced, being issued to regular forces as well as SOE. In addition to being easily portable, the Clam looked reasonably anonymous. The F Section agent Harry Rée reported a hair-raising incident when a Clam, falling from the pocket of a member of his 'Stockbroker' circuit, was handed back to him by a German! More exotic were the camouflaged devices developed by Station XV, notably those resembling dead rats or animal droppings. Such curiosities might easily be perceived as treading dangerously near that thin line which is said to divide genius from lunacy; however a fairer view might simply regard them as tokens of the relentlessly inventive spirit which permeated SOE's research establishments.

Plastic Explosive featured again in MD1's Gammon Grenade (No. 82 Grenade). This was rather more of an offensive weapon than a sabotage device, being essentially an impact fuse attached to a bag which could hold a kilogram of PE. When thrown it made a fearsome ambush weapon. An early and extemporized bomb, based on the same precepts, was issued to the assassins of the prominent Nazi Reinhard Heydrich.

Incendiary devices were also provided to SOE agents. MD1 offered a thermite filled 'Firepot', while Station IX devised a pocket incendiary complete with its own internal delay, working on the same principle as the Time Pencil. Station IX also developed an incendiary brick, which produced its own oxygen as it burnt, thus keeping the flames fuelled, even in a confined space. Perhaps the most ingenious of Station's IX's creations did not explode or burn at all, but worked in a more insidious way. This was abrasive grease, made with finely ground carborundum, which could play havoc when applied to vulnerable points such as vehicle axle-bearings. By use of this grease F Section of SOE scored one of its most notable successes. Prior to D-Day, members of the 'Pimento' circuit doctored the axles of tank transporting rail-cars which were earmarked to carry the tanks of the 2nd SS Panzer Division. The breakdown of these cars when called into action after the Allied landings, was the catalyst for a sequence of SOE-inspired resistance activity which delayed this powerful division's arrival at the front for a fortnight (contrary to what the film 'Saving Private Ryan' would have us believe!).

Having described this catalogue of interesting devices, it should not be forgotten that proper training was essential if they were to be used to good effect. Instruction in sabotage techniques was given to SOE agents notably by George Rheam at Station XVII in Hertfordshire. This included tuition in recognizing the most vulnerable parts of likely targets. The great advantage of sabotage work was that, unlike aerial bombing, significant damage could be done to the enemy's productivity and infrastructure without hazarding many lives and expending vast quantities of munitions. Careful selection of what to sabotage was the key. If a number of machines or vehicles were to be attacked, then the same part was destroyed on each; thereby preventing repair by cannibalization. The destruction of certain machines in factories could bring the whole works to a halt. In April 1944 work at the Dunlop factory at Montluçon was halted, due to a mere 2 lbs. of PE placed by F Section's Maurice Southgate. Likewise, a propeller plant at Figeac was brought to a standstill by the destruction of six crucial machine-tools by the 'Footman' circuit.

Instructional pamphlets were supplied with the various specialized sabotage devices. In addition, as early as 1939, Jefferis of MI(R)c had produced a pamphlet entitled 'How to Use High Explosives'. This might be considered a basic primer for would-be saboteurs. Hundreds of thousands of copies were distributed world-wide by SOE, in numerous translations. The widespread dissemination of such dangerous knowledge was certainly novel, and the implicit concept that everyone has the potential to be a saboteur (or indeed terrorist, if post-war developments are considered) could be said to be one of SOE's most influential and lasting legacies.

Agents' weapons

As I can testify from the enquiries and visitors which I regularly receive, the weapons issued to SOE agents are, for many, a source of unending fascination. Primarily, attention tends to be focused on the specialized firearms developed at Station IX. Some of these, although very interesting, did not see full-scale production; notably the Welpen .22 firing device and the innovative Welgun submachine-gun. More successful were the Welwyn laboratory's ventures into silenced firearms.

From the outset SOE experimented with silenced pistols, these being modifications of standard weapons. One of these was a silenced version of the American High Standard .22 pistol. So successful was this that a version was later ordered direct from High Standard for use by the United States' Office of Strategic Services (OSS). With a .22 calibre weapon, however, lethality was somewhat marginal unless the user was a skilled shot. Consequently, in 1943, Station IX went on to develop the Welrod. This was a repeating pistol (i.e. it was magazine-fed but the bolt required manual manipulation to reload and re-cock after each shot) with an integral silencer. Despite its primitive looks it was both quiet and accurate. It was produced in both 7.65mm and 9mm calibres; the former being more popular due to its smaller size. Precise information regarding its production remains classified to this day.

From late 1942 onwards, Station IX was also working on a silenced version of the Sten submachine-gun. They achieved this by adapting a silencer which had been put forward by some Polish designers, of whom there were several at work in wartime Britain. The Sten with Welsilencer went into operational use in June 1943. The silenced Sten was very much an offensive weapon, for use against guards and sentries, or for assassinations. It was not intended to be used for automatic fire except in emergencies, as this would speedily destroy the interior of the silencer.

At the risk of digression, this might be the place to make reference to the mythical powers which are often attributed to silenced firearms. This is necessary I feel, because the question of how silent a firearm is will naturally colour our perceptions of how it might have been used. In point of fact 'silenced' (more properly, 'suppressed') firearms are not very silent! Their report, as I can vouch from personal experience, is clearly audible over some distance. On the other hand, the noise is considerably less than that of an un-suppressed weapon. The reduction is typically in the region of 20–30 decibels. While this may appear marginal, it should be remembered that three decibels represent an order of magnitude of sound; consequently an un-suppressed weapon can be as much as ten times louder than a suppressed weapon firing the same cartridge. Therefore, while clearly audible in quiet conditions, the report of such weapons would have been difficult to identify as a gunshot when heard against the background noise of a town, seashore or railway yard. In silenced weapons of the type used by SOE, gasses released by firing were bled off into a system of baffles through holes bored in the barrel. This has the side-effect of reducing the muzzle velocity of supersonic ammunition to subsonic levels thereby avoiding the tell-tale crack made by a supersonic bullet in flight.

While silenced weapons and disguised firing devices have captured the public's imagination, agents who carried firearms were more usually equipped with unmodified self-loading pistols. From the early days of Section D and MI(R), it was realized that agents in the field might need to be equipped with pistols which could not readily be identified as being of British origin. The procurement of such weapons became the responsibility of the Arms Section. A paper written by a member of the Arms Section in 1945 bemoans the fact that 'We in this country, unlike most other European countries and America, are most un-gun-minded', consequently the necessary quantity of pistols could not simply be purchased in Britain. Apart from employing suitable captured weapons, the Arms Section tapped a surprising variety of other sources. From 1941 onwards American pistols, both new and second-hand, were purchased via the Ministry of Supply. In 1944 an unknown, but 'large', quantity of pistols was purchased from the Spanish firm of Gabilondo y Cia, makers of the Llama brand. At the same time a consignment of 8,000 .45 calibre Ballester-Molina pistols were acquired from Argentina. It is highly likely that this latter procurement involved the despatch of lend-lease steel from the USA to Argentina, as wartime shortages meant that such high grade metal was not locally available to fill export orders.

In an effort to exploit sources within the United Kingdom, three 'pistol drives' were mounted, in conjunction with Scotland Yard and the Home Office. Firearms owners were contacted by the police and encouraged to give up suitable pistols, either as a gift or in return for compensation. The first of these drives, in 1942, yielded 7,000 pistols; the second, a year later, produced 3,000. The last, in 1945, was specifically aimed at acquiring German commercial pistols – evidently in anticipation of their use within Germany itself. Throughout the war gunsmiths and military ordnance depots were scoured for suitable weapons, and even the Air Ministry was able to assist by passing on pistols from the estates of deceased airmen. The Arms Section laid claim to having 'sent to the field' over 100,000 pistols of non-standard types. Nevertheless, almost until the end of the war in Europe, there was a permanent shortage of such weapons and, to an extent, their ammunition.

Agents who decided to carry pistols (and there were many who did not) were generally provided with readily concealable pocket pistols. Most popular among these was the Colt Pocket Hammerless, available in either .32 (7.65mm) or .380 (9mm Short) calibres. Alternatively .25 (6.35mm) calibre pistols of the type commonly found on the Continent could be used. These were of course far less lethal, but were easier to hide and, if found, did not by themselves identify the carrier as a British agent. These types were primarily weapons of self-defence. One further item outwardly resembled a fountain pen, but was used to fire a .38 calibre tear-gas cartridge. Surviving examples bear a US patent number, and it would seem likely that they were acquired by the Arms Section via commercial channels in America. Wing Commander Yeo-Thomas of RF Section was carrying one, along with a .32 Colt, when he was arrested in Paris in March 1944.[5]

For more offensive purposes larger pistols could be issued. Peter Wilkinson of the Czechoslovak Section arranged for Colt .38 Super pistols to be issued to the assassins of Heydrich, specifically because of their killing power. Curiously the two agents did not choose to use them, either during the attack, or to defend themselves when later surrounded. Agents operating in the *maquis*, or with partisans in the Balkans, or with the hill tribes of Burma, would of course have been able to carry whichever firearms took their fancy, concealment not being a consideration. The Imperial War Museum is fortunate enough to have a silenced .22 High Standard (Model B) and a .32 Welrod that were owned by David Smiley of SOE's Albanian and Siamese Sections. We also have a collection of his photographs, which testify to the popularity of the Thompson submachine-gun among SOE operatives in Albania. More esoteric were the 9mm UD M42 Marlin submachine-guns issued to some SOE personnel in the Eastern Mediterranean theatre of operations. These were supplied from a small shipment of this rare firearm received from the USA.

Agents' weapons were not limited to firearms. Coshes, knuckledusters and a variety of knives were also made available to them. The most well known of these hand-to-hand combat weapons was the Commando knife designed by Captains Fairbairn and Sykes. These two former Shanghai policemen were responsible for training SOE personnel in close combat techniques. Their knife was designed purely for killing and, as shown in Fairbairn's manual *All-In Fighting*, could be used for stabbing, or to slash vital arteries. A heavier edged weapon was also developed. The Smatchet, as it was known, possessed a formidable, leaf-shaped blade, which could be used to deliver a variety of cuts, chops and stabs. At the other end of the scale, a number of small, concealable blades were produced. These included a variety of bodkin-like stabbing weapons and the 'thumb' or 'lapel' knife. The latter was a stubby, hilt-less knife, which could be easily hidden. It was provided with a small leather sheath, which could be sewn into an agent's clothing – typically behind the conveniently wide lapels of the era. As with the firearms discussed above, there are few reliable accounts of the use of these items in the field. One is tempted to echo the following comment, made by M. R. D. Foot on the thumb knife: 'Like so many of these ingenious, almost toylike, agents' tools, this was something for which a theoretical case could be made out; but was anyone ever vicious enough to use it?'[6] Agents had also to be aware that killing with such knives inevitably involved the spilling of large amounts of blood, and bloodstained clothing is never an easy thing to explain away.

Perhaps the most significant close combat tool in the SOE agent's armoury was the psychological superiority imbued by the training received from Captain Fairbairn. This, according to one agent 'gave us more and more self-confidence which gradually grew into a sense of physical power and superiority that few men ever acquire. By the time we finished our training, I would willingly enough tackled any man, whatever his strength, size or ability'.[7] Even if, at the moment of crisis, the actual methods inculcated by Fairbairn were forgotten, this psychological strength appears to have remained. Two prime examples of this are Harry Rée's fight to escape arrest and Frank Pickersgill's doomed attempt to escape the Gestapo while held in the Avenue Foch in Paris. In both cases these men had no hesitation in setting about armed Germans. Coincidentally, both found that the nearest weapon to hand was a bottle.

Arms supplies

As previously mentioned, until 1943 the Arms Section was responsible for supplying standard army-issue weapons to resistance forces operating in conjunction with SOE. This work was transferred elsewhere (presumably within the SOE Supplies Directorate) when the organization's worldwide commitments became too large for the Arms Section to handle. The statistics regarding arms supplied through these means, while somewhat fragmentary, are extremely impressive. It should be noted that this achievement was greatly assisted by the high priority enjoyed by SOE in the scheme of military procurement.

Pride of place among the weapons supplied must surely be awarded to the Sten submachine-gun (or Machine-Carbine, to employ the contemporary British term). This weapon, designed in response to an urgent need for automatic firepower which had not been envisaged before the fall of France, was the brainchild of the Royal Small Arms Factory (RSAF). The brutal simplicity of its fully developed form might be viewed as the apotheosis of wartime austerity. Despite this, it worked. It did receive a reputation in some quarters for unreliability, although this was due largely to variable standards of magazine manufacture. Furthermore, it required a certain care in handling. The failure of Josef Gabčik's Sten gun, as he took aim at Heydrich is well known; a similarly melancholy incident occurred on the Andaman Islands in March 1943, when an SOE agent was killed by the accidental discharge of his Sten. Notwithstanding these problems, which were hardly unique to the Sten, it was an ideal guerrilla weapon and was cheap enough to be distributed in vast quantities. Over one million were supplied by SOE during the course of the war. The majority of these were the Mark II model, which offered the useful facility of being easily broken down into three parts: barrel, body and butt.

In addition to Sten guns, SOE was responsible for providing large quantities of other weapons suitable for ambushes and assassinations. Prominent among these was the No. 36 Grenade, better known as the 'Mills Bomb'. Revolvers, either British-issue Webleys and Enfields, or their Colt or Smith & Wesson-made US counterparts, were also distributed in huge quantities. Although not as sophisticated as some of the more modern self-loading pistols, and not able to use captured enemy ammunition, these were robust and reliable weapons.

As the war progressed, SOE became increasingly involved with aiding open, armed resistance in several regions. Where this occurred, more substantial armaments needed to be supplied. Consequently, SOE distributed Lee-Enfield rifles (primarily the No. 4), Bren light machine-guns, Boyes anti-tank rifles, PIAT anti-tank rocket projectors and even 3-inch mortars. It is interesting to note the effect on morale that the arrival of such supplies had on their recipients. Both M. R. D. Foot and Pierre Lorain record the pleasure of French *résistants* at receiving rifles which, apparently, made them feel that they were being treated as true soldiers.[8]

Supply of these weapons was particularly important in South-East Asia, where the general absence of profitable sabotage targets meant that the main work of SOE was in the raising of irregular forces. Drawn largely from the hill tribes of Burma, these guerrillas were the beneficiaries of one of the Arms Section's more unusual procurements. In 1942, soon after the Japanese advance to the borders of India, a requirement was perceived for an easily handled and maintained weapon which could be issued to native forces in the region. The Arms Section's response was to redirect a shipment of 2,800 Greener Police Guns, which had been intended for the Egyptian police. This entailed making suitable arrangements with the Egyptian government, via the War Office. The Greener gun was a single shot, 12 bore shotgun which employed the falling-block principle (wherein a lever was manipulated to work the action). It boasted heavy wood and metal furniture, which was intended to aid the breaking down of doors or chastisement of rioters. Interestingly, it was designed to fire only a dedicated Greener cartridge. This had been intended to prevent its use if stolen from the police, but must have caused problems with ammunition supply once in service in Burma. In South-East Asia as a whole, SOE arms supplies comprised 25,000 small arms, 1,300 Bren guns, PIATs and mortars, 60,000 grenades and 30 tons of explosive.

Whether in Europe or Asia, delivery of these weapons was conducted primarily by air-drop, although boats and overland smuggling were used where applicable. Arms were parachute-dropped in various loads, either in packages, or packed in containers. The standard loads were identified by code letters, and varied according to the mission which they were intended to supply. For instance, the 'MD' load, suitable for saboteur groups comprised:

6 containers with:

509 lbs. of explosive
10 Sten guns with 3,000 rounds of ammunition
27 revolvers with 775 rounds of ammunition
20 Mills Bombs
8 Anti-tank grenades
15 Anti-tank detonators
13 Railway charges

Conversely, a load might be intended for use in an armed uprising; for example the 'OW' load, which comprised:

2 Bren guns with 2,520 rounds of ammunition
18 Sten guns with 9,400 rounds
27 revolvers with 575 rounds of ammunition
40 Mills Bombs
76 Anti-tank grenades
27 Anti-tank detonators
206 lbs. of explosive

The above are large loads, but numerous smaller quantities could be provided, either as packages, or as individual 'cells' within a container. Therefore, by using the relevant code letters, agents in the field could swiftly send requests by radio for whatever combination of arms and equipment they might require.

Conclusion

It is not the purpose of this chapter to make judgements on the overall success of SOE in employing its amazing armoury of weapons and devices, nor to assess the strategic impact of such success. However, in researching the facts presented herein, the scale of the achievement of those involved in the design and provision of this equipment became abundantly clear. When war came, clandestine operations and irregular warfare were very new and unfamiliar concepts. Nevertheless men and women were found who were able to rise to the challenge and provide the tools with which this unexpected form of warfare could be undertaken. Some criticism might perhaps be levelled at the somewhat Byzantine manner in which the various research and design departments were organized. This of course engendered some duplication of effort. The example of MI(R)c's 'L' Delay and Station IX's Time Pencils has already been cited. Additionally, while the Welwyn 'lab' was labouring to produce a silenced Sten, an equally effective version was being designed at the Royal Small Arms Factory at Enfield. Moreover, even such an obscure item as the Welpen firing device had an Enfield counterpart – the Enpen! It should of course be remembered that the independence of 'The Firs' and the RSAF were not the result of any policy decision by SOE. Furthermore, competition between design teams can be a positive thing in terms of the inventiveness it inspires. This is a policy which was traditionally and successfully employed in the Soviet Union's military-industrial complex.

I have previously alluded to the fact that much of what is written on SOE equipment tends to concentrate on the more exotic devices and the more unusual or gruesome weapons. This should not be allowed to cloud the truth of the matter, which is that, despite considerable difficulties, SOE was able to put into the hands of its agents the means of doing their job. Just as importantly, it was able to distribute vast amounts of weapons and equipment among those who wished to resist the Axis occupiers of their countries. This had an obvious harmful effect on the occupying forces, but perhaps its most important aspect was the morale effect on those who received the arms. The political climate of the post-war world would surely have been very different if SOE had not provided the opportunity for the occupied peoples to play an active role in their own liberation.

Notes

1 This chapter was written before the release of the files relating to the design and production of SOE's weapons and equipment. However, the SOE Adviser was able to furnish information from the then closed archive. Some works have recently been published on the subject drawing upon the now declassified files these include Mark Seaman (Introduction), *The Secret Agent's Handbook of Special Devices*, Richmond: Public Record Office, 2000 and Fredric Boyce and Douglas Everett, *SOE: The Scientific Secrets*, Stroud: Sutton Publishing, 2003.
2 Stuart Macrae, *Winston Churchill's Toyshop*, Warwick: Roundwood Press, 1971.
3 Ibid., pp. 148–55.
4 Ben Cowburn, *No Cloak No Dagger*, London: Jarrolds, 1960, pp. 165–79.
5 Mark Seaman, *Bravest of the Brave*, London: Michael O'Mara, 1997, p. 136.
6 M. R. D. Foot, *SOE*, London: BBC, 1984, p. 73.
7 Ibid., p. 64. The F Section agent was George Langelaan.
8 Ibid. and Pierre Lorain, *Secret Warfare*, London: Orbis, 1984.

3

SOE AND SEA
COMMUNICATIONS

Sir Brooks Richards

In the summer of 1940, when SOE was created, nobody knew whether, or on what scale, air transport would be available to it. It had inherited commitments to the Poles and the Czechoslovaks which could not be tackled at all without RAF help, but it looked as though sea communications were all it could hope for to penetrate France and Western Europe.[1] A paper put up to its chief executive in the first month of its existence argued that one of its main tasks would be to recruit and train a select body of saboteurs to operate exclusively against targets on, or near, the sea. In March 1941, however, there had been a parachute operation to Brittany as well as one to Poland. Brigadier Gubbins, its Director of Training and Operations, wrote that 'all the parties of men we are now training … may well have to be landed by sea as no other means exists'.[2]

Churchill's mandate to set Europe ablaze led SOE to see itself as a striking force whose blows would help to convince the world that we were fighting on, neither beaten nor cowed. They saw sea communications as necessary for seaborne raids as well as for transport of agents and stores. SIS regarded this as a threat to their interests. From June to September 1940 the coast from the Hook of Holland to Brest lay wide open but, as German controls and defences grew, they found that agents were more safely landed and picked up east of the Scheldt or west of Cherbourg. They were the senior service and their operations enjoyed priority. At a meeting on 16 December to co-ordinate the activities of SIS, SOE and the Commandos their representatives said they were 'against Raiding Parties as they might interfere with their organization for getting agents into enemy-occupied territory'.[3]

SOE was indeed forming and training a small-scale amphibious raiding force on Poole Harbour. Its commander, Gus March-Phillipps, a dashing, high-handed and romantic Gunner, had requisitioned a 65-ton Brixham trawler yacht and told Baker Street he wanted to try out such a vessel for the type of morale-raising raid they had in mind. When he put up a detailed plan worked out with SOE's Dutch Section, the Admiralty, no doubt after consultation with SIS, turned it very firmly down. He was eventually allowed to sail *Maid Honor* out to West Africa, where, with the help of civilian volunteers from Nigeria, he organized a cutting-out raid

33

on the neutral Spanish island of Fernando Po, taking prize an 8,500-ton Italian cargo liner and two German tugs.[4] By the time he got back to England in the spring of 1942 the Channel coast of France was heavily defended. SIS knew by then that what interested them for landing and picking up agents was Brittany. Gus was allowed to raid the Casquets lighthouse off Alderney, but he and all his raiding party were either killed or captured in September in an operation to Normandy. Pinpricks though they were, these raids infuriated Hitler, who issued his infamous secret order that the perpetrators, when caught, should be executed.

Infiltration of agents to France and the Low Countries was proving difficult. Commander F. A. Slocum, who had set up an Operations Section for SIS, used whatever fast craft he could find or borrow from the Navy. On 2 August 1940 he landed two Free French agents in Normandy but after that he had nothing but failures on the north coast for 13 months: 16 of those failures were for SOE. He was greatly handicapped by having to work with borrowed Coastal Forces craft: it was insecure, they might not be available when wanted, could not be fitted with special navigational equipment and their crews could not be trained for the job, including landing small boats on open beaches.

Although Slocum was the only person working in the Home Waters who could call upon naval resources for clandestine transport, both the Free French and Commander W. H. Dunderdale, one of his SIS colleagues, had used refugee fishing boats for missions to Brittany. SOE, feeling desperately let down, decided in October 1940 to do likewise. One of their officers named Gerry Holdsworth, who had worked as an agent in Scandinavia for Section D and knew about boats and the sea as a keen member of the Royal Cruising Club, was put into naval uniform, authorized to select twelve Royal Naval Patrol Service ratings and given £1,000 to fit out chosen French vessels from among the many lying in British ports. He set up a small base on the Helford River in Cornwall. The RAF gave him an exiguous 41-foot seaplane tender, RAF 360, in the hope that it might be the means of rescuing shot-down airmen. With Slocum's blessing and support, Holdsworth and the author of this chapter made contact in this little vessel on 11 September 1941 off the Ile-de-Batz with an even smaller local boat carrying intelligence mail for SIS. The operation took place in bright moonlight and involved very precise timing. We were lucky: five subsequent attempts to contact this valiant old man again, using much larger Motor Gun Boats (MGBs) borrowed by Slocum, failed. We, meanwhile, had done another successful operation with RAF 360, returning to his home waters at Aber-Benoît a young Free French agent named Joel Le Tac, a parachute-trained veteran of the Norway campaign, of SOE's first parachute operation to France and of their first industrial sabotage in France – an attack on the transformers supplying current to the U-boat base at Bordeaux. He was to establish a group to which other operations by sea could be organized from Helford. RAF 360 had a hard return passage home. She was far too small for winter operations across the widest and most exposed part of the Channel. Holdsworth said so, hoping it would strengthen his plea for two, 63-foot RAF Air-Sea Rescue Launches. Slocum ruled that '360' must not be used except perhaps in the summer, when we all knew she was far too slow to make the double crossing under cover of darkness. SOE must make use of whatever Coastal Forces craft were available to him. He had at the time a good Class-C Gunboat, which did three further operations to Le Tac and other work for SOE from Dartmouth. Holdsworth did not take too kindly to being relegated to the role of passenger on other people's boats.

Dunderdale's and the Free French operations to Brittany had come to an end with the capture of two of the boats they were using, but Slocum's interests had widened considerably. He sent the only real Q-Ship he employed, HMS *Fidelity*, to the Western Mediterranean twice in the course of 1941 looking for easier ways into and out of France. She landed agents for SOE on both occasions. He organized a series of successful rendezvous at sea between fishing boats working for a Quimper-based group of Dunderdale's agents and British submarines on watch for any attempt by the *Scharnhorst* and *Gneisenau* to put to sea from Brest. The first of these operations brought out a young Breton agent named Daniel Lomenech who had an impressive knowledge of the Breton fishing industry. Lomenech persuaded Slocum that it would be far better to use Breton motor trawlers fitted out in this country for such meetings, rather than submarines. Slocum was attracted by his arguments, fitted out a vessel of the type Lomenech recommended and issued a directive bringing SOE's Helford ships under his operational control. After various fits and starts and a couple of very unsuitable choices of skipper, Steven Mackenzie, a foundation member of Slocum's staff, and Lomenech inaugurated what became, for the next 16 months, an almost regular monthly service to Rémy's 'Confrèrie Nôtre Dame', the largest and most productive of de Gaulle's intelligence networks. The growing importance of this remarkable link to SIS doomed SOE's hopes of conducting fishing-boat operations to the Bay of Biscay. First they were told that their boats – chosen 18 months previously, in the light of what was then known – were of the wrong types. Then, when they had been replaced with Slocum's help and an operation to Quiberon laid on, Slocum placed an indefinite ban on all SOE operations to the west coast of France on the ground that the SIS link to Rémy had, with the German occupation of the French Mediterranean shore in November 1942, become so important that nothing could be allowed to imperil it.

Slocum had, indeed, been out to Gibraltar at Christmas 1941 seeking alternative sea routes into France. He found that the Poles, who had been running operations to Morocco to evacuate their own servicemen interned by Vichy, wanted to conduct similar operations to the then almost undefended south coast of France, but were unable to undertake such long voyages because they could not repair and re-engine the felucca they wished to use. Slocum helped them surmount this obstacle and sent a trawler to back them up. SOE contributed a second, 47-foot felucca with a Polish crew which had been on loan to them from Sikorsky. *Sea Wolf* and *Sea Dog* between them carried out 36 separate operations to France in the course of 11 round voyages from Gibraltar, landing or embarking 52 passengers for SOE, as well as three large groups of British evaders and escapees and sundry other agents, in addition to some 500 Poles. This valuable service was brought to a halt when the Germans occupied Southern France and fortified its coast in response to the Allied landings of November 1942 in French North Africa.

The planned link to Le Tac at Aber-Benoît had been aborted by a wave of arrests in Brittany and there was now nothing to keep Holdsworth at Helford. At the beginning of December 1942 he sailed with two of SOE's fishing vessels and most of the flotilla's operational personnel to serve SOE's sea transport needs in the Western Mediterranean. Thereafter, the Baker Street French Country Sections turned almost exclusively to the RAF for arms deliveries to the field – a more appropriate solution in the case of a country with a heavily defended coastline.

Conditions in Brittany improved from the agent's point of view as 1943 drew to a close: German controls grew easier to avoid and agents were trained for SOE's DF Section (which ran land lines) to work with the flotilla of MGBs which Slocum had at last been able to form at Dartmouth. A line of communications was established to St-Cast, close under one of the largest enemy coastwatching radar stations at Cap-Fréhel. This pinpoint had to be abandoned after MGB 502 was spotted and fired on just before Christmas, but the agents re-established themselves further west and a considerable number of agents including François Mitterrand, future President of the Republic, were carried to or from the field. This was important because SOE's Independent French Section had, at the time, to give up Lysander pick-ups because the loyalty of Déricourt, their organizer, had come under suspicion.

Christmas Day 1943 brought a moment of glory to SOE's Helford Base – little more than a training establishment since Holdsworth's departure to the Mediterranean a year earlier. MGB 318, from the Dartmouth Flotilla, had been engaged in a protracted and trying series of operations to Aber-Benoît, where an SIS network had collected no less than 27 candidates for evacuation, including a Flotilla Officer and five ratings left on shore in bad weather a month earlier. The SOE Base was called upon to provide a Coxwain and boat's crew to embark these people as they were the only team who had trained in the large, 24-foot 9-inch SN2 surfboat – far too big to be carried on the deck of a gunboat, but towed over and used on this occasion. Their efficient rescue of this large party is commemorated by an annual cross-Channel yacht race.

At the northernmost extremity of the United Kingdom, operations by sea to Norway developed quite differently.[4] Norway has, it is said, a coastline as long as that of the rest of Europe put together. The Germans never attempted to fortify or control it as they did by building the 'Atlantic Wall' in France and the Low Countries. Clandestine operations for both SIS and SOE flourished to and from it between 1940 and 1945 in conditions that could, apart from the ever-present risk of bad weather, hardly have been more favourable. But though the deeply indented Norwegian coast lent itself to work of this nature, the mountainous hinterland made travel inside the country difficult for agents and others who did not want their baggage or their papers closely examined, since the number of ferries and bridges across which a traveller must pass made control an easy matter.

At the outbreak of war Norway possessed some 50,000 fishing vessels and boats of sizes ranging from the big steel-built whale catchers that worked in the Arctic and Antarctic to the little 30-foot coastal smacks. The greater part of this huge fleet consisted of wooden-built drifters 60–70 feet long, with semi-diesels and speeds of 6 to 10 knots. A number of such boats arrived in the Shetlands early in 1940 and a constant stream of refugees continued to arrive there in the next 12 months. This meant that a large number of craft from all parts of the country were available in the United Kingdom for reversing the procedure and landing parties of agents and saboteurs at chosen points along the Norwegian coast. Owing to the difficulty of travel inland, agents had to be maintained by sea with supplies of all sorts and the number of operations called for was high, as each group needed to be serviced individually.

Realizing the potentialities, SIS sent an army officer named Mitchell to Lerwick in the summer of 1940. He collected 10 of the best refugee vessels and formed them into a flotilla for clandestine transport, manned by Norwegian volunteer crews recruited among the refugees themselves. The procedure for operations was simple enough: an agent who had been recruited and trained to return to Norway would want to be sent to his own district. He would know of a local pilot for the area, if indeed he was not himself qualified in that respect. The expedition would them be built up on a 'family' basis – the skipper being chosen by members of the crew – and would sail from the Shetlands in the most suitable ship. The ship would sail straight into the fjord nearest to the agent's home and remain there, openly, while he made enquiries on shore. If these were satisfactory, the agent returned to the Shetlands. This happy state of affairs continued during the winters of 1940–41 and 1941–42.

During the winter of 1940–41 SOE began to build up, in conjunction with its Norwegian counterpart, a series of sabotage and paramilitary resistance groups. In the spring of 1941 these operations became extensive. In some cases Norwegians were recruited in Norway itself and brought over to the Shetlands for training before being returned to their homes with arms and explosives. SIS viewed these heavily increased SOE activities as a considerable threat to the security of SIS-sponsored agents passing through Lerwick. Rightly or wrongly, they considered that the Norwegians had the highest alcohol consumption and the worst sense of security of all our Allies. Though steps were taken to deal with the worst offenders, SIS decided that an alternative base was necessary to avoid the inevitable mixing of agents delayed by weather in the Shetlands. Their choice fell on Peterhead, where a small flotilla of five boats was formed with Norwegian naval crews to cater exclusively for SIS ventures.

The SOE base at the remote Lunna Voe in the Shetlands was run by David Howarth, a Norwegian-speaking officer. In the second half of the 1941–42 winter there was a series of SOE-sponsored operations from this base. Four areas, ranging from south of Bergen to the island of Bremanger in the mouth of the Nordfjord, all had three, four or five visits and most of these operations were successful. In April 1942 the five Lunna ships completed ten operations and on two or three days in the middle of the month they were all at sea or in Norway at once. In the winter of 1941–42 this small flotilla made 40 trips, landing 43 agents and picking up nine. They landed 130 tons of arms and equipment and brought out 46 refugees. But this proved the high point for operations by fishing boat: as stocks of diesel oil fell, fishing off the Norwegian coast decreased. At the same time, enemy air patrols increased and the first casualties from this increased enemy vigilance became inevitable as soon as the nights became too short to allow slow-moving vessels to make an offing of 100 miles or more in the darkness. In April 1942 the *Aksel* was twice attacked but landed six men and 14 tons of material before returning safely. But that same month the *Mars*, veteran of nearly 20 voyages, and the *Froya* were sunk by enemy aircraft while making voyages for SIS. Operations were halted for the summer months: three other vessels had been lost that winter, two driven ashore by gales while in Norway and one sunk without trace in heavy weather with 35 passengers on board.

Against this background, the winter operating season was started in September 1942 with considerable misgivings. Owing to unsatisfactory refits in Scotland, only half the SOE boats were ready, but in October four big new boats – *Bergholm*, *Brattholm*, *Andholmen*, and *Sandøy* – Arctic whalers which had taken refuge in Iceland in 1940 – were handed over. From a new base at Scalloway, fishing boat operations for SOE were resumed. But the open boat *Sjø* was captured while on a reconnaissance trip on 22 August. At the end of October the now-legendary Leif Larsen set out in the *Arthur* with two submersible 'Chariots', hidden under a cargo of peat, and six RN personnel for a planned attack on the *Tirpitz*, then lying far up in Trondheim Fjord. This was frustrated after they had successfully passed through a German inspection. The 'Chariots' had been put into the water and were being towed, submerged. When only five miles short of the target, *Arthur* rounded a bend in the fjord and ran into a strong head wind and rough water: the tow-ropes snapped and the 'Chariots' were lost. Larsen scuttled the *Arthur* according to plan. The crew, except for one British naval rating, killed by a frontier guard, returned safely via Sweden. Then, in December, the disaster which had earlier struck the SIS boats befell the SOE flotilla. The *Aksel* was lost 200 miles north of the Shetlands on her way back from the far north. Only a few days later the *Sandøy*, which had made half a dozen trips to Træna on the Arctic Circle, was sunk with the loss of all hands, probably as a result of an attack by aircraft. Then the *Feie* was lost on the short crossing to the islands south of Bergen. Twenty-four out of a total of 60 men serving in the SOE flotilla had been lost in three months, but still volunteers came forward and still the disasters continued. On 17 March Larsen sailed from Scalloway in the *Bergholm* to Træna. They were attacked by aircraft on the return trip: the wheelhouse was shot to pieces around the intrepid and imperturbable skipper but, before the boat sank, Larsen patched up the holes in the lifeboat and transferred the surviving members of the crew to it. They were 350 miles north of the Shetlands and 75 miles from the Norwegian coast. Larsen headed for Ålesund, 150 miles away, which they reached by rowing: they were later picked up by a Motor Torpedo Boat (MTB). On 24 March the *Brattholm* sailed to the Tromsø area to land four men and an arms cargo. She was intercepted and sunk by an enemy war vessel on arrival. Only one member of the crew escaped.

Operations were once again suspended during the summer of 1943. Everyone had concluded that the days of the fishing boat were over and the search for an alternative began. By the beginning of the 1942–43 winter season, SOE had obtained, through the good offices of the American OSS, three 110-foot US submarine-chasers. Manned by Norwegians and based at Lerwick, these vessels took the place of the fishing boats for SOE traffic. They proved excellent seaboats, somewhat slow by MTB standards but far faster, of course, than the fishing vessels previously employed. Their reliability and high endurance were outstanding, while their impressive armament meant that, though often inspected by enemy aircraft, they were never attacked. These qualities, together with the available knowledge of the Norwegian coast, made operations relatively easy. During their first winter season, they completed 34 operations, two of which were for SIS.

After the usual summer close season, a sudden spate of SIS operations came forward and continued until the spring of 1945. Twenty-seven of these missions were carried out by the SOE submarine-chasers, which performed a total of 75 operations during the last winter of the war. Of the 114 operations carried out by these vessels, *Hitra*, *Hessa* and *Vigra* in the last two winters of the war, 29 were for SIS and all the rest for SOE.

David Howarth, though to his great regret never allowed to go on operations, pointed out in his book *The Shetland Bus* that, though the Scalloway base ran quite formidable war vessels over great stretches of ocean, they remained until the end quite independent of the Royal Navy. They steamed 90,000 miles in the last four winters of the war and in that time only four strange vessels were sighted.[6]

Norway was uniquely dependent on clandestine sea transport: her weather being what it is, communications by air – so important to SOE in other parts of German-occupied Europe – were on a very limited scale since aircraft de-icing equipment was still at an early stage of its development. The ships crossed and re-crossed the most exposed part of the North Sea, always in winter, benefiting from the darkness but enduring appalling weather. It was the weather that was the worst enemy and the feats of seamanship performed by their Norwegian crews showed that the spirit of their Viking ancestors was very much alive among the fisher-folk of the Norwegian seaboard.

An eleventh of the 700 tons of material sent into Denmark by SOE went in by sea. Fifty tons of this was landed at Lysekil on the Swedish coast from one of the five high-speed merchant vessels of the series that had been converted at Southampton from MGB hulls for the blockade-breaking 'Bridford' run from Hull to Gothenburg to fetch ball-bearings. A party of well-disposed Swedish policemen accompanied this cargo of arms southwards by rail and made sure nobody interfered with it until it could be quietly slipped across the Sound into Denmark.

In the course of 1943 SOE became interested in the idea of using the Danish fishing fleet, on the Dogger Bank from January to November each year, to supplement by seaborne operations the airborne supply of arms and explosives to

Denmark. Slocum had been working on the possibility of such a sea line for a Polish intelligence requirement that had fallen through. The original vessel he selected developed chronic engine defects but a second ship was commissioned as MFV 2043 and sent to Blyth, ostensibly as a minewatching boat. After a false start in January 1944 and further delays caused by a breakdown in W/T communications with Denmark, two new vessels were recruited in Frederikshavn. Once again this operation failed but a new system, profiting by earlier failures, led to a successful rendezvous at the end of August. Four tons of arms and six tons of fuel were transferred in bad weather by slinging the cases overboard in a trawl which was then hauled aboard the Danish craft. The operation was completed overnight, taking ten hours. A second expedition was carried out in September; but none in October as the fishing season had reached its close.

Somewhat unexpectedly, the two Frederikshavn boats arrived in the United Kingdom as refugees, having narrowly escaped arrest for resistance activities unconnected with these operations. But replacements were found and on 21 March 1945, MVF 2043 met the new Danish vessels near the Outer Silver Pit and transferred four tons of stores. On 17 April she did even better, meeting two other Danish boats and transferring to them 136 packages, 15 drums of fuel oil, lubricating oil, comforts etc. in 2 hours, 25 minutes.

Though SOE was not initially involved in George Binney's blockade-running operations from Sweden, they were, by 1943, a direct SOE responsibility and Binney himself was a member of SOE's Danish Section. They were an important achievement.

Binney was already well known before the war as an Arctic explorer, having taken part in three expeditions from Oxford, two of which he led. He went out to Sweden in December 1939 as representative of the British Iron and Steel Control. His mission was to place orders for and to ship to the United Kingdom, special steels, machine tools, ball-bearings and Swedish iron, which was essential to the war effort, particularly at a time when the US economy was not fully engaged in its support. When the German occupation of Denmark and Norway in April 1940 imported a blockade on the Skagerrak, he was instructed by Sir Andrew Duncan, Churchill's Minister of Supply, that it was of paramount importance for us to receive all the war stores on order in Sweden: he must at all costs get them to England. After exploring all the alternatives, Binney and his chief Swedish associate concluded that, although both belligerents claimed to have closed the Skagerrak by mining, the so-called Norwegian Channel along its northern side was so deep that it was probably impossible to lay mines there.

There were a number of Norwegian merchant ships immobilized in Swedish ports by the blockade and, in a camp which Binney had organized, were the masters and crews of four British iron-ore carriers captured by the Germans at Narvik but released and evacuated to Sweden when the Allies re-occupied the town. In the face of untold difficulties, Binney set about organizing a blockade-running operation code-named 'Rubble' – one of the most daring and successful enterprises of the war. In the last week of January 1941 five vessels under Binney's command slipped through the Norwegian Channel under cover of darkness and were escorted by the Royal Navy to the Shetlands. 'Rubble' added 43,000 tons to the Allied merchant fleets and delivered 25,000 tons of urgently needed war materials to British ports. Hitler was reduced to carpet biting, Binney was knighted, turned down the offer of a cushy job in Washington and, although suffering from jaundice, was flown back to Sweden to mount a second operation. The Swedes came under intense German pressure to prevent any such repetition.

SOE were, from this point, increasingly involved and they partly conducted the new operation, code-named 'Performance'. Ten further Norwegian ships were prepared and loaded with material that could not be obtained from the USA. The Germans exerted every possible pressure on the Swedes to prevent these ships sailing, they indulged in legal harassment to the same end. It was not until the 17th March 1942, when the hours of darkness were becoming dangerously short, that a favourable verdict by the Supreme Court removed this judicial obstacle. The Swedish Navy played what Peter Tennant, SOE's man in Stockholm, called an inglorious part in preventing Binney's ships moving up the coast to hide in a fjord from which they might escape undetected, by escorting them with fully-lighted ships, in forcing them out on to the guns of the waiting German armed trawlers and making it impossible for them to take refuge in territorial waters. Six of the ships had to be scuttled and their crews were captured. Two, carrying 27 per cent of the cargoes by value, reached the United Kingdom: two, the *Dicto* and the *Lionel* returned to Gothenburg with 47 per cent for subsequent shipment. Other methods of blockade-running had become necessary.[7]

The air-lift to Scotland was expanding: between November 1943 and March 1944, 88 tons were carried in heroic circumstances, but air transport alone could not cope with the volume and weight of materials awaiting shipment. Binney and SOE had got down to planning a new form of blockade-running by sea. A flotilla of five, fast, merchant vessels was created out of hulls originally built as motor gunboats for the Turkish Navy. These vessels, allocated to SOE and sailing under the house-flag of the Ellerman-Wilson line belonged to the same series as the four MGBs allocated to Slocum and could each carry 50 tons of cargo. Like their half-sisters at Dartmouth, they suffered from somewhat unreliable Paxman diesels, but regular runs were made from Hull to Lysekil, where the *Dicto* and *Lionel* served as base ships, between 27 October 1943 and March 1944, with the loss of one ship captured by the Germans. Binney himself made four round trips, but suffered a severe heart attack and had to be invalided out of the operation, to his intense disgust, but with the consolation of a DSO. His place in the flotilla was taken by Brian Reynolds. The winter's operation, code-named 'Bridford', had, with the air service, exceeded the target of 400 tons of valuable freight and 347 tons of this was carried by SOE's 'Grey Ladies'.

From September 1944 to January 1945 bad weather made resumed passages from Hull impossible. It was from a new base at Aberdeen that the 50 tons of material destined for Denmark was landed at Lysekil. By this time, the Swedes were far more cooperative.

SOE Cairo, which worked under different cover at different times, was operating small craft both in the Red Sea and the Eastern Mediterranean early in 1941. Their man in the Red Sea was an Anglo-Irish Moslem called Lieutenant-Commander Abdullah Bey, RN, who had left the Royal Navy as a Sub-Lieutenant and lived between the wars as a Red Sea dhow captain with Somali crews, trading, no doubt, like his French counterpart, Henri de Montfried, in pearls, arms and hashish. As the East African campaign drew to a close and General Platt's British and Indian troops closed in on Massawa, the Royal Navy foresaw that Axis shipping lying in the port would try to slip by night through the Bab-el-Mandab straits in Vichy-controlled territorial waters off Djibouti. Unable to mount a regular watch there themselves, they got SOE to organize it with two engineless dhows: these, operating from Perim, anchored each night in neutral French waters. Abdullah Bey himself sank an escaping 8,000-ton German merchantman with a 2-pounder gun of the type fitted to naval steam picket boats in the 1890s and took prisoner her crew of nearly 40. SOE Cairo's man in the Mediterranean was Michael Cumberledge, son of an admiral, who had been professional skipper of a large, American-owned ketch before the war and knew the Aegean well. With a crew which included his cousin and a young Cambridge don named Nicholas Hammond, a future headmaster of Clifton College and Professor of Classics, he and his armed caique, HMS *Dolphin*, took part in SOE's preparations for a Cretan resistance movement in the mountains after the withdrawal of General Freyberg's forces. Thereafter, SOE's communications with Crete were, from late 1941 until the spring of 1943, entirely by caique or submarine. The caiques *Escampador*, *Porcupine* and *Hedgehog* were captained by sailors of extraordinary skill and courage such as John Campbell and Mike Cumberledge. The latter was captured late in 1942 while trying to mine the Corinth Canal. He was shot as Flossenburg concentration camp at the very end of the war. Admiral Cunningham withdrew the RN submarines after what Antony Beevor describes as a 'disastrous incident at Antiparos'. Thereafter the service to Crete was maintained by the Greek submarine *Papanikolis* and a flotilla of B-class Fairmile Motor Launches, operating from Derna, Bardia, Mersa Matruh or even Alexandria as the ebb and flow of the desert war dictated.

The caique flotilla persisted. It consisted of 13 boats when Captain Slocum descended on Cairo in April 1943, determined to amalgamate all 'private navies'. In this he was unsuccessful: the so-called 'Levant Fishery Patrol' continued to be operated by SOE for its own requirements. It still remained under British command when the two other flotillas formed to work for the SIS and various raiding forces had been handed over to the Greek Navy. At the end of the war Slocum had the grace to pay tribute to its 'fine traditions and great experience of the Aegean'.

The Allied landings of 8 November 1942 in French North Africa turned the Western Mediterranean into a major theatre of war. SOE had not worked in Algeria, where the Americans prepared clandestine support for the invasion, but they helped over W/T communications with Gibraltar and attempted to smuggle 10 tons of arms to the Algiers resistance. The expedition used Slocum's largest and fastest ship, but they found no reception at either of the pinpoints indicated by Robert

Murphy, Roosevelt's personal representative in North Africa. The resistance managed all the same to make the landings at Algiers far easier than at Casablanca and Oran. SOE had sent a small mission with the invasion force and, a week later, the same vessel carried a group of French volunteers eastward to support the British First Army in Tunisia.

A second and larger SOE mission codenamed 'Massingham' arrived in Algiers hard on the heels of the other to prepare a base for operations to Corsica and Italy. Slocum had received similar instructions and there was a predictable, but unnecessary row between SOE and his representative at Gibraltar about coordination and control of sea operations from the new North African base. It was an unnecessary wrangle in that neither party had the operational vessels required, which were submarines: fortunately these were made available for SOE's requirements from the 8th Submarine Flotilla, whose depot ship, HMS *Maidstone*, had moved up from Gibraltar to Algiers. Slocum's mixed collection of Spanish feluccas and other small local craft proved unable to re-start operations to Corsica or the south coast of France, now in German hands, while the French submarine *Casabianca*, which had escaped from Toulon when the rest of the French squadron there scuttled itself, opened new sea lines both to Corsica and to Provence. With technical help and training from 'Massingham' she managed, among other feats, to land, first, 11 tons and a month later, 20 tons of arms for the Corsican *maquis*.

In April 1943 Slocum, who was in the process of transforming his SIS post into a genuine Admiralty appointment as Deputy Director Operations Division (Irregular) – DDOD(I) – visited the Commander-in-Chief Mediterranean. Admiral Cunningham accepted the proposed change, which would give, in theory at least, Slocum authority to call upon overseas commands for necessary help, but made it clear that irregular operations did not interest him, though he would suffer them.

As the invasion of Sicily progressed, the demand for intelligence from Italy increased. The scarcity of fishing activities in Italian waters made operations by fishing vessels inappropriate, but, with Sicily in Allied hands, it seemed that a solution might be found by employing fast craft out of Palermo. Preliminary arrangements were made with the American Naval Commander to use United States PT craft from that port, which was under complete American control. In July, Slocum visited the area to obtain permission from the British naval authorities. In spite of American willingness to cooperate, Cunningham categorically refused to release any craft possessing offensive capabilities for clandestine operations. Slocum returned to London but subsequent suggestions and requests from the Admiralty achieved nothing. Irregular operations had been brought to a standstill.

The deadlock continued until October, when, after the Italian armistice, Senior Officer Inshore Squadron, the ever helpful Captain N. V. Dickenson, was faced with the problem of what to do with the considerable number of Italian MAS boats lying idle at Maddalena in Sardinia: they obviously could not be used on offensive patrols against their erstwhile enemy and even less so against their own countrymen still fighting on the German side. He offered them to Patrick Whinney, Slocum's representative who had been sent to investigate the possibility of conducting operations from Bastia. It was a risky policy, but Slocum eventually agreed, there being really no alternative. Gradually the ban on the use of Allied fast craft was relaxed and over the next eight months there were over 100 successful operations from Bastia to Elba, the Italian mainland and south eastern France.[8]

'Massingham' had always intended to use Corsica, once it was in Allied hands, as a base for operations by sea; and had sent forward a highly-qualified amphibious unit called 'Balaclava' under command of Major Andrew Croft, well known before the war as an Arctic explorer. Croft provided the landing facilities for 24 successful operations, many to difficult pinpoints: he on one occasion landed a mixed group of 10 SOE and SIS agents between two machine-gun posts guarding the Ansaldo shipyard on the outskirts of Genoa. There was much German coastal traffic at night: two of Croft's admirably trained and equipped men, left behind when their mother ship was driven off by E-boats, rowed their rubber boat nearly 100 miles to get home.[9]

The Italian armistice had been negotiated on a 'Massingham' agent's W/T link and Holdsworth, appointed commander of SOE's 'Maryland' mission to Italy, the first sent to operate from ex-enemy territory, lost no time in getting there, sailing one of his own vessels to Monopoli, just south of Bari. By the time DDOD(I)'s African Coastal Flotilla's (ACF) reconnaissance party got there, SOE, MI9 and OSS had each organized what Slocum termed scornfully 'private navies' for their own use. As the British Admiral at Taranto had approved these arguments, the best he could do was to appoint an officer to the Admiral's staff to coordinate Special Operations. Lieutenant Levy, holder of the new post, found that SOE Cairo had already organized an arms supply service from Italy to Albania and, in due course, he himself helped them to establish a similar one to western Greece and the Ionian Islands, in most cases using Italian naval vessels and landing craft for that purpose.

Over the next 18 months Levy, coordinated and recorded no less than 250 Special Operations in the Adriatic. Users included 'A' Force, MI9's local organization, which had large numbers of former Italian prisoners of war to collect, OSS (Brindisi), OSS (Naples), ISLD (i.e. SIS), the SBS, the SAS and Lieutenant-Commander Douglas Fairbanks Jnr., USNR of Task Group 80.4 (the deception organization). But SOE was by far the largest single user. The ferry service to the Dalmatian coast via the island of Vis, was so big and so open that Staff Officer, Special Operations (Adriatic) did not even record it. This was undoubtedly an SOE supply commitment even if Fitzroy Maclean preferred to regard himself as directly responsible to the Prime Minister. The Senior Naval Officer at Vis was Lieutenant-Commander Morgan Morgan-Giles, a future Captain of HMS *Belfast*, Admiral and MP for Winchester. The arms and ammunition, largely salvaged from the battlefields of Tunisia and Sicily by SOE, were ferried over in Special Service MLs and Landing Craft. A trawler of Slocum's African Coastal Flotilla carried hundreds of Allied and Partisan troops and many tons of supplies between Italy and Komiža. She also escorted the small island convoys and towed broken down LCTs (Landing Craft, Tank). She was joined by an ex-Fiume/Pola ferry boat and an Italian-built Motor Fishing Vessel. Morgan-Giles had a forward liaison officer,

Lieutenant-Commander Merlin Minshall RNVR, with the Partisans and in contact with Maclean. It was he who arranged for the Partisans' navy, which consisted of local schooners and caiques, to collect supplies from Vis. The total tonnage delivered to Yugoslavia by all means was 17,000 tons – far greater than SOE sent into any other occupied country – and it seems clear that a large proportion of this went by sea.

DDOD(I) and his local representatives were still longing to abolish the 'private navies': it was what they described as the 'highly irregular sailing of an SOE vessel' on the west coast that finally brought matters to a head and led to all private craft employed on clandestine operations being placed under the control of Senior Officer, African Coastal Flotilla (Adriatic). I know all about this incident: it was a misplaced piece of private enterprise by a picaresque character recommended to Holdsworth in 1940 by Ian Fleming, then special assistant to the Director of Naval Intelligence: but that is a story in its own right.

To redress the balance, it should be recorded that, from a small ACF base set up at Leghorn in December 1944 mainly for SOE's needs, an operation was successfully mounted by SOE to sink the Italian aircraft carrier *Aquila*, a prospective blockship lying in Genoa harbour. MGB 177 and the Italian MS.74, each towing one SOE Mobile Transport Submarine (MT S/m), proceeded to a position five miles off Genoa harbour. The MT S/ms then towed SOE 'Chariots' to within one mile of the harbour, which was entered without opposition. The limpets were attached to the aircraft carrier and the 'Chariots' left to rejoin the main force outside the harbour, still without encountering any enemy opposition.

All in all, SOE, with Force 133's commitments to Greece, Albania and Force 399's to Yugoslavia, was by far the largest user of clandestine sea communications in Italian waters.

Although this chapter primarily deals with SOE's activities in Western Europe and the Mediterranean, brief mention must be made of naval operations in the Far East. SOE's missions in India and Australia, confronted by the vast distances of South-East Asia, used submarines in early attempts to get operational parties ashore in the Japanese-occupied Andamans, Malaya and Sumatra. The first group to return to Malaya, led by John Davis, a former Malayan police officer who had sailed a small vessel to Ceylon after the fall of Singapore, was landed by a Dutch submarine and picked up a month later in June 1943. Ivan Lyon's 'Jaywick' attack on Japanese shipping in Singapore harbour was mounted from a local vessel named *Krait*. His disastrous follow-up operation 'Rimau', in which he and 27 brave men were lost, sailed from Fremantle by submarine and should have been picked up by submarine had all gone well. There were also sea-borne raids by SOE on Japanese oil depots in Java using an SOE submarine named *Witch*. This vessel could be set to submerge itself and to re-surface at a pre-determined time.

In conclusion, all in all, for a predominantly military organization and for all its feuding with Slocum, SOE was a far greater user of communications by sea than is generally known and recognized.

45

Notes

1   The late Brooks Richards's original paper did not include end notes and he died before these could be completed. The editor has sought to identify sources but the reader is encouraged to consult Brooks's seminal work on the subject for further illumination. Brooks Richards, *Secret Flotillas, Clandestine Sea Lines to France and French North Africa 1940–1944*, London: HMSO, 1996. Reprinted in two volumes, *Secret Flotillas, Volume I Clandestine Sea Operations to Brittany 1940–1944, Volume II Clandestine Sea Operations in the Mediterranean, North Africa and the Adriatic 1940–1944*, London: Whitehall History Publishing/Frank Cass, 2004.
2   M. R. D. Foot, *SOE in France*, London: HMSO, 1966, p. 62.
3   Ibid., p. 66.
4   TNA HS 3/87, HS 3/91-3 and HS 3/96.
5   Brooks Richards, 'Britain and Norwegian resistance: clandestine sea transport', in Patrick Salmon (ed.) *Britain and Norway in the Second World War*, London: HMSO, 1995, pp. 161–6.
6   David Howarth, *The Shetland Bus*, London: Thomas Nelson, 1951.
7   Peter Tennant, *Touchlines of War*, Hull: The University of Hull Press, 1992.
8   Patrick Whinney, *Corsican Command*, London: Patrick Stephens, 1989.
9   Andrew Croft, *A Talent for Adventure*, Hanley Swan: SPA, 1991.

4

CHURCHILL AND SOE

David Stafford

In the spring of 1942, the best selling wartime English-language parable of European resistance, John Steinbeck's *The Moon is Down*, was published in Britain. One of its most eager readers was Winston Churchill. The novel tells the story of a small town overrun by foreign occupiers. At first peaceful, the troops turn violent when they encounter resistance. The mayor is taken hostage, then shot. Young men flee across the sea to Britain. 'Let British bombers drop big bombs on factories', the mayor pleads before they leave, 'but let them also drop us little bombs to use, to hide, to slip under the rails, under tanks. Then we will be armed, secretly armed.' A few weeks later British planes drop thousands of small explosive devices by parachute, which the town's population collect and hide away like so many Easter eggs.[1]

Enthused by the image, Churchill dashed off a letter to Lord Selborne, the minister in charge of SOE, asking if such an operation could be carried out on a wide scale across Europe. After due deliberation, Selborne told him 'no': such a programme should only be initiated on the eve of Allied landings, to be targeted on railways and with the imminent arrival of Allied forces to protect civilians against reprisals.[2]

Churchill had earlier, in his now legendary and much-repeated phrase, urged Selborne's predecessor, Hugh Dalton, 'to set Europe ablaze'. This metaphor, along with his *The Moon is Down* vision of resistance, has presented an easy target for critics of both SOE and Churchill. The distinguished military historian John Keegan, for example, has damned SOE's programme of subversion, sabotage and resistance as 'a costly and misguided failure' whose price was paid by very great suffering on the part of the brave patriots whose actions must be judged, Keegan concludes, as 'irrelevant and pointless acts of bravado'.[3]

The patriots of Europe, and those who fought with them, will certainly have answers of their own to this view, so redolent of the traditionalist military objections that dogged SOE from its birth. My concern here is with Churchill. In his defence, I would say the following: his rhetoric is no sure guide to his actual beliefs or policy, or indeed those of SOE. As Selborne's response to Churchill's *The Moon is Down* idea makes clear, it was *not* SOE policy to promote mass popular uprisings. Critics should know whereof they talk. SOE had multiple dimensions, and thus many criteria by which it may be judged. Here I shall focus mainly on Churchill and SOE in Europe.

Churchill had always been an enthusiast of secret intelligence and unconventional warfare. In Cuba, celebrating his 21st birthday, he admired the role played by first-rate intelligence in the effectiveness of the Cuban guerrillas fighting the Spanish army – a valuable force multiplier for those weak in conventional arms and resources. Similar observations marked his experiences with British imperial forces on the North West Frontier, in the Sudan, and in South Africa. Dramatically escaping from the Boers, he added personal experience of survival behind enemy lines to add to his repertoire of expertise. It is noteworthy that when, as a Conservative Member of Parliament after the 1900 General Election, he supported stringent economies in army expenditure, he excepted the Intelligence Department from his demands. Subsequently he provided unwavering support for the new Secret Service Bureau, founded amidst a spy scare in 1909. As Home Secretary he introduced the practice of granting MI5 general warrants for the secret surveillance of the mails, and as First Lord of the Admiralty threw his considerable energy and weight behind the efforts of Vernon Kell and the spymasters to unmask the German spies; they were, he feared (quite wrongly) preparing the way for a German invasion. No sooner had war broken out than he approved the formation of Room 40, the Admiralty's special decoding centre; subsequently he wrote its first charter and hungrily devoured the intelligence it delivered on German fleet, submarine and airship movements. For the rest of his political life, in whatever office, he demanded and expected to see secret intercepts as part of his daily ministerial fare. Without them, he felt disarmed.

Alongside his appreciation for such intelligence, he also demonstrated an extraordinary faith in the ability of secret agents to change the course of political events. After 1917, in his passionate hope that the Bolsheviks could be overthrown, he looked to Russian dissidents such as Boris Savinkov, and to British agents such as Sidney Reilly, to raise the banner of revolt against Lenin. His involvement with this subversive campaign was more profound than ever he admitted. Its failure did not deter him from hoping for better when it came to Hitler.

Section D, the SIS forerunner of SOE, was formed in 1938, when Churchill was still in his 'wilderness years' and out of office. Characteristically, as soon as he entered the Admiralty in September 1939, he hoped it could help him. Determined to halt Swedish iron ore supplies reaching Germany, he looked to a sabotage operation to do the job. When Stewart Menzies, contrary to Churchill's preference, was appointed 'C' in November 1939, his first official appointment was with Churchill. Perhaps he hoped to mend fences, but he also carried with him details of the special Section D operation against Swedish iron ore for Churchill's approval. For the rest of his time at the Admiralty, Churchill agitated for the operation to go ahead.

On becoming Prime Minister, Churchill determined to harness the secret services more closely and effectively to Britain's needs. An immediate result was the creation of SOE.

Fiery rhetoric surrounded its birth. Hugh Dalton spoke ambitiously of creating movements in occupied territory comparable to the Sinn Fein in Ireland, to the Chinese guerrillas operating against the Japanese, to the Spanish irregulars who had helped defeat Napoleon, even to the Nazi 'Fifth Column'. Much of this was for Cabinet consumption.[4] But those who actually ran SOE were often no less ambitious. Colin Gubbins developed the idea of SOE organizing and equipping secret underground armies that would, like Dalton's unmilitary workers, undermine the Nazis from within, a concept that coloured much of SOE's early planning. 'The underground fighters,' Dalton himself said, 'should do all they can to prepare a widespread underground organisation ready to strike hard later, when we give the signal.'[5]

But if SOE was to give the signal, what did the rest of the timetable look like, and were all the passengers ready to board the train? That those running SOE were keen for the trip is readily understandable. What about those, like Churchill, actually making strategic decisions?

Here too, in 1940/41, there was ambitious talk, much of which was grasping at straws. After the collapse of France, these were at a premium. SOE was conceived at a desperate meeting of the British Chiefs of Staff on 19 May 1940 when French defeat was already visible. Bracing their morale, they decided that economic warfare, a bombing offensive and popular revolt could still deliver victory. 'We regard this form of activity as of the very highest importance' they concluded, 'a special organisation will be required. ...'[6] The War Cabinet concurred on 27 May. Bickham Sweet-Escott, one of SOE's heavyweights, later described it as 'no more than a hopeful improvisation devised in a really desperate situation'.[7]

Churchill had to yield to political pressure from his Labour Party partners in placing Hugh Dalton in charge, a man he detested.[8] Their relationship was unhappy, although it seems unlikely that this seriously damaged SOE. Dalton, who admired Churchill and yearned for his acceptance, complained bitterly that the Prime Minister 'did not focus well on SOE'. It would be more accurate to say that Churchill did not focus well on Dalton. 'Keep that man away from me' he is reported as ordering his aides, and over the winter of 1940/41 the files bulged with complaints by Dalton that Churchill is refusing to see him. Yet, when he finally invited Dalton to Chequers, in March 1941, Churchill showed himself very well briefed on SOE's plans and operations, and keen to support them. The Yugoslav coup later that month undoubtedly helped, because Churchill rationed his time and energy. Until Dalton could show results, he was reluctant to spend time with him.

It was often felt in Baker Street, and has been oft repeated since, that Desmond Morton, Churchill's long-time confidant and personal intelligence adviser, was an 'enemy' of SOE in Downing Street. Morton, of course, came from SIS and retained close links with it and, as we shall see, many of his SIS colleagues remained resolutely hostile to SOE throughout its life. One recently released file in the Public Record Office (now the National Archives) supports this negative view.

Soon after becoming Prime Minister, Churchill gave Morton *carte blanche* to deal directly with any matters concerning the intelligence services. On 15 February

1941 Gladwyn Jebb, SOE's Chief Executive Officer, complained to Morton that he (Morton) was contacting people inside SOE independently of (i.e. behind the backs of) himself and SOE's Executive Director, Sir Frank Nelson. Two days later Nelson received a stormy call from Morton denouncing Jebb's complaint and proclaiming that Churchill had authorised Morton 'to see the files'. Then, as a still smarting Nelson carefully recorded in a file memorandum, Morton launched on a diatribe:

> the sense of which was that the Prime Minister hated Dalton, hated Jebb, hated me, hated the entire organisation and everybody in it, and that it was only through the efforts of Major Desmond Morton (who felt that the organisation was an important one and was serving an important purpose) that it had been allowed to continue as long as it had; but that if he was to be indicted on matters of this description he would wash his hands of the whole affair and so far as he was concerned he would cease to help us directly or indirectly, individually or generally.

'At this point', noted Nelson laconically, 'he put down the phone and the conversation ended.'[9]

It is hardly surprising, then, that Morton acquired he reputation he did in Baker Street. Later on, as we shall see below, during the major crisis for SOE over the winter of 1943/44 precipitated by the *Englandspiel* disaster, he was to be found agitating for a return of special operations to SIS.

But two points should be made here. First, suspicion of SOE *as an organization*, or jealousy and dislike of those who ran it, did not mean Morton was opposed to special operations themselves. As a major actor in the 1924 Zinoviev affair and one-time SIS handler of Sidney Reilly, as he has recently been revealed to have been,[10] he was obviously no mean disciple of subversion himself. Indeed, as another wartime episode illustrates, he could outdo even SOE in pressing for drastic 'dirty tricks'. This was the case with Vichy-controlled Madagascar which, until its capture by Allied troops in May 1942, was a constant source of anxiety in London. As chairman of the Whitehall coordinating committee on French resistance, Morton consistently urged and supported SOE subversive activities in Madagascar. It was Morton's committee that first recommended SOE control of subversive operations there and approved the employment of its first secret agent in the island, and it was Morton, too, who in May 1941 pressed SOE to be even bolder than it had contemplated. To the same Gladwyn Jebb he had savaged only three months before, he urged that SOE should do more than simply assist a Free French coup on the island. 'Is there not a dim possibility' he urged, '[that] ... by bribery, corruption, murder ... you may even be able to bring about a change of regime in Madagascar without the external aid of armed force?'[11] This, of course, was a double-edged comment that also carried a criticism of SOE, and doubtless his enthusiasm here was experienced as meddling in Baker Street. Until the end of the war he was regarded at best as an uncertain and sceptical ally in Downing Street.

Second, insofar as Morton was opposed or hostile to SOE, this did not necessarily influence Churchill. Indeed, on the recorded occasions when Morton was to be found opposing SOE, Churchill demonstrated that he was perfectly able to discount his adviser's preference and make independent decisions of his own quite contrary to Morton's wishes. By the end of the war, indeed, Morton's influence with Churchill was heavily on the wane – a matter that as early as mid-August 1943 prompted an astonishing and bitter private verbal attack against the Prime Minister by Morton in which he intemperately denounced his relationship with Roosevelt as 'almost homo-sexual'. This outburst, recorded in the diary of a Secret Intelligence Service officer, has only recently come to light.[12] Morton was an ubiquitous and undoubtedly influential figure, and, as Jebb and Nelson discovered, he could be abrasive and daunting. But he was not as powerful with Churchill as he both hinted and as others believed.

SOE was a hopeful improvisation, certainly, but one that Churchill residually clung to for some considerable time. Even after Pearl Harbor a year-and-a-half later, while en route to Washington to meet Roosevelt, he envisaged SOE-inspired resistance playing a significant strategic role in the liberation of Europe. 'It need not be assumed that great numbers of men are required', he wrote, 'If the incursion of the armoured formation is successful, the uprisings of the local populations, for whom weapons must be brought, will supply the corpus of the liberating offensive.' Even after Anglo-American talks officially quashed such strategic ideas, they lingered on in Churchill's imagination. 'We must look to the revolt of the conquered territories ... no nation or region overrun should relax its efforts for the day of deliverance ...', he told the Canadian Parliament on 30 December 1941.[13]

But long before what I have elsewhere termed 'the detonator concept' – the notion that small Allied landings would detonate a decisive uprising of the captive peoples[14] – disappeared from Churchill's strategic thinking, the harsh realities of priorities, resource allocation and logistics had revealed the limits of SOE. Hopes that subversion should be recognized by the three Fighting Services as an independent Service was a non-starter, and SOE quickly lost control of propaganda. Even in its reduced form, SOE never had permanent representation on the Chiefs of Staff committee.

Moreover, preliminary attempts to infiltrate agents by sea into Europe proved only their virtual impossibility, and as Bickham Sweet-Escott later recalled, 'the revolutionary belief was thus gradually forced on us that the only hope we had of doing our job in Western Europe lay in the parachute'. Initially, as Sir Brooks Richards' chapter makes clear, SOE had thought that 'sea communications were all it could hope for to France and western Europe.'[15]

The problems of infiltration by sea made SOE dependent on aircraft from Bomber Command and meant that agents would have to be more highly trained than anticipated, and severely limited the scale of operations.[16] Thus its operational capacity in the first year was virtually nil, except for the Balkans. It was no wonder that Sir Frank Nelson reported in September 1940 that he saw 'no possibility of any quick results of a major type'. Dependence on SIS for communications exacerbated the situation, and was so bad as 'to make CD's activities in many cases almost impossible'.[17]

SOE's first strategic directive from the Chiefs of Staff, in November 1940,[18] was outwardly broad and ambitious, a necessary bureaucratic weapon in the struggle for resources. Yet already realities were coming home. It warned strongly of the need to avoid premature uprisings and focused on immediate areas where sabotage could help, both inside and outside the occupied countries. Implicit was a down-grading of SOE's role as a grand strategic player, and by focusing on sabotage as the most immediately effective objective it placed subversion and the secret armies on the back burner – thus further eroding the notion of the Fourth Arm of warfare. These harsh practical realities are themselves sufficient to explain why Churchill saw little point in spending time with Dalton over the winter of 1940/41. As the excellent monograph on Colin Gubbins by Peter Wilkinson and Joan Bright Astley emphasizes, virtually everyone, from Churchill downwards, severely under-estimated the time it would take to launch effective operations.[19]

We can trace the inexorable story of the waning of Churchill's initial grand conception for SOE and behind-the-lines resistance through all subsequent directives from the Chiefs of Staff. In May 1942, for example, their directive, entitled 'SOE Collaboration in Operations on the Continent', prepared with Anglo-US operations in western Europe in 1942 and 1943 in mind, envisaged SOE building up and equipping paramilitary organizations to support conventional forces by interrupting enemy signals communications and transport, counter-sabotage, attacks on enemy aircraft and air personnel, and 'the disorganization of enemy movements and rear services by the spreading of rumours'. Gone were any references to secret armies, liberating offensives, or large-scale subversion.[20]

By 1943, the subordinate role of SOE in British strategy was even more explicit. The directive for that year instructed it to work to the maximum extent in support of agreed Anglo-American strategy, and in particular to focus on current activities rather than on long-term preparation. 'Any activities which are unrelated to this strategy,' it ordered, 'should be severely curtailed.' Against this background, SOE activities should be concentrated on, first of all, sabotage.[21] As for guerrilla activities, these too should be subordinated to immediate strategic directives.

That Churchill and the Chiefs of Staff were containing SOE tightly within the parameters of what, since the entry of the Soviet Union and the United States, was being transformed into a massive conventional war that would be won by largely traditional means, did not, of course, mean that SOE activities were either diminishing overall or were of no considerable significance in some sectors.

On the contrary, SOE in 1943 was far more active than in 1942 or 1941, operating in more countries with a far greater number of agents and more resources than before. Furthermore, this very 1943 directive gave SOE a major role to play in the Balkans. 'An intensified campaign of sabotage and guerrilla activities in the Balkans,' decreed the Chiefs of Staff, 'is of the first strategic importance in order to impede the concentration and consolidation of German forces on the Eastern Front.' The high and significant level of SOE activity on the Balkans from this point on, and Churchill's foremost role in prompting and encouraging it, is a matter of record that does not have to be further elaborated here.[22]

The 1943 directive also makes explicit the second major factor that limited SOE's role in ways unimagined on its creation in 1940. Namely, its clear subordination to the requirements of Britain's capture and exploitation of high grade enemy intelligence ('Ultra'), which came under Menzies's control. 'The requirement of SIS,' dictated the Chiefs of Staff in March 1943,

> should in general be accorded priority over your own operations in Norway, Sweden, France and the Low Countries, and, if the appropriate Commander-in-Chief agrees, on the mainland of Italy and in Sicily. In other areas care should be taken that your activities do not clash with SIS and that the latter's sources of information are not imperilled.[23]

Churchill, an avid reader and exploiter of 'Ultra' – again a story too well known to need further elaboration here – did not challenge his Chiefs of Staff on any of these issues.

The subordination to SIS interests went back to the origins of SOE. In its early life it depended heavily on Broadway (SIS Headquarters), where Churchill's separation of Section D from SIS created considerable bitterness.

SIS's previous relationship with Labour in power, in the 1920s, had been unhappy,[24] and Dalton's high-flown rhetoric about SOE's role in Europe only fed its anxieties. References to creating underground and guerrilla movements in Europe threatened SIS's need for the painstaking reconstruction of intelligence networks, and the situation was aggravated by the fact that SOE, theoretically separate from SIS, was still heavily dependent upon it for personnel, communications and other forms of technical assistance. All these made it vulnerable to SIS pressure. Under an agreement reached in September 1940, all SOE's W/T traffic was to be handled through SIS, which was given the right to accept or reject it. This dependence lasted until March 1942, giving rise to suspicions that SIS sometimes obstructed SOE operations of which it disapproved. The SOE-SIS rivalry of the early years of the war focused for the most part on this issue and late in November 1940, for example, the communications situation was regarded as so serious in Baker Street 'as to make CD's activities in many cases almost impossible'. An effort was made to gain independence, but in April 1941 SIS defeated a demand by SOE to be allowed its own codes and signals network.[25]

The situation persisted. In January 1942, when Dalton had a personal tête-à-tête with Mountbatten, communications and the related rivalry with SIS topped his agenda.[26] Further, under the same agreement of September 1940, all intelligence collected by SOE as a by-product of its operations was to be passed to SIS, even before it was circulated within SOE. This in itself created hard feeling in SOE, but mutual recriminations intensified when SIS was forced to recognize that SOE in Denmark had access to far better intelligence than itself. For SIS this was humiliating, and worsened the climate.[27] Finally, SOE was to consult SIS in the recruitment of all agents. SIS, on the other hand, was bound by no reciprocal obligation, and made no commitment to provide SOE with any intelligence at all.

This asymmetrical arrangement over intelligence, which lasted for the duration of the war, was crucial to the relationship between the two organizations.[28] It meant, for example, that 'Ultra' was sometimes not passed on to SOE at all, even when it directly concerned SOE. Stewart Menzies, 'C', mistrusted SOE's security and, quite correctly anxious to safeguard 'Ultra', rationed it rigidly, sometimes with effects bitterly resented inside SOE. On one occasion, for example, Section 17M of the Naval Intelligence Division (NID) noted from intercepts of Abwehr communications in Norway that the Germans had gone on alert along parts of the Norwegian coast. This information was passed by NID to SOE, in case the latter was planning to land agents ashore. This apparently sensible move incurred Menzies's wrath, however, for it breached a strict SIS rule forbidding NID to pass Special Intelligence material to anyone outside the Navy. SIS alone would pass such information on, Menzies said. But, as NID was well aware, 'the liaison between the appropriate one of "C's" officers and the "named officer" in SOE to whom some Special Intelligence was passed was "not too efficient".'[29]

A similar situation reigned in Cairo. For a long time, intercepts revealing the extent of Partisan activity in Yugoslavia never reached SOE. It seems to have been only by accident that these began to circulate to SOE Cairo at the beginning of 1943, an affair that has now become almost legendary.[30]

That SOE's activities would be seen as a threat to SIS interests, and that the former would be subordinated to the latter, was made clear very early. In December 1940, for example, SIS opposed SOE activities in the coastal areas of northern and western France 'as they might interfere with their organization for getting agents into enemy-occupied territory'[31]; and no SOE sea operations were ever attempted on the north French coast as a consequence.

So far as Churchill was personally concerned, the tension between SOE and SIS reflected the tug between heart and head, between his emotional commitment to immediate unconventional war on the one hand and his rational appreciation of the eventual power of the big conventional battalions on the other. No mention was made in SOE's first directive of any priority in SOE-SIS relations. But in the spring of 1942 the question became acute because it was then that Anglo-American plans for continental landings were beginning to take shape. It also coincided with what Bickham Sweet-Escott recalled as 'one of the periodical waves of feeling in Whitehall that it was time to give SOE a real shake up'. In this, SIS played a leading role.[32] In February 1942 Churchill had shifted Dalton to the Board of Trade and replaced him with his old friend and Tory ally, Lord Selborne, and in the following month SOE finally acquired its independence from SIS in codes and communications.[33] Broadway responded by launching a campaign to bring SOE under stricter control, inaugurating a period of turmoil in its affairs. When it all finally landed on Churchill's desk, however, he gave total backing to Selborne and SOE's continued independent existence.

Two days after a personal meeting with Selborne on 6 April 1942, Churchill bluntly told Foreign Secretary Anthony Eden, who had joined in the hostile chorus demanding fundamental reform, that he expected him to work with Selborne and sort out their jurisdictional differences (mostly over SOE operations in neutral countries). In doing so, Churchill also brusquely dismissed Desmond Morton's suggestion that SOE should 'not be directly under any Minister'. Instead, he asked Selborne to prepare a defence of SOE and then, having read it, ordered it circulated to the War Cabinet and Defence Committee. The report dismissed complaints against inefficiency and extravagance against SOE as 'baseless calumnies'. Churchill also dismissed Morton's suggestion that he himself (Morton) should lead an enquiry into SOE. Instead, the job went to John Hanbury-Williams, managing director of Courtaulds, assisted by Sir Edward Playfair, of the Treasury. The former concluded that Baker Street had been 'as much sinned against as sinning'.[34]

SOE was not yet completely out of the woods, however, and later that month the Joint Intelligence Committee recommended that SOE's activities be more strictly coordinated with and subordinated to the interests of SIS. In the words of the Committee:

(a) We recommend that closer coordination between SIS, SOE, and CCO [Combined Operations] be maintained at all stages in planning. The activities of SOE increase the alertness of the local authorities and greatly hamper the work of our intelligence. It is necessary that such activities should be avoided in areas where this adverse effect outweighs the results which these activities may be expected to produce. This applies especially to areas where larger operations are likely to take place.

(b) It is most difficult for the organisations concerned to determine by agreement where the balance of the advantage lies, since their duties inevitably conflict. Until some adequate arrangements are made to eliminate this conflict, we recommend that the Chiefs of Staff should appoint someone to decide all such issues on their behalf.[35]

The Chiefs of Staff accepted the recommendations on 1 May 1942 and instructed the directors of plans to report on the best method of coordinating SOE and SIS activities. Stressing how fundamental the conflict of interests between SOE and SIS was, they recommended their amalgamation into a single service under the direction of the Chiefs of Staff.

Churchill dismissed this proposal, too, although shortly thereafter a liaison committee under Sir Findlater Stewart was set up to resolve SOE-SIS disputes.[36] But it was short-lived, and subsequent coordination and liaison appears to have reverted to the ad hoc arrangements of the past, supplemented by regular meetings between SOE and the Foreign Office at which SIS was represented. Aware of SOE's narrow escape, and of Churchill's crucial role in saving it both then and undoubtedly in the future, Selborne prudently began sending him regular reports. 'As my Department works more in the twilight than the limelight', he told Churchill, 'I should like to keep you informed regularly of the progress of the brave men who serve in it.' The files reveal that Churchill took pains to read and comment on them and that those who passed them on were duly impressed. Reacting to Selborne's first quarterly report, for example, which covered the period March–June 1942 and reached Churchill's office in mid-July, John Peck, one of his private secretaries, noted that 'the achievements of SOE in Norway, the Balkans and Madagascar are very impressive. And so,' he added, 'is the part played in the death of Heydrich'. SOE trained the agents involved and Selborne claimed that SOE agents had earned 'the gratitude of mankind by his removal'.[37]

Not surprisingly, Churchill's alternating enthusiasms often heightened bureaucratic friction between Baker Street and Broadway. After the 'Torch' landings in November 1942 precipitated German occupation of the whole of France, for example, Churchill dashed off a note to Selborne reminiscent of his response to *The Moon is Down*.

It seems most important to intensify the operations in the newly occupied regions of France in order to make the relations between the torpid French and the German invaders as unpleasant as possible. Pray let me know what you propose to do.[38]

Predictably, Churchill's urge to action sparked deep anxiety from Menzies, who demanded that SOE should keep in close touch with SIS, which was attempting to build up its own networks in France. 'I should be most grateful,' he told Churchill, 'if ... you could see fit to state [to Selborne] that the closest touch should be maintained with "C" in order to avoid imperilling his Secret Service.' Churchill did as he asked, but this failed to prevent extensive sniping between the two agencies over the recruitment of agents in France.[39]

Churchill directly intervened again in the summer of 1943, when he demanded more aircraft for SOE and urged that supplies to the Balkan guerrillas be increased to 500 tons a month. Portal, Chief of the Air Staff, argued that a distinction should be drawn between SOE work in the Balkans and that in western Europe. In the Balkans, SOE activities should receive full support: 'they accord with our strategic plans, they exploit our present successes and should give us good and immediate results'[40]; but in western Europe resistance movements were of potential value only and could not merit any diversion of aircraft until nearer the invasion date. Although SOE contested this view, the Chiefs of Staff, meeting on 27 July, accepted Portal's argument and agreed that 'we should support SOE activities in the Balkans as far as possible and at the expense, if necessary, of supply to the resistance groups in western Europe'. To back his case, Portal presented a Secret Intelligence report indicating that a number of resistance groups in France had been penetrated by the Germans. 'At the present moment,' it noted, 'resistance groups [in France] are at their lowest ebb and cannot be counted on as a serious factor unless and until they are rebuilt on a smaller and sounder basis.'[41]

What better evidence could have been presented to reinforce the Air Ministry's case? That SIS and the Air Ministry had collaborated to produce the evidence at this opportune juncture seems clear, revealing graphically that the SOE and SIS rivalry remained acute. Not surprisingly, the Joint Intelligence Committee deplored, once again, the failure of SOE-SIS coordination and the lack of symmetry in their respective relationships to the directing centres of British strategy: for whereas 'C' (SIS) was, through permanent representation on the JIC, an integral part of the Chiefs of Staff organization, 'CD' (SOE) was not, despite the fact that SOE's role was operational.[42] This was despite Churchill's own suggestion that friction could be smoothed out if the heads of SIS, SOE and MI5 met monthly with Desmond Morton. Although such meetings began, only two were actually held in the first six months of 1943.

The culmination of SIS-SOE rivalry came in December 1943, marking the climax to a train of events which had begun with the July-August crisis over aircraft.[43] In September, SOE's handling of the Greek resistance had so alienated the Foreign Office and its representatives and allies in Cairo that it precipitated a special meeting of ministers, chaired personally by Churchill on 30 September. Once more, he made a robust defence of SOE, and the meeting reaffirmed it 'would preserve its integrity under the Ministry of Economic Warfare'. But Sir Charles Hambro, Nelson's successor, was forced to resign and, after Churchill agreed, he was replaced by Gubbins.[44]

This September decision was only a truce. The Foreign Office, which had never regarded SOE with benevolence, was now deeply hostile, and in December the opportunity arose to join hands with SIS and elements of the regular military establishment to rid themselves of it. These forces were encouraged to act, moreover, by Churchill's prolonged absence from London, first for the Teheran Conference and then because of his serious illness and convalescence in North Africa.

The crisis was precipitated by the *Englandspiel* disaster.[45] On 1 December 1943, Air Marshal Bottomley alerted the Chiefs of Staff that the Commander-in-Chief, Bomber Command (Harris), had suspended all SOE flights to occupied Europe. Even more serious, Bottomley claimed that 'SIS had warned SOE, on more than one occasion that there was a danger of what had in fact occurred, but SOE had refused to accept their advice'. There followed a full-scale enquiry into SOE operations in Europe. This took several weeks, and it was not until mid-January 1944, in Churchill's continued absence in North Africa, that the Defence Committee met under Attlee's chairmanship to consider the results. While any changes in SOE's relationship to the higher command were deferred until Churchill's return to London, and it was revealed that the SOE organization in Holland had been penetrated and operated by the Germans for over a year, the situation elsewhere in Europe, with minor exceptions, was deemed satisfactory. It also became clear that SIS's role in the Dutch affair was little better than that of SOE. As Sir Archibald

Sinclair, the Secretary of State for Air, himself admitted: 'there had been a great deal of wisdom after the event in this matter. SIS has been consulted and in the summer of 1943 had been unable to produce any evidence of penetration of the SOE groups in Holland.'

Nonetheless, SOE's independent future rested on a knife-edge. Sir Alan Brooke, the CIGS, believed that 'SIS and SOE should be brought under one ministerial head'. Ideally, both should be placed under the Minister of Defence, but if SIS could not be removed from Foreign Office control, then 'he would rather see SOE come under the Foreign Secretary than that the present situation should continue'. He persuaded his colleagues on the Chiefs of Staff Committee to support this view, and they duly recommended it to Churchill. Morton, too, seized the moment to pounce. 'I have always held the view' he told Churchill, 'that on technical as opposed to political grounds at least part of the work for which SOE is now responsible should always have been carried out by C.'[46]

Once more, however, Churchill reaffirmed the status quo. Temporarily consumed by a passion for the *maquis*, he dismissed SIS rumblings of discontent as being the result of Bomber Command machinations. He was clearly prepared to live with SOE, and took a broader and more resigned view of the scene than those most closely involved. 'The warfare between SOE and SIS,' he told Ismay in February 1944, 'is a lamentable but perhaps inevitable feature of our affairs.'[47]

Two months later Churchill illustrated how tolerant of SOE he could be. Following a personal protest from Soviet Foreign Minister Molotov against SOE activities in Romania, he exploded in anger: '... it does seem to me,' he protested, 'that SOE barges in in an ignorant manner into all sorts of delicate situations ... It is a very dangerous thing that the relations of two mighty forces like the British Empire and the USSR should be disturbed by obscure persons playing the fool far below the surface.'[48] Nonetheless, SOE survived his outburst and continued in being until the end of the war.

Churchill's attitude to SOE's survival into the peace was hesitant. On the one hand he agreed with Lord Selborne that a government that neglected special operations in peacetime would be 'like an admiral who said he did not require submarines'. On the other, he failed to provide any strong direction in the internecine Whitehall battles as to who would control such activities. Perhaps, by now, he was thoroughly weary of the bickering and prevarication was his way of tackling it. In the end, SOE did not survive. Instead, it sank into the turbulent waters of coalition politics where the Labour leader and Deputy Prime Minister, Clement Attlee, was opposed to anything that resembled 'a British Comintern'.[49] Like the Moscow version, SOE was formally dissolved. Yet, like communist subversion in reality, special operations lived on, to be embraced vigorously by Churchill when he returned to Downing Street in 1951; most notably in helping overthrow the Iranian government of Mohammed Mussadeq, a classic SOE-type operation in which a former SOE officer, Monty Woodhouse, played a significant part.

Churchill's spirit embodied that of SOE itself: bold, adventurous, unconventional and determined. His personality and own life experience lent force to the view that the fight should be taken to the enemy with behind-the-lines action, and that it should be enriched by first rate intelligence. *Without* Churchill there would have been no SOE, which owed its creation to his energy, determination and highly personal approach to war. His direct interventions on operational matters were often impetuous and ill-thought out, but on all the crucial issues vital to SOE's survival he was the indispensable saviour. *With* his support it survived several attempts at bureaucratic sabotage and assassination. This, no doubt, is why most Baker Street veterans still regard Churchill and SOE as virtually synonymous.

Notes

1   John Steinbeck, *The Moon is Down*, London: Heinemann, 1942, p. 118. This episode, along with others relating to Churchill and SOE touched on here, are discussed more fully in David Stafford, *Churchill and Secret Service*, London: John Murray, 1997.

2   David Stafford, *Britain and European Resistance 1940–1945; A Survey of the Special Operations Executive, with Documents*, London: Macmillan, 1980, p. 100.

3   John Keegan, *The Second World War*, London: Hutchinson, 1989, pp. 483–5.

4   See David Stafford, *Britain and European Resistance 1940–1945*, p. 25.

5   Ibid., p. 32.

6   Ibid., p. 23.

7   Bickham Sweet-Escott, 'SOE in the Balkans', in Phyllis Auty and Richard Clogg (eds), *British Policy Towards Wartime Resistance in Yugoslavia and Greece*, London: Barnes and Noble, 1975, p. 5.

8   M. R. D. Foot, *SOE: An Outline History of the Special Operations Executive 1940–1946*, London: Pimlico, 1999, pp. 19–20.

9   Nelson, file memo 17 February 1941, TNA HS 6/309.

10 Gill Bennett, *'A Most Extraordinary and Mysterious Business': The Zinoviev Letter of 1924*, Foreign and Commonwealth Office, History Notes No. 14, February 1999, pp. 30–1.

11 E. D. R. Harrison, 'British Subversion in French East Africa, 1941–42: SOE's Todd Mission', *English Historical Review*, Vol. CXIV, No. 456, April 1999.

12 See David Stafford, *Roosevelt and Churchill: Men of Secrets*, London: Little, Brown, 1999.

13 Stafford, *Britain and European Resistance*, p. 81. For Churchill's speech to the Canadian Parliament, see David Stafford, *Camp X: SOE and the American Connection*, London: Viking, 1986, p. 62.

14 David Stafford, 'The Detonator Concept: British strategy, SOE and European resistance after the fall of France', *Journal of Contemporary History* 10(2) (April 1975), pp. 185–218.

15 Bickham Sweet-Escott, *Baker Street Irregular*, London: Methuen, 1965, p. 49. Sir Brooks Richards, 'SOE and sea communications', in this volume.

16 For SOE-Bomber Command fights over aircraft, see M. R. D. Foot, *SOE in France*, London: HMSO, 1966, pp. 74–5, 165, 235, 352.

17 Stafford, *Britain and European Resistance*, p. 46.

18 'Subversive activities in relation to strategy', COS(40)27(0), TNA CAB 80/56. Full text provided as Document 2 in ibid., pp. 219–24.

19 Peter Wilkinson and Joan Bright Astley, *Gubbins and SOE*, London: Leo Cooper, 1993, p. 79.

20 'SOE Collaboration on Operations on the Continent', COS(42)133(0), TNA CAB 80/62. Full text in *Stafford, Britain and European Resistance*, Document 6, pp. 246–7.

21 'Special Operations Directive for 1943', COS(43)142(0), TNA CAB 80/68. Full text in ibid., Document 7, pp. 248–57.

22 Among many sources, see especially Auty and Clogg (eds), *British Policy Towards Wartime Resistance in Yugoslavia and Greece*; Elisabeth Barker, *British Policy in South-East Europe in the Second World War*, London: Macmillan, 1976; Basil Davidson, *Special Operations Europe*,

London: Gollancz, 1980; Mark Wheeler, *Britain and the War for Yugoslavia 1940–1943*, New York: Columbia University Press, 1980; Nigel Clive, *A Greek Experience 1943–1948*, Norwich: Michael Russell, 1985; Michael Lees, *Special Operations Executed*, London: William Kimber, 1986; and Richard Clogg, 'Negotiations of a complicated character', in this volume.

23 Stafford, *Britain and European Resistance*, p. 249.

24 Christopher Andrew, *Secret Service: The Making of the British Intelligence Community*, London: Viking, 1985, pp. 298–338.

25 F. H. Hinsley *et al.*, *British Intelligence in the Second World War*, Vol. 1, London: HMSO, 1979, p. 278.

26 Record of a meeting between Dalton and Mountbatten, 9 January 1942, Dalton Papers, British Library of Political and Economic Science.

27 Hinsley, *British Intelligence*, p. 278.

28 David Stafford, 'Secret Operations versus Secret Intelligence in World War II: the British Experience', in Timothy Travers and Christon Archer (eds), *Men at War: Politics, Technology and Innovation in the Twentieth Century*, Chicago: Precedent, 1982, pp. 119–36 *passim*.

29 Ewen Montagu, *Beyond Top Secret Ultra*, New York: Coward, McCann, 1978, pp. 94–5.

30 See Auty and Clogg (eds), *British Policy*; and Davidson, *Special Operations Europe*, *passim*.

31 Foot, *SOE in France*, pp. 66–7; Brooks Richards, 'SOE and sea communications', in this volume.

32 Sweet-Escott, 'SOE in the Balkans', pp. 123–4.

33 F. H. Hinsley *et al.*, *British Intelligence in the Second World War*, Vol. 2, London: HMSO, 1981, p. 14.

34 See numerous documents in TNA PREM 3/409/4, 'Enquiries into SOE, April 1942', and Wilkinson and Bright Astley, *Gubbins and SOE*, p. 101.

35 JIC(42)156(0) (Final), 29 April 1942, TNA CAB 84/85.

36 Hinsley, *British Intelligence*, Vol. 2, pp. 14–15. See also Stafford, 'Secret Operations versus Secret Intelligence'.

37 Peck to Prime Minister 23 July 1942, and other correspondence, TNA PREM 3/409/5.

38 Churchill to Selborne, Prime Minister's Personal Minute No. M.527/2, 13 November 1942, TNA PREM 3/409/7.

39 'C' to Prime Minister, 13 November 1942, and Churchill to Ismay, 14 November 1942, in TNA PREM 3/409/7. See also Hinsley *et al.*, *British Intelligence*, Vol. 2, pp. 15–16.

40 COS(43)404(0), 25 July 1943 TNA CAB 80/72.

41 COS(43)178th(0), TNA CAB 79/63.

42 JIC(43)325(0), 1 August 1943 TNA CAB 79/63.

43 Stafford, 'Secret Operations versus Secret Intelligence', pp.129–31.

44 Wilkinson and Bright Astley, *Gubbins and SOE*, pp.140–41.

45 See M. R. D.Foot, 'SOE in the Low Countries', in this volume. For a recent insider's perspective on the disaster, see Leo Marks, *Between Silk and Cyanide*, London: Harper Collins, 1999, *passim*.

46 Morton to Churchill, 6 January 1944, TNA PREM 3/408/4.

47 Churchill to Ismay, 10 February 1944, TNA PREM 3 185/1.

48 Elisabeth Barker, *British Policy on South-East Europe in the Second World War*, p. 140.

49 Stafford, *Churchill and Secret Service*, pp. 308–9. Wilkinson and Bright Astley, *Gubbins and SOE*, pp. 217–37, are particularly helpful on Selborne's fruitless attempts to persuade Churchill of his case.

5

HUGH DALTON, POLAND AND SOE, 1940–42

Terry Charman

At 6 pm on Tuesday 14 May 1940, five days after the German invasion of the Low Countries, Hugh Dalton, then at the Labour Party Conference in Bournemouth, received a telephone call from Winston Churchill. 'Your friends tell me that you have made a considerable study of economic warfare,' the new prime minister said. 'Will you take that ministry?' Dalton's response was both immediate and affirmative, 'I should be very glad to,' he replied, telling the premier that, 'I am very proud to serve under you.' Two months later, on 16 July 1940, the day that Hitler gave the orders to prepare for Operation 'Sealion', Churchill gave Dalton ministerial responsibility for the new secret organization, the Special Operations Executive (SOE), with the famous injunction: 'And now set Europe ablaze'. In his memoirs Dalton recalled, 'I accepted the Prime Minister's invitation with great eagerness and satisfaction', adding, '… for the next 18 months until I moved to the Board of Trade, the running of SOE absorbed an ever-increasing part of my time and energies'. Those energies, as both Dalton's friends and enemies could testify, were formidable.[1]

Dalton, the son of Canon John Dalton, tutor to the future King George V, was born on 16 August 1887 and educated at Eton and King's College, Cambridge. It was while at Cambridge, where Rupert Brooke was among his circle of friends, that Dalton became a Fabian socialist and was thus forever after regarded by his Tory political opponents as a 'class traitor' or 'Etonian renegade'. During the First World War he served with the Army Service Corps on the Western Front before transferring to the Royal Artillery in January 1917. Assigned to the Italian Front, Dalton was awarded Italy's Bronze Cross of Valour for his part in saving the guns during the retreat following the disastrous Battle of Caporetto of October 1917. By the end of the war he had decided on a political career, writing later:

> I am of that generation which during the Great War was massacred in droves upon the battlefields. Like many millions of others, I served in the Army and, unlike most of the best friends of my youth, I survived the

war. It was belief that politics, rightly handled, can put an end to war, which, more than anything else, drew me into the life of active politics when the war was over.

Dalton's revulsion at the mass slaughter of the Great War did not, however, turn him into a pacifist and in the 1930s he built up a formidable reputation as an anti-appeaser. He was also the principal architect in changing the Labour Party's essentially pacifist stance at the beginning of the decade to one which, by the end of 1937, encompassed armed deterrence, collective security through the League of Nations and bitter opposition to Chamberlain's appeasement of Hitler and Mussolini.

This, despite a very abrasive and bullying personality that won him few friends among his colleagues. Fellow Labour minister Emanuel (later Lord) Shinwell considered him to be 'the most wicked man in politics I've ever known', while political opponent and ministerial rival Brendan Bracken described him as 'the biggest bloodiest shit I've ever met!' Dalton's great admiration for Churchill was not reciprocated. 'Dr. Dalton, as he calls himself, though I have yet to hear of a patient that he has cured,' was one of the premier's *bons mots* at the expense of his Minister of Economic Warfare. On another occasion he remarked, 'Keep that man away from me. I can't stand his booming voice and shifty eyes'.

Dalton had established himself as an expert in foreign affairs with the publication in 1928 of *Towards the Peace of Nations* which was partly inspired by a six-week visit to Poland that he had made in 1926. Dalton recalled in his memoirs:

> I came away aware for the first time of this most gifted and romantic nation, so brave so gay, with so much good looks and personal charm in both sexes ... It was this visit to Poland which finally determined me to try and re-write the foreign policy of the Labour Party.

Dalton argued that most Labour Party foreign policy experts thought that

> as for Poland, she was picked up, like much else, in their silly syllogism, 'Everything that came out of the Allied victory in the war, and the Treaty of Versailles, is bad. Poland came out of all that. Therefore Poland is bad.' But few of these 'experts' had ever visited Poland or met typical Poles.

Dalton set about rectifying this anti-Polish bias especially when serving as Parliamentary Under-Secretary of State at the Foreign Office during the 1929–31 Labour Government. Ten years later in his Penguin Special, *Hitler's War*, Dalton recalled :

> putting on paper ... the argument, in opposition to the views held by others, that on the grounds of justice and in the light of all the facts there was no reason why we should back German claims against Poland, and

that, moreover, it could not be in British interests to aggrandise at Polish expense a Germany who had been, and might again become, what Poland would never be, a grim menace to this country.

Dalton pursued this pro-Polish line throughout the 1930s, often meeting with fellow socialists from Poland as well as maintaining more official contacts with their London Embassy under Ambassador Count Raczynski. These contacts became more frequent as the crisis over Danzig and the Polish Corridor heightened during the summer of 1939. With the German invasion on 1 September 1939 Dalton threw himself wholeheartedly into support of the beleaguered Poles, inveighing against the lack of action on the part of Britain and France to come to the aid of their ally. 'To sacrifice an Eastern front altogether is a tremendous price to pay for whatever advantages are supposed to result from air inactivity in the West', he recorded in his diary on 11 September 1939.

In a meeting on the same day with the Secretary of State for Air, Sir Kingsley Wood, whom he was 'shadowing', Dalton, in what appears to have been a highly emotional outburst, actually offered to fly to Poland himself. In his memoirs he recalled telling the Air Minister:

It was impossible to justify our treatment of the Poles. We were letting them down and letting them die while we did nothing to help them. I said that I would gladly fly myself, in any British aircraft flying to Poland, either by direct or indirect route. My name, I said was well known in Poland as a friend of their country. If I arrived in Poland now or even if I tried and failed, I thought this would help their morale and be a symbol of the reality of our Alliance against Germany.

Kingsley Wood was not enthusiastic and later that day told Dalton that the scheme was 'not considered advisable'.

For the rest of September 1939, Dalton continued to put pressure on government ministers, including the new First Lord of the Admiralty, Winston Churchill, to give the Poles active assistance, especially in the air, but to no avail. On 27 September 1939 Warsaw capitulated and a week later all organized open resistance ceased with the surrender of General Franciszek Kleeberg's army at Kock. However, irregular operations led by Major Henryk 'Hubal' Dobrzanski continued in the Kielce district until his death in battle in May 1940, while at the same time guerrilla warfare was waged by the 'Jedrusie' partisans commanded by Wladysaw Jasinski in the area around Sandomierz.

Throughout the 'Phoney War' Dalton kept up his contacts with the Poles, dining at the Embassy on 12 October 1939 to meet government minister August Zaleski, and again on 18 November 1939. Among his fellow guests that night was Colonel Colin Gubbins who had served as GSO1 and chief of staff of No. 4 Military Mission to Poland during the September 1939 campaign and who had managed to escape via Romania. Gubbins, described by Dalton as 'pro-Pole and pro-Czech and intelligent', made a highly positive impression on the Labour politician. So much so, according to Dalton, that:

> next year when I was Minister of Economic Warfare, and looking for a good soldier to help me to plan, and train personnel for, Special Operations in Europe, somebody mentioned Gubbins. At once I remembered this Polish dinner party and, after much battling with other claimants for his body, I got him.

Gubbins reported to his new minister on 18 November 1940: 'He makes a very good first impression', Dalton noted in his diary, 'He too is very quick and dynamic'.

For his part Gubbins, according to his biographers:

> like everyone else … at times found Dalton exasperating, but admired the singleness of purpose with which he fought SOE's battles in Whitehall and certainly did not share the view of some of Dalton's Etonian contemporaries that he was a traitor to his class. Besides they both liked and admired the Poles.

After the war Gubbins said of Dalton, 'He drove himself and his leading figures in SOE equally hard'.

A month after joining SOE, Gubbins with Dalton, and the latter's Chief Executive Officer Gladwyn Jebb – another old Etonian – spent Christmas 1940 as guests of General Sikorski on an inspection tour of Polish units stationed in Scotland. On the trip, Dalton delighted in making speeches to the Polish troops whom he thought to be 'fine soldiers and attractive human beings'. At the same time, the three men were able to take advantage of the trip to discuss the capabilities and potential of SOE including its Polish Section.

This had been established in late 1940 and was initially run by Bickham Sweet-Escott and then by Captain Harold Perkins who before the war had run a light engineering firm in Bielsko, spoke fluent Polish and was au fait with the country's history and customs. Perkins was subordinate to Major Peter Wilkinson who had served alongside Gubbins with the military mission to Poland. Contacts, which included a British military mission in France which Gubbins headed, with Polish resistance organizations had been formed before the establishment of SOE and early British support had been made via Section D. Liaison with the British on the Polish side was initially undertaken by Professor Stanislaw Kot, the Minister of the Interior in the government-in-exile, and his assistant, Jan Librach, a diplomat.

With the establishment of SOE's Polish Section direct contact was made with the Polish General Staff's Sixth Bureau, which was responsible for home affairs intelligence. In 1962 at a conference at St. Antony's College, Oxford, on Britain and Europe Resistance 1939–45, historian H. T. Willets gave the following succinct definition of the work of SOE's Polish Section:

The responsibilities of the Polish Section of SOE consisted of helping the Polish Sixth Bureau in preparing and developing communications with Poland and in operational training, of obtaining equipment and arranging the flow of equipment and personnel. Much of the work consisted in liaison between the Poles and interested British authorities.

This remained the case long after Dalton's departure to the Board of Trade in February 1942 for:

until the very last days of the war no British military mission as such, landed on Polish soil, and the operations technically organised by SOE from Britain to Poland were essentially conducted by the London Poles acting as an independent power.

Dalton's own view of the role of SOE had been given in July 1940 in a letter to Foreign Secretary Lord Halifax in which he wrote:

We have got to organise movements in enemy-occupied territory comparable to the Sinn Fein movement in Ireland, to the Chinese guerrillas now operating against Japan, to the Spanish irregulars who played such a notable part in Wellington's campaign ... the 'democratic international' must use many different methods, including industrial and military sabotage, labour agitation and strikes, continuous propaganda, terrorist acts against traitors and German leaders, boycotts and riots.

Dalton, who throughout his life entertained a strong streak of socialist romanticism, saw his new organization's primary task to be the mobilization and encouragement of left-wing opinion throughout Axis-occupied Europe into a mass movement that would spontaneously revolt against the Nazis, their Italian allies and satellites. In Dalton's view and, it must be acknowledged, those of many others in Whitehall at that time, 'occupied Europe was smouldering with resistance to the Nazis and ready to erupt at the slightest support or encouragement'.

This we now know to be a gross miscalculation of the actual situation. As John Lukacs states in his brilliant book *The Last European War*:

All of those who attempted to record, and later to reconstruct, the state of public opinion and of popular sentiment in the summer of 1940, agree: The majority of the peoples of Western Europe were willing to adjust their thoughts to the new order of things, and to embark on some kind of political collaboration with the Third Reich – with what it was, and with what it seemed to represent.

Lukacs goes on to point out that what resistance there was to the Germans during the first months of occupation came not from left-wing activists but from the right:

65

in Holland, Belgium, Luxembourg, and Denmark, the first demonstrations against the New Order were those by people who asserted their demonstrative allegiance to their royalty. The first Socialist demonstrations against local Nazis occurred in Amsterdam in February 1941, and in Brussels in March 1941.

The one exception to this 'placid lying down of the people in submission', as Churchill put it in a broadcast on 14 July 1940, was Poland where the population, from the very start of the occupation, had felt the full ferocity of Nazi racial policy. In Poland no attempt was made by the Germans, as they did initially in Western Europe, to hide the iron fist inside the velvet glove. To the Nazis the Poles were an *untermensch*, fit only to labour for the greater glory of the Third Reich. According to Himmler, Poles were just to be taught 'to count up to 500, to write their name, and to know that by divine order they owed obedience to the Germans'.

All Poles under the Nazi occupation lived in constant fear of arrest, torture, transportation or extermination. Poles were arrested and killed for the most trivial of reasons; for being out after curfew or for selling goods on the black market. No Pole leaving home in the morning could be sure of returning home safely in the evening.

> After all, it made no difference whether your papers were in order or not, whether you were guilty or innocent. The German terror was incalculable and the fact of being a Pole a deadly sin in itself – so you left it at that

observed Jozef Retinger, Sikorski's right-hand man, who himself parachuted into Poland in early 1944.

Any sign of repression was brutally suppressed. On 3 November 1939, barely a month after Warsaw's surrender, two women, Eugenia Wlodarz and Elizabeth Zahorska, were shot for tearing down an anti-British poster. But such terror failed to cower Polish resistance, the groundwork for which had already been laid before the end of the September 1939 campaign. One of its first planned operations was an attempt to assassinate Hitler during his visit to Warsaw to review a victory parade on 5 October 1939.

Instructions formalizing this armed resistance – The Union for Armed Struggle – were issued by the Polish government-in-exile, then based at Angers in France, on 4 December 1939, and they reached Warsaw by special courier on 1 January 1940. On 14 February 1942, a week before Dalton's responsibility for SOE ended, the Union for Armed Struggle changed its name to the Home Army. Its commander was General Stefan Rowecki who was later captured and shot, on Himmler's direct order, at Sachsenhausen concentration camp on 3 August 1944.

A pre-war friend of Dalton's, Mieczyslaw Niedzialkowski, a Socialist Party leader and member of the political council of the resistance, had been an earlier victim of Nazi terror. On 18 November 1939 Sikorski told Dalton that he would like to include Niedzialkowski in his government, but before he could be got out of Poland, Niedzialkowski was arrested on 23 December 1939 and shot in Palmiry Woods on 21 June 1940.

During the 'Phoney War' many Poles assumed that their liberation was only a short matter of time. 'We imagine … a dais raised in front of the Pontiatowski monument, and Sikorski standing on it, smiling, accompanied by Polish, French and British generals. Tanks roll by their French and British crews waving to the assembled crowds,' wrote one Warsaw resident at the beginning of May 1940.

Two months later, after the success of Hitler's offensive in the west, the same Pole recorded not only his fellow countrymen's disillusionment with France following that country's collapse, but their still unshakable belief in a British victory: 'which has become the last hope, not only for us, but for so many nations in Europe … that bastion will not be captured.' Gubbins himself was of the opinion, as he told a post-war audience that 'only the Poles, toughened by centuries of oppression, were spiritually uncrushed'. But at the same time as their offensive in the west, the Nazis also launched their infamous 'Aktion-AB', the cold-blooded hunting down and murdering of Poland's intellectual elite, the potential leaders of resistance.

The fall of France had radically altered the status of Polish resistance as Sikorski himself recognized. The Germans would now be able to redirect thousands of police and troops to combat any acts of resistance by the Union for Armed Struggle and to take even more savage reprisals against the civilian population as a result of such acts. Sikorski accordingly sent a telegram on 18 June 1940 to Rowecki ordering that armed resistance by the Union for Armed Struggle should cease. Two days later in a second telegram Sikorski ordered the cessation of sabotage, describing it as both 'pointless and provocative'.

From henceforth and until further notice, resistance activities were confined to espionage, intelligence and propaganda. Sikorski's orders, combined with a number of mitigating factors, caused a decrease, for a time, both in anti-Nazi activity by the Poles and in membership of the underground which fell from 75,000 in June 1940 to 54,000 in the spring of 1941. Nonetheless, as Gubbins's biographers point out, the Polish resistance connection during the autumn and winter of 1940 was undoubtedly seen as the best horse in the SOE stable and its 'principal asset'.

During this period Dalton, at the suggestion of Desmond Morton, Churchill's intelligence expert, was having regular meetings with Professor Kot. After the sixth meeting on 11 November 1940 Dalton wrote the next day to Churchill reporting progress. The letter, in which with no false modesty Dalton told the Premier 'my own personal relations with the Poles have long been good, much better than their relations with one another', was accompanied by a copy of the minutes of the meeting of 11 November 1940 when aerial communications with Poland were discussed. Dalton also sang Gubbins's praises to the Prime Minister – 'the outstanding man for my purpose' – besides dealing with wireless communication and aerial leaflet problems. In a fairly terse reply Churchill told Dalton, 'I am glad to think that you are smoothing out all (*sic*) your difficulties'.

Since their arrival in Britain after the fall of France the Poles had been anxious to renew contacts with the resistance movements back home. The Sixth Bureau selected and trained a small group of Polish volunteers, mainly officers, who were to be parachuted back into Poland to act as couriers. Initial support for this venture had come from No. 4 Military Mission in a memorandum to the Director of Military Intelligence dated 7 August 1940. Later in the year Colonel Josef Smolenski of the Sixth Bureau enlisted Captain Perkins's support in trying to obtain from the Air Ministry aircraft to undertake the operations. Direct approaches to that ministry by the Polish Air Force had proved unsuccessful as Perkins recorded in a memorandum of 28 December following a meeting with Colonel Smolenski:

> It was very pleasurable to note that Smolenski said that he had taken the matter out of the hands of the Polish Air Force and their connection with the Air Ministry, whom he blamed for the failure of the first attempt, and wished to deal exclusively with us.

In their discussion, Perkins noted,

> Smolenski told me exactly where he wished the parachute jumping to take place in Poland and asked me at the same time to let him have a decision as soon as possible as to whether this could be done or not.

The two men ended their discussion by discussing minor matters related to the operation, but Perkins in conclusion noted that the 'main thing is to get a decision as to the possibility of the operation as a whole'.

Given the magnificent contribution of the Polish squadrons in winning the Battle of Britain, combined with pressure from SOE and the Prime Minister himself, the Air Ministry finally agreed to releasing aircraft for the operation. The only available aircraft at the time for such missions were obsolescent Armstrong Whitworth Whitleys. These were twin-engined bombers which had undertaken the bulk of the leaflet raids during the 'Phoney War'. On 15/16 March 1940 Whitleys of No. 77 Squadron had even got as far as Warsaw on such a mission, an 11-hour round trip from their base at Kinloss in Scotland.

In order to undertake the agent dropping to Poland the Air Ministry agreed to modify a Whitley by fitting an auxiliary fuel tank in the rear of the fuselage. Captain Perkins, in cooperation with the RAF helped to draw up specifications for cylindrical containers attached to parachutes which could be released from the Whitley's bomb bays. The containers which were designed to carry weapons and explosives were constructed by SOE's technical section. With slight modifications suggested by the Polish resistance these containers became standard equipment for the rest of the war, and were also used by British airborne units.

Plans were made for the first flight to Poland to take place before Christmas 1940, but there was a last minute postponement because further modifications had to be done to increase the range of the aircraft. There were two other false starts, but these did not prevent Dalton, Gubbins and Jebb toasting the mission's success at a party on 31 January 1941 at Retinger's flat at which Sikorski and Kot were both present. Dalton noted in is diary:

> Retinger produces some bottles of Polish vodka of which, both liking it and desiring to be friendly, I drink a good deal ... I leave the Poles with every appearance of dignity and propriety, but my dignity might have suffered a little had they spent the next hour in my company!

Just a fortnight later on the night of 15 February 1941 the mission finally went ahead. General Sosnowski, one of Sikorski's ministers, told the three young couriers Stanislaw Krzymowski, Jozef Zabielski and Czeslaw Raczkowski before departing for take off: 'You are flying to Poland as our advance guard. Your task is to prove that we are able to maintain liaison with the home country.'

The team were flown to Poland in Whitley Z6473 captained by Flight Lieutenant F. Keast of the Royal Air Force's No. 419 Flight. The round trip of 1,800 miles which took 11 hours and 20 minutes, turned out to be Keast's last successful flight as he was shot down over Belgium the following night. Unfortunately the team were dropped sooner than planned as Keast was unable to locate the dropping zone and the low reserves of fuel precluded him from circling to find it. As a result Raczkowski and his companions landed not in the General-Gouvernement area of occupied Poland, but in the part of the country annexed to Germany in October 1939 – the Warthegau ruled by the infamous Arthur Greiser – some 60 miles from their original destination.

The parachutists were further handicapped by the loss of all their equipment and Lieutenant Zabielski also seriously injured his legs on landing. With the help of their fellow countrymen, however, all were able to eventually reach Warsaw and start their resistance work. The Germans made a great psychological blunder at this point by issuing posters announcing their arrival, describing them as 'three exceptionally dangerous bandits' and calling on the local population to join in the search for them. The posters proved counter-productive for, as Professor Jozef Garlinski records,

> The effectiveness of the grapevine was such that from the moment these posters appeared the whole of German-occupied Poland knew that the men in question were members of the underground army ... Polish hearts beat faster and hopes rose higher – the Western Allies were at last making their presence felt.

Dalton was elated. Here, at last, was the first liaison with occupied Poland and its resistance organization on which so many of his hopes were pinned. Here, too, was a tangible recognition of Poland's effort which, on the very morning of the flight, Sikorski had complained to him was not being fully recognized by the British government. It appears that Dalton, perhaps with the politician's eternal dream of quick and easy results, and the Poles failed to appreciate both the enormous difficulties of the air operation, and the absolute impossibility of supplying the Polish resistance with sufficient arms and equipment by air from British bases. Dalton's optimism was infectious and in both London and Warsaw planning started for massive air support for the Polish underground army which would lead to the launching of a full-scale airborne operation when the time came for an open revolt against the Nazis. His biographers record that Gubbins took a more realistic view of the situation but 'he nevertheless could not afford at this stage to discourage the Poles from planning operations on the greatest scale'.

As things turned out, the next successful flight to Poland did not take place for many months, indeed not long before Dalton had departed to the Board of Trade. 'Dr Dynamo', as some of his more sycophantic officials called him, was reluctant to sever his SOE ties when Churchill telephoned him on 21 February 1942 with the offer of promotion to President of the Board of Trade. 'Handing over SOE twangs my heart strings', he wrote in his diary the following day, 'and I shall feel very desolate and unfriended if I lose the daily presence of those who have been for 21 months my trusted inner circle.'

Dalton's new post meant that he now dealt exclusively with home front issues, but he nevertheless retained a great interest in Polish affairs, meeting regularly with members of the government-in-exile especially Retinger. He proudly recorded in his diary on 2 August 1944, 'I am regarded by the Poles as their best friend in England ... my name is known and loved throughout their Underground.' Despite this, on the vexed question of Polish-Soviet relations which bedevilled the alliance against Hitler, Dalton took a pragmatic approach.

Hugh Dalton went on to become Chancellor of the Exchequer in the 1945 Labour Government although he had hoped to become Foreign Secretary, the post that went to Ernest Bevin. He retired from active politics in 1958, was created a life peer in 1960 and died two years later on 13 February 1962. In his memoirs he had looked back on his pre-war visit to Poland and recalled, 'I could not know how close was to be my future relationship with many Poles at critical hours in the life of our two peoples.'

Notes

1 The bulk of SOE's Polish files are to be found under HS 4 in the National Archives and details are given in Louise Atherton, *SOE in Eastern Europe. An Introduction to the Newly Released Records of the Special Operations Executive in Czechoslovakia, Hungary, Poland and Russia*, Kew: PRO, 1995.

6

SOE AND MILORG

'Thieves on the same market'[1]

Ivar Kraglund

When Norway was occupied the king and government established themselves in Great Britain along with numerous other toppled regimes. There were, however, important differences between the Norwegians and other exiles. The Norwegian government was very strong both constitutionally and economically – it was even able to pay for itself. The question soon arose how best to participate in the struggle for freedom. This chapter will concentrate on the relationship between the Norwegians and one of the secret agencies involved with resistance and arguably the most active and prominent, the Special Operations Executive. I will also use one particular SOE mission, 'Anvil', as a generic example of the numerous problems experienced through this long-lasting relationship.

Milorg

For the benefit of some readers I will say a few introductory words about Norwegian resistance. It is quite common to divide the resistance into a civilian and a military side. We shall naturally concentrate on the latter. The organization later known as the Milorg (military organisation) grew right out of the defeat in 1940. These resistance pioneers came from many different parts of society. Officers maintained the military tradition, and the first organization followed the principles of the old army, dividing the country into five districts. In 1942 this was changed and a complete revision of the structure implemented. The country was split in some 14 districts and this later rose to 23 as a number of the originals were split. At the liberation this 'Secret Army' numbered about 40,000 trained 'soldiers' who were equipped largely thanks to the SOE.

ANCC

When the Anglo-Norwegian Collaboration Committee (ANCC) had its first meeting on 16 February 1942 it was to be the formal start of a process aimed at achieving a smooth and effective relationship between Norwegian and British authorities, both on the civilian and military side. The need for such a body had been clearly proven through numerous episodes both in Britain and in occupied Norway where several 'thieves' operated on the same 'market' to organize and execute resistance activities of various kinds. It was mainly a question of liaison between SOE and the Norwegian authorities. The former was represented by Sir Charles Hambro and Colonel John Skinner Wilson and the latter by Leif Tronstad and Thore Boye from the Norwegian High Command and the Forsvarets Overkommando IV (the branch of the military concerned with resistance).

What kind of resistance?

A major concern for the ANCC was to agree upon and lay down the *principles* for resistance in Norway, to establish a *joint policy* for the work and develop *trust* between the different actors in the play. There was some way to go and the creation of the ANCC was only the start of this process. Serious trouble between the allies followed as a result of British raids in Norway, in particular the 'Anklet'/'Archery' operations.

Before we continue, we must briefly mention that SOE was not the *only* British organization to carry out clandestine operations in Norway. The Secret Intelligence Service (SIS) established throughout the period a widespread network involving numerous Norwegian agents. Other British bodies were also active during the first years, such as the Directorate of Combined Operations (DCO) and the predecessors of SOE, Section D and MI(R). Nevertheless, for all practical purposes, SOE became *the* organization responsible for operations in Norway.

1942 is described as the 'great year' in Norwegian resistance. This is generally correct but it was also the year of serious setbacks. These were largely the consequence of SOE activity. One can argue that any action involves a certain risk and no risk means no progress. This is not quite enough to give absolution to SOE in this period. Anyway, the ANCC spent most of 1942 trying to synchronize the policies of SOE and Norwegian resistance. The result was eventually a good one. It has been written that as a partner in a greater alliance, Norway had to undergo a trial period.[2] By 1943 this was over and Norway emerged completely integrated in the alliance.

For Milorg the prevailing policy was to rebuild and reinforce the organization, especially considering the numerous setbacks of 1941. Further, the intention was to create an organization ready to be activated during an Allied invasion of Norway. Such an invasion would have to be a major one and encompass most of the country and not a limited attack on a limited part of Norway. It was not the policy of Milorg to embark on an offensive embracing sabotage and other related activities at this stage. This was not just theory but a realistic assessment of Milorg's capabilities at the time.

The policy advocated by the Norwegians was not exactly music to the ears of SOE. The active stance was, from the very start, more or less the organization's trademark and their *raison d'être*. The enemy was to be constantly put under pressure in the occupied countries. Through various measures the cost of occupation should be raised, and the Germans should be forced to keep large forces to control the occupied areas. At the same time the resistance organizations were to be consolidated. The resistance had to be armed and trained to be able to assist the Allied invasion forces effectively at the right moment.

The views referred to above were not simply *the* Norwegian and *the* British ones. Norwegian military sources in the High Command's office for resistance matters, the FO IV, supported both views. 'The Milorg view' was maintained by Captain Jens Schive; operations were not to be launched during the build-up period and Milorg was only to be activated in connection with a major Allied invasion of Norway. This judgement did not represent a *total* ban on all offensive activity but, as a general rule, such operations were to be avoided.

The opposite views were expressed by Professor Leif Tronstad who did not feel comfortable sitting on the fence in a world conflict; it was necessary for Norway to play a part and also to be willing to sacrifice something in the struggle. According to Tronstad, it was not morally right to expect liberation to come without substantial Norwegian participation in its prelude.

Tronstad's thoughts corresponded largely with those of SOE and the British. Another complication was the desire of the Norwegian government both to influence and be informed of military activities on Norwegian territory. The previous year had indeed been troublesome regarding this. The three British raids carried out against northern and western Norway were planned and implemented almost without Norwegian political participation and, to make things even worse, included the use of Norwegian personnel. Arguments about their military value did not ease the tension, but pointed out the necessity of a closer cooperation between the British and Norwegians.

A close shave – 'Anvil' first phase

On 29 January 1942 the following instructions were issued for Operation 'Anvil': 'Object: To establish W/T and Organised Guerrilla Groups in Lillehammer'.[3] These seemingly uncomplicated instructions were to be a serious setback in Anglo-Norwegian relations. I will try to tell the details of this operation in its first phase and comment on the difficulties. I will further sketch the consequences and the experiences gained from this and other SOE operations in the period.

'Anvil', whose real name was Jon Gunleiksrud, was to leave London on the last day of January for Shetland and sail to Norway between the 2nd and 3rd February 1942. His estimated arrival in Norway was scheduled for the night of 4th/5th at Silda Island on the North-west coast, some 100 miles south of Ålesund. The reason for landing there was that members of the crew came from that place, and a transport route was established to channel the agents northwards to Ålesund and beyond. Gunleiksrud was to carry the identity card and border zone card of 'Jens Thorsen' issued in Oslo and Bergen respectively. He was also to bring with him a fair number of weapons and supplies as well as 22,000 Norwegian crowns and 1,000 Swedish crowns. After a short delay the fishing smack *Siglaos* left the Shetland base at Scalloway on 5 February at 1600 hours. The next day Gunleiksrud landed safely at 2330 on Silda. From then on very little went according to plan.

The crew of the *Siglaos* were to introduce the agent to a Rasmus Silden and, together, they were to hatch a plan for the concealment of an arms dump at or near the landing place at Silda. This dump was intended as a reserve for the 'Anvil' organization to be drawn upon at a later stage. Only 'Anvil' himself and the keeper of the cache were to know the location of the dump and the password to gain access to it. The password was 'Maskinsolar' – 'Engine-fuel'. Gunleiksrud's orders also said that he should inform his contact (Rasmus Silden) that a W/T operator was to arrive a few weeks later by boat bringing a transmitter which was to be the main contact for the forthcoming organization.

In the beginning of 1942 the situation in the area was a very tense one. One of the most dangerous Norwegian Gestapo agents, Henry Rinnan was working in the Ålesund district with severe results for the resistance in the area. It was into this hot spot that 'Anvil' had landed and through which he was to proceed to the Lillehammer area without raising the suspicions of either the Gestapo or the local resistance. It soon became clear that the situation was difficult and 'Anvil' found it necessary to get rid of his papers, which were burnt. After his landing he established contact with a member of the local police force who was able to house him during the first period. It is somewhat unclear whether this contact was part of the original plan. The SOE papers say that 'Anvil' was to stay at the landing site until a messenger turned up to guide him to Lillehammer. This messenger was first to approach Rasmus Silden with the message 'Do you know my Uncle Myckelbust?' and Silden was to answer 'Yes, I know his daughter Sarah'. The result of this conversation was to be that the messenger should ask to be introduced to Jens Thorsen and, after further checkouts, by Silden the messenger was to meet 'Anvil'.

The policeman who was hiding 'Anvil' introduced him to a local teacher, Kåre Viken, knowing he was from Lillehammer. Viken furnished 'Anvil' with an introductory note to his brother-in-law, Sigmund Kleiven, in Lillehammer. Gunleiksrud left the Ålesund area for Lillehammer and went straight to Viken's brother-in-law. The day after his arrival there, Kåre Viken was arrested and this fact was reported to the resistance network in Lillehammer and to Kleiven. Simultaneously, the central leadership of Milorg issued a warning against an informer, Finn Kaas. It so happened that Gunleiksrud looked a bit like the notorious Gestapo informer. When the SOE man appeared, suspicions were raised about his identity. We must at this stage bear in mind that 'Anvil's' instructions clearly prohibited any contact with the local Milorg and he was also forbidden to disclose his real identity. He was taken by the resistance to the local hospital and placed in isolation until his identity was verified. Unfortunately, he acted in accordance with his British orders and was very reluctant to cooperate. With the aforementioned informer in mind, Milorg gave very serious consideration to liquidating the SOE agent. Luckily it did not go quite that far. In the meantime the local resistance tried to check his real identity.

After eight days of interrogations the increasingly impatient Gunleiksrud told his 'captors' he had a brother in Oslo, and a courier was despatched to verify this. When the courier appeared in the home of the alleged brother he noticed a portrait of Gunleiksrud on a shelf. When asked about the picture he was given the answer that he was in Britain. 'No, he's not' replied the courier. 'He's in Lillehammer, and you are requested to positively identify him there.' When his brother entered the room at the hospital 'Anvil' rose in bed and called out his brother's name. Feeling betrayed, he approached the courier, accusing him of breaking a promise of not involving his family. The reply was that it had been absolutely necessary. Indeed it was. The resistance was on the brink of liquidating 'Anvil' if the confrontation had proved unsuccessful. The doctor carried a lethal syringe for that purpose and the courier had a concealed weapon.

Thus a very dramatic situation came to a close. The main problem, however, remained. 'Anvil's' instructions were unsuitable and very poorly adjusted to realities in occupied Norway and in particular in a district with a scattered population and fairly transparent social networks. 'Anvil' was released from hospital and entered talks with the local resistance leadership concerning his future tasks in the district. The central leadership of Milorg sent their 'inspector' for the area, Helge Motzfeldt, to Lillehammer, and he met Gunleiksrud on several occasions. Simultaneously, a prominent representative from the Norwegian High Command, Jacob Schive, was in Norway to clear up the situation between FO and the central leadership. 'Anvil' was taken to Schive and after some time persuaded to cancel his instructions to organize independent groups. Instead he was invited to train the *existing* groups in the area. Schive promised to explain the change of plans to SOE when he returned to London. The decision was a fortunate one for the resistance movement. Gunleiksrud proved very efficient and served numerous groups covering a wide area. In mid-July he crossed into Sweden and was rapidly transferred to Britain. He was later parachuted back into Norway to resume his work in the area.

The 'Anvil' team's W/T operator, Finn Bjørn Johnsen appeared in Norway in late March. Having established contact with Rasmus Silden, like his predecessor, he quickly made his way to Lillehammer. On 27 April, exactly one month after leaving Shetland, the first message was received in the United Kingdom from the new station. Johnsen became one of the most successful W/T operators in Norway staying on the air under different signatures, and from various places for more than three years until liberation in May 1945.

One may also chose to view the 'Anvil' operation as symbolizing the relationship between Milorg and SOE. The initial difficulties which almost led to the death of the agent were gradually overcome and the final result was trust and mutual benefit.

Two reports

The 'Anvil' operation is only one example of the effects of a different attitude and policy regarding the resistance work. We have already stated that SOE wanted a more offensive line in Norway. We shall return to 1941 to examine important guidelines for later development that were laid down in the course of that year. The central leadership of Milorg was not quite ready for this, and the previous year a message arrived in Britain saying that the resistance did not want any weapons at present.[4] This rather strange attitude was explained by saying that the organization preferred a silent, consolidating period and any weapons should be received simultaneously or immediately prior to an Allied invasion. Sabotage in any form was strictly to be avoided. The Norwegian resistance leadership was concerned not to evoke reprisals from the Germans. Premature attempts at mobilizing Norwegian youth for military purposes would only be catastrophic in a struggle against overwhelming German forces. It was also maintained that the leadership had so far acted as a self-appointed body without any formal acknowledgement from the Government.[5] Norwegian resistance was still quite young, and it may be seen as understandable that its capabilities and aspirations were limited in an initial phase. This cautious attitude was of course not acceptable for British authorities including SOE.[6]

The SOE answer opened in a very accommodating tone:

> On the whole the plan put forward by the Military Organisation in the Report under reply is extremely satisfactory, and too much stress cannot be laid upon the importance of this work and the desire of the Norwegian authorities outside Norway and of the British authorities working through and with them to assist in its development.

The report continued along a more critical line, although it was partially 'giftwrapped'. It pointed out the unrealistic approach to the question of arming the resistance. To expect a massive supply shortly before an invasion was definitely not possible and wishful thinking. Any resistance organisation would obviously need an extensive period of weapon training.

> Any large-scale attempt to bring in arms just before the day when it is ordered to use them would not only be certain to result in a large part of the forces involved being without arms and equipment at the critical time, but would also be likely to jeopardise the success of the entire plan because it would be impossible to transport in a short period and even with unlimited aircraft the arms required without the operation being detected.

Consequently, Milorg had to adopt a much more realistic attitude towards this type of warfare.

> The plan which must be adopted is to send samples of arms concerned to Norway in the near future in sufficient quantity for training purposes. Thereafter every attempt will be made to create dumps by landing arms from the sea and by dropping arms and supplies from the air, and we must look to the Secret Organisation to spread these arms throughout the country to the points where they must be stored until they are needed. It

is particularly important that no impression should be held that when the Norwegian people are called to arms an unlimited number of aircraft will be available for distribution of supplies. This may by no means be the case, as air transport will be needed in many places by the regular forces.

SOE reminded the Norwegians that, unlike many other countries, major operations were about to be executed in the foreseeable future. These were plans to precede a final Allied invasion. Because of this, Milorg had to prepare for action on very short notice, at least in certain parts of the country like Northern Norway. What SOE perhaps did not take into account was the paucity of the population in that part of the country. SOE stated:

> It is noted that the Military Organisation does not seek to have connection with Northern Norway, but it is doubtful whether this is the right policy. At the present time there is little if any Military Organisation north of Trondheim, and it is particularly unfortunate as the point at which Norway is most vulnerable and the enemy weakest is the Northern area.

The question is whether SOE in its evaluation neglected the massive build up of German forces in the north for the warfare against the Soviet Union. In many communities in the north-east there were at least seven Germans to each Norwegian. This somewhat deplorable situation tended to affect the possibilities of a potential resistance.

Milorg's opinion on sabotage was also rejected. The importance of tying up large German forces by sabotage was regarded as a necessary part of the work.

> The question of acts of sabotage during the waiting period requires careful study. It is entirely agreed that such acts must be vigorously controlled and that indiscriminate or ill-planned sabotage can do nothing but harm because of the reprisals which are bound to follow and the consequent effect on morale. On the other hand it is important to cause the Germans in Norway as much trouble as possible and to force them to keep large garrisons there, and properly planned sabotage can be most effective in these respects. Sabotage of the right type, if skilfully performed, can do great damage and at the same time give the appearance of genuine accident, and it is suggested that plans should be prepared for this type of sabotage to be carried out either by special sabotage groups in Norway or by gangs sent in from the United Kingdom to do a specific job and then escape out of the country.

The question of who was to carry out the sabotage was also spelled out in the document and the answer was not in accordance with Milorg's lines. It can, of course, be argued that the latter generally rejected sabotage at this stage but SOE stated that:

The local sabotage groups should be recruited quite separately from the Secret Army and no member of a sabotage group should ever be connected with or have any particular knowledge of the Secret Army. It will generally be found that the ideal group will consist of seven men of whom one is both instructor and leader.

These principles may have been theoretically sound and even proven feasible under other conditions. In Norway, they proved to be somewhat impractical. The 'Anvil' story is just one example to illustrate this.

It is fully realised that the large organisation which is being so successfully created in Southern Norway must have a governing body, but it is necessary to make it quite plain that His Majesty King Haakon cannot recognise such a body as a Government. He is only prepared to recognise the properly constituted Norwegian Government appointed by constitutional means which serves him at present and which is now in the United Kingdom. Further, it must be clearly understood that it will not be for any governing body in Norway to decide when the military machine now being created is to function. This can only be done by the Officers in Command of the Norwegian Forces in the United Kingdom acting in conjunction with and under the direction of the British General Staff. It must be remembered that any military operations by the Secret Army are bound to fail unless they are coordinated with arrangements for the landing of Norwegian and British troops from outside the country and probably also with simultaneous risings all over occupied Europe by the Secret Armies of every territory dominated by the Germans. Premature or uncoordinated rising can only lead to disaster and must be avoided at all costs.

Despite its rather friendly introduction, it was clear that SOE watched Milorg's present policy and activity with grave displeasure. SOE was certainly *not* the organization for peaceful and slow development. It is, however, worth remembering that the summer of 1941 was not exactly the turning point of the war and the signals from SOE may at that time have been regarded as somewhat premature. Still, it was not the task of SOE to present a defensive strategy for clandestine warfare.

I have quoted quite extensively from this SOE response because it is undoubtedly very important. It laid down a number of principles for the clandestine warfare that gradually became reality. It is, however, not a 100 per cent SOE piece of work. The exact process is not fully clear but John Rognes is known to have participated in the work. He felt strongly that the June report from the Council gave a somewhat incorrect picture. The SOE proposal was presented to the new Norwegian Foreign Minister, Trygve Lie, before it was sent back to Norway. What SOE identified and shed light upon was the disagreement concerning the resistance policy amongst its members. The most fundamental question was, of course, whether one should carry on the 'lie low and wait for the day' policy or adopt an activist line hitherto unknown in Norway except for the communist resistance. The policy of the latter corresponded in some ways with that of the British, only without any governmental backing. For Milorg, the communist line was of growing concern as the rank and file were attracted by their activity.

As a whole, the SOE proposal became a catalyst to the problems facing the Norwegian resistance. It did not *solve* any, but was instrumental in putting them on the agenda.

As previously mentioned, several Norwegians also rejected the views held by the Council. As late as October 1941 Schive explained that Milorg wanted to thoroughly discuss these matters throughout the organization.[7] The resistance establishment was not yet fully apprised of the realities of warfare. Active combat against the invaders was not widely accepted. Despite this, SOE still wanted to escalate the warfare in occupied Norway. The problem was that such a policy only could effectively be pursued in cooperation with local groups.

From large scale raids to smaller operations

1941 was the year of British raids on different parts of the Norwegian coastline. The Lofoten Isles were struck twice with Operation 'Claymore' in March and Operation 'Anklet' in December. Both times there was Norwegian participation organized through SOE although this had not been fully discussed with the Norwegian Government. A later raid, 'Archery', included an attack on Måløy on the island of Vågsøy and resulted in the unfortunate loss of Captain Martin Linge, the leader of the SOE unit, Norwegian Independent Company No. 1 (NORIC). His death triggered a crisis in the relations between Britain and Norway and subsequently gave birth to the ANCC. A few words must be added regarding NORIC. This unit *was* more or less SOE in Norway. The British understood from the beginning that any activity in occupied Norway must rely heavily on local participation. With this in mind, SOE recruited Norwegians in Britain from day one. This was of considerable concern for the Norwegian political and military authorities as they were eager to maintain control over Norwegian citizens in Britain. After all, Norwegian forces were being established in that country with the purpose of being able to participate in the future invasion and liberation of Norway. NORIC (which later, informally, was labelled the 'Linge Company') posed a threat to the principle of Norwegian control of their own forces. The discussions and problems related to NORIC are described in various places and shall not be scrutinized here.

By the beginning of 1942, the large-scale raids of the previous year were mainly discarded. SOE did not, however, give up Norway as an arena for offensive operations. A major question was the proposed 'Second Front'. Plans were made to cut Norway in two and the resistance was instructed to prepare for this. Particularly in mid-Norway and on the south coast the activity was escalated. The

Allies had already decided to opt for North Africa but wanted, of course, to tie down the German forces in Norway by indicating operations against this territory. The ANCC did little to discourage several SOE missions against selected targets especially in the last half of the year. It was nevertheless an operation in the spring that had the gravest effects on the Norwegian population. A fishing smack *Olaf* landed operations 'Penguin' and 'Anchor' in Telavaag outside Bergen. The two agents were discovered by the Gestapo and, in a subsequent gunfight, two Germans were killed. The result was the destruction of a whole small community and numerous executions including the SOE agents. The remaining population was deported, and Telavaag became for Norway what Lidice is in Czech history.

Once again voices called for closer cooperation with SOE. In the autumn the operations 'Kestrel' and 'Knotgrass-Unicorn' struck industrial targets in Trøndelag and Nordland. These were combined operations with a mixture of British and Norwegian participants. Once again German reactions were very uncompromising, although the Gestapo was not directly involved. German fears of an invasion in the region may have played an important part. A state of emergency was imposed in the Trondheim area on 6 October, and, after three days, 34 hostages had been executed by the Germans. These measures paralysed the organized resistance in the region for almost two years. Combined with the difficulties created by the highly effective gang of Norwegian informers led by Henry Rinnan, the results were devastating.

Another attempt by SOE to organize their own groups was the activity of 'Cheese' and 'Biscuit', Odd Starheim and Andreas Fasting. They were the first agents to be parachuted into occupied Norway on 2 January 1942. Their goal was to organize resistance in the southernmost part of the country. Starheim worked in parallel with a branch of Milorg, headed by Major Arne Laudal. Gradually the two organizations merged. Their plans were based upon the assumption that the invasion of Norway was at hand, and this short-term perspective influenced their work. British signals strongly pointed in that direction. But through various means the Gestapo closed in and finally struck in the beginning of December the same year. Laudal was arrested and was finally executed in May 1944. Starheim himself nearly made it but died when he tried to assist Operation 'Carhampton' the seizing of merchant vessels. Seventeen men took control of the *Tromøsund* but it was spotted by a German plane and sunk. Starheim's body was later washed ashore.

'Cheese' operated in improving cooperation with Milorg but it was clear that resistance still had to be carried out in the light of local conditions. Forcing the pace of the build up of activity in certain regions proved disastrous. These lessons were learned by SOE and from 1943 onwards the operations were, as a whole, more adopted to the prevailing situation. Added to this was the increased stiffening of local resistance and the people's reaction to resistance in general. A more thorough understanding of the necessities of war spread out through the resistance networks.

In late 1942 another operation with tragic consequences was attempted by SOE. It was decided to destroy the heavy water facilities at Vemork in Telemark. After discussions in which the Norwegian authorities were involved, a daring plan was hatched involving both Norwegian SOE personnel and British soldiers. An advance party of Norwegians, 'Grouse', was to receive two gliders carrying 34 volunteers from the Royal Engineers, 'Freshman'. This particular operation is, to put it mildly, well known and there is no need to elaborate on it here. The result was 41 British personnel killed when the Horsa gliders and one Halifax towing aircraft crashed. The Gestapo murdered the survivors, some only a few days after their capture, and the rest in January 1943. The follow-up 'Swallow/Gunnerside' team success-fully destroyed the target in late February the same year. Although this was mainly an SOE operation it was carried out in close cooperation with the Norwegians and also involved the local resistance network to some extent. This was to become the established rule.

Numerous groups of NORIC personnel were sent home to Norway with orders to work with Milorg. A very fruitful cooperation developed and 'UK-guys' proved invaluable in training and leading Milorg networks in Southern Norway. In a way this was very close to what had been suggested in the July 1941 reply, only now the mutual trust had been fully established. Milorg itself was eager to take up a more active role as security, experience and capabilities grew. The early 1941 idea of 'no weapons please' was discarded in favour of frequent heaven-sent 'gifts' when air operations by Special Duty squadrons delivered containers and parcels by the thousands. Adding to this were considerable supplies brought across the North Sea by the 'Shetland Bus'.

Conclusion

In the history of Norwegian Resistance SOE plays one of the main roles. The relationship was transformed from distrust to close cooperation. This was not only the case between SOE and Milorg but also on a more general level between the two countries. It may be argued that SOE/Milorg relations served as an indicator of this. I have not discussed personal relations in this picture. Certainly a number of appointments on both sides contributed to the success by bringing the right people together. It is tempting to conclude on a joyous note – 'All's well that ends well' – but the struggle was a costly one, and all too many did not live to tell the tale. However, the ties between Norway and Britain were definitely stronger than ever before. A major contributor was the Special Operations Executive.

Notes

1   The title 'Milorg and SOE' was used by Arnfinn Moland in his article for Patrick Salmon (ed.) *Britain and Norway in the Second World War*, London: HMSO, 1995. I have chosen a somewhat different approach and concentrated on SOE.
2   Olav Riste, *Londonregjeringa*, Vol. 1, Oslo: Det norske Samlaget, 1973, p. 220.
3   The following is mainly taken from the SOE archives at Norway's Resistance Museum. These archives are invaluable for the study of SOE activity in Norway and they are accessible observing the normal rules for Norwegian public records. SOE files at the National Archives are to be

found at HS 2 and a detailed outline of them is provided in Louise Atherton, *SOE Operations in Scandinavia. A Guide to the Newly Released Records in the Public Record Office*, London: PRO, 1994.

4 Report by the military 'Council' of the Milorg to HM the King, 10 June 1941, Reidar Omang (ed.), *Regjeringen og Hjemmerfronten under Krigen*, Oslo: Aschenhoug, 1948, pp. 42–4.

5 This situation was rectified on 20 November 1941 when Milorg was 'authorized' by the Government. All military resistance in Norway was to be out under the Milorg command as part of the Norwegian Armed Forces.

6 SOE's answer to the 10 June report is dated 17 July 1941. Omang, *Regjeringen og Hjemmerfronten*, pp. 45–9.

7 Report by Jacob Schive, 28 October 1941.

7

SOE IN THE LOW COUNTRIES

M. R. D. Foot

For a generation after the war, what SOE had done wrong in Holland was a set text in all the world's spy schools: how not to do it. It then turned out that what the Abwehr (working for once in collaboration with the Sicherheitsdienst) had done for 18 months to SOE – collecting *all* their agents as they arrived, nearly 50 of them – had been done by MI5 against the Abwehr, on a still grosser scale, all through the war. Every single agent the Germans sent to wartime England, bar one, was captured; most agreed to change sides; those who did not were tried and hanged. The one exception committed suicide before he started work. Masterman's matchless account of exactly how this sort of thing is done emphasizes the incessant attention that it needs at the deceiving end.[1] Technically the German achievement was remarkable; MI5's success even more so.

How had the Germans managed to do so well in Holland? Accepting the world-wide myth of the infallibility of English secret services, many Dutch now take for granted that the agents must have been sacrificed on purpose, to suit a deception plan so deep that the reason for it has never surfaced. The truth is more mundane: the agents were the victims of sound police work on the German side, assisted by Anglo-Dutch incompetence in London.

The Dutch government-in-exile consisted of the queen, the cabinet and those officials who had also managed to get away in a hurry at the moment of catastrophe in May 1940. Active external resistance settled as the responsibility of a marine colonel called de Bruyne who had never himself known occupation, while intelligence came under the queen's personal confidant, Mr van't Sant, a professional police officer.

This was an unlucky decision from SOE's angle. Many eminent Dutchmen got out of Holland, reported to the queen, and offered to go back; she referred them all to van't Sant; who detested the first head of SOE's N Section, R. V. Laming, and therefore mistrusted SOE. Laming, a Dutch-born Englishman, came from a shipbroking family and had long been a diplomat – he rose to commercial counsellor at The Hague; he and van't Sant had taken opposite sides during an espionage case in Rotterdam in 1916 and had never forgiven each other. Van't Sant therefore kept almost all the best Dutchmen away from SOE, which had to make do with whom it could find.

Laming hoped to insert agents by sea; all his attempts to do so failed. He quarrelled with his superiors in SOE, who would not believe him when he assured them that Holland was too densely populated for the sort of activities that SOE then favoured; and went back to diplomacy early in 1942. He was succeeded by a businessman turned diplomat, called Blizard, who had also been on the legation staff in 1940. Under Blizard, troubles began to multiply, and they got worse under his abrasive successor early in 1943, Bingham.

Two agents, young mechanics, had been put in by parachute in September 1941. They took with them several addresses, provided by Laming, of people who might help; none of whom did. They had to sleep somewhere; so they broke a rule instilled during training, and went to stay with the uncle of one of them at a small tobacconist's in The Hague: a man called Martens.

One was arrested soon after; the other took a canoe for England, and never appeared – presumed drowned, possibly a prisoner. Two more agents went in, also by parachute, in November 1941: Taconis and Lauwers. Taconis was a half-Indonesian graduate student from Leyden; Lauwers, the wireless operator, had been working for years in the rubber trade in the Far East, and had come back from Manila to volunteer to serve.

The arrested agent, Homburg, though sentenced to death (without trial), did a classic escape, and managed to stow away on an Ijmuiden trawler of which he persuaded the captain to sail to England. He had laid on a code word with Martens the tobacconist, and had a mass of intelligence to report.

Lauwers could not make his set work till early 1942 (it had a wiring fault), but by late February was often on the air to Home Station; until he was caught by direction-finders in The Hague on 6 March 1942.

A few days before Lauwers was caught, Taconis made a slip: only a small slip, but one in this game is more than enough. He confided to a friend that he needed a lorry, to get some stores away from a parachute drop. The friend introduced him to a friend named Ridderhof who owned a lorry, who was a paid-up double agent working for the Abwehr. The Abwehr planted a fragment of naval intelligence on Taconis, which they reckoned he was certain to pass on to London.

On being arrested, Lauwers maintained a stolid silence while an Orpo officer worked away, at a side table, on the three coded messages Lauwers had had in his pocket at the moment of arrest – another small slip with awful results. After 20 minutes this officer remarked, 'Ah, I see the *Prinz Eugen* is in Schiedam' – the planted nugget of false intelligence. Lauwers, who had recently encoded a telegram to just this effect, supposed his code broken on sight: which it had not been – the German was bluffing. But the bluff worked: Lauwers at once admitted that he was a parachuted wireless operator, and moreover at once gave away his code.

He kept quiet about his security checks, which he never used again; but they were infantile checks, of no real use. N Section, like F Section, paid no attention to them, anyhow. After a few days' pause, Lauwers consented to send his messages after all and resumed what London thought to be normal traffic. He was induced to do this by a promise from Giskes, of the Abwehr, that his and Taconis's lives would be spared if he did so (Taconis had been pulled in as well): a promise that went the way of most Nazi promises in the end, but meanwhile worked.

Before long, Lauwers sent a message, answering one from London, that gave a new dropping zone; onto which another agent was dropped; who, on being received by his enemies, talked, only too volubly. The Germans rapidly built up a mass of information about N Section's training schools, staff and training methods; and used it to bedazzle each fresh arrival. By the time they could describe the colour of the walls in the classrooms at Beaulieu, it was hard to believe that they did not know everything.

Giskes and Schreieder, his SD opposite number, took a relaxed, informal attitude with each new captive, assuring them that this style of reception was habitual, because they had a friend in London who kept them informed. The friend in London was notional but the emotional shock to each newly arrested agent was severe. It contrasted so sharply with what he had been led to expect, at Beaulieu, about the behaviour of the Gestapo that it answered German purposes well.

N was not fool enough to send all his agents through a single channel: he sent two more pairs, and two singletons, to Holland separately in spring 1942, one singleton came by sea (the only insertion by sea) and the rest by parachute. Unperceived by him, the Germans managed to weld all but one of these parties together. One singleton came back, over a year later, having achieved nothing ('not a resourceful agent' was London's comment); the rest appeared to be busy.

The Germans amalgamated the parties by deft police work. London told Taconis, through Lauwers, to go to 'the tobacconist in The Hague' to meet one of the agents who had come separately. Schreieder, chatting to Taconis in his cell about this and that, threw in a chance question about whether he knew of a tobacconist at The Hague; got the name of Martens; looked up the address in the telephone book; and sent another double agent round, who found Andringa the agent, sitting at the back of the shop; and, through indiscretions by him and his friends, collected all but one of the rest.

Thereafter, at the insistence of the London Dutch, N continued to send agents in to reception committees, never realizing that all of these were supplied by the Germans and their double agents, until November 1943 when two extra enterprising captured agents, Ubbink and Dourlein,[2] who had managed to escape from the seminary near Tilburg where they were all kept prisoner, turned up in Switzerland.

For six months past, there had been no more drops to Holland, not because N had spotted that anything had gone wrong but because the RAF resented the high casualties – one aircraft in every six sent – that they encountered there. The ban on flights to Holland continued until the spring of 1944; and when they restarted, it was too late to get much done to arm a Dutch resistance that might have proved itself more formidable than it did.

The captured agents, meanwhile, had been packed off to Germany, where in the end most of them were butchered in Mauthausen concentration camp in early September 1944, as part of the panic that followed the fall of Brussels. The tireless

Simon Wiesenthal eventually tracked down the NCO who had organized this massacre and got him arraigned in front of an Austrian court, which acquitted him.

The case of Belgium was parallel to that of Holland; not quite so black, but by no means spotless. The Belgian government-in-exile took much longer to get going than the Dutch; only two ministers were in London in the earliest stages, and one of them was disavowed by his colleagues. The prime and foreign ministers did not turn up until late October and, notoriously, the king stayed behind to share his people's sufferings instead of continuing the fight.

The truth seems to have been that the government-in-exile had severe doubts about whether the Allies were going to win the war, until the war's main tide changed in the winter of 1942–43. A series of more or less sharp quarrels between it and SOE resulted in August 1942 in a complete, though temporary, break in relations; repaired before Christmas. Some of these quarrels were personal, some institutional.

The first head of T Section, which was to look after Belgium, was Eric Dadson, former manager of the Antwerp gas works. He fell out with SOE's security authorities, and resigned, to spend most of the rest of the war in the Political Warfare Executive (PWE). He was succeeded by Claude Knight, then a young major in the Coldstream Guards with beautiful manners who knew no more of clandestine war than Dadson did. In mid-1943 Knight was discarded, also to PWE, to appease the Belgians, who mistrusted him. The Section was taken over, provisionally at first, by Hardy Amies the couturier who always felt himself a fish out of water in a secret service, but at least knew something of what he was up against: he had worked for some years in Nazi Germany. Amies's chief assistant, Ivor Dobson, succeeded Bingham as head of N early in 1944.

Dadson and Knight were both bamboozled by their German opposite numbers; Amies was cannier and more successful, perhaps because he was less self-confident. Again, the German break-ins to SOE's working resulted in part from agents' indiscretions, in part from Baker Street's inattention to detail.

The command structure in London was faulty. The Belgians insisted on their security section knowing everything but SOE long refused to agree this. The security section accordingly took care, according to Knight, to make sure that those of SOE's parties of whom it knew got into trouble. This point was not resolved until late in 1942 but by then, out of more than 50 agents dispatched, hardly any were at work, and all the wireless operators were operating under German control (or, more usually, were being imitated by clerks in the Orpo) – unknown to T. This was before the days of 'fingerprinting', and before Marks had reinvented the one-time pad.

The role of accident, as usual, was predominant. For instance, Tromme, one of the earliest agents to be parachuted in (on 12 May 1941) was dropped, by aircrew error, 20 miles from his drop zone – inside Germany, and, worse, inside a prisoner of war camp. Moreover, the navigator of the Whitley forgot to press the switch that released his container, so he had no wireless set and no change of clothes.

He escaped, and turned up three months later in Brussels where he easily fell into touch with another SOE wireless operator, who found him a set; at which the Germans soon arrested him. Both in Belgium and in Holland, the small-country syndrome worked against adequate security for any secret service's agents: many of these men had trained together, most of them knew each other at least by sight, and if one changed sides, it boded ill for his acquaintances.

Parachute accidents were in those days quite common; T encountered several. An early wireless operator, who had demanded to be shriven on the way to Newmarket airfield, and had to confess to his organizer, a Jesuit priest who had so far kept his clerical identity secret, had a parachute that never opened, and was towed back dead to Newmarket by his Whitley. Armand Campion, who had won a croix de guerre with the Foreign Legion in Norway, broke his ankle badly on landing near Mons in August 1941. He was well looked after locally, recovered and began work but was arrested at his set and proceeded to denounce every single person he had worked with since his arrival, his own sister, brother-in-law and nieces included, except for the *curé* who had found him his original doctor. Knight went on sending messages, even messengers, to Campion for over a year. Campion was killed by an Allied bomb – the same bomb that killed the heroic Baron Greindl of the 'Comet' line – in 1943.

Unhappily, there were several parallel cases – none were quite so black. To relieve the scene, there were also a few undoubted successes: notably, Groupe G, a don's dream come true of how to conduct sabotage efficiently and unobtrusively. Jean Burgers took an excellent degree in electrical engineering in the free university of Brussels in the autumn of 1940. He consulted discreetly with his professors, recruited a few entirely reliable friends and set out, gradually, to discompose the Germans' supplies of electric power in Belgium. He got essential help from André Wendelen, who did three missions into Belgium for SOE by parachute, and had been fully trained in sabotage technique. Wendelen provided technical advice and supplies of explosive and detonators, Burgers and his friends did the work.

They did their best to check German efforts to bleed the Belgian national grid for the benefit of the industries of the Ruhr. Once, in January 1944, by a set of simultaneous cuts, they brought much of Belgian industry to a standstill for a week in which they reckoned they cost German war industry 15,000,000 man-hours of work. This coup brought severe reprisals, which culminated in Burgers's own arrest. The Germans soon murdered him but his security was fine, he said nothing he should not have said, and his young wife and his friends kept the circuit going. Wendelen survived to become a Belgian ambassador after the war.

While they were volunteering for service in SOE, prospective agents in western Europe were warned that they were putting their lives on the line: the odds were then thought to be about evens whether they came back alive or not. In brute fact, half the agents sent into Holland, and a third of those sent into Belgium (and about a quarter of those sent into France) never returned.

'Jedburgh' casualties were much lower but no 'Jedburgh' teams went in before Normandy D-Day, 5/6 June 1944. Half-a-dozen teams who were standing by to go to Belgium never left, because the country was so rapidly overrun. This was one of the fastest advances in modern military history, of which the speed was partly due to the efforts of Belgian resistance on the spot, much assisted by SOE: or so General Horrocks said to the SOE adviser at his elbow, in Brussels, on the evening of 3 September 1944.[3]

The following day, 4 September, was Belgian resistance's proudest: it marked the counter-scorching of Antwerp, which fell into Allied hands all but intact. SOE had a lot to do with this, behind the scenes. The Comte de Liedekerke, who was correctly picked on by Knight as an agent likely to appeal to upper-class circles into Belgium, like Wendelen carried off three missions into Belgium by parachute, and returned safely from each of them overland through France and Spain. On one of these he was sent jointly by SOE and Belgian security to look into the problems of Antwerp. He found on the spot a Belgian army engineer subaltern called Urbain Reniers who had been studying the problem since 1940 and with great good sense, although Reniers belonged to a body of which the Sûreté disapproved, encouraged him to carry on. Reniers worked through the port authorities, who continued to appear to appease the Germans but had in fact by the spring of 1944 changed sides; caught the Germans off balance; and managed to make their efforts to destroy the port ineffectual. He got all the supplies he needed by parachute, arranged through two brothers called Waddington who were SOE radio operators, and who told the intelligence officer of the 23rd Hussars exactly where the German defences were when the Hussars reached the city on the afternoon of 4 September. That no use was made of this port until late November was not SOE's fault.

Four 'Jedburgh' teams went in with the Allied airborne forces on operation 'Market Garden' into Holland on 17 September. One other team, 'Dudley' under Major Brinkgreve, had jumped into Overijssel on 11/12 September, knowing nothing of what was about to come. A single agent, Harvey A. Todd of the United States Infantry, got right through to Arnhem bridge and helped Colonel Frost defend it for several days. He was wounded, taken prisoner, and survived the war. Brinkgreve was less lucky. He was shot dead in a scuffle with an SS man who searched the farm at which he was staying, as late as 5 March 1945.

At Arnhem, some of SOE's earlier troubles came home to roost. One of the worst snags for the troops on the ground was that their wireless sets did not work. The local resistance had, standing by, a secret telephone service in full working order.[4] But SOE's troubles, coming on top of SIS's troubles at Venlo early in the war,[5] had bred such suspicion of Dutch resistance in official military circles that no useful contact between the telephone net and airborne troops was achieved; and the soldiers, who were expected to hold out for two days before Horrocks relieved them, withdrew – or rather, the survivors withdrew – after nine.

Two more 'Jedburgh' teams went into Holland in the closing stages, in the spring of 1945, when the Dutch resistance in the eastern parts of the country did what it could to imitate the Belgians by harassing the retreating Germans and keeping the advancing Allies informed of where they were. They were aided in this task both by the 'Jedburghs' and by SAS and a few N agents; but 'too little, too late' has to be the verdict on SOE's achievement in Holland after the worst troubles with the German security services were wound up.

A word may be allowed in conclusion on the always sensitive business of inter-secret-service relations, and the always interesting one of books. In its early years, SOE had considerable troubles with jealous junior competitors in SIS; nothing more probable considering that the two services were often trying to operate on the same ground with different objects and with SOE's agents attracting the attention of the policemen whom SIS wished to avoid.

As so often, personalities counted for more than formalities. Late in 1943 Philip Johns, formerly SIS's man in Lisbon, was posted to London to take charge of T Section, and moved up in February 1944 to the new post of DR/LC, responsible under Robin Brook for both Holland and Belgium. He knew how to tackle Broadway tactfully and by midsummer was able to report that, at least in his field of work, SOE and SIS were working as parts of a single team: a proper intelligence community had at last been forged.[6]

Johns's own book is admirable alike for its discretion and for what it does reveal; and Giskes's account, now 50 years old (it first appeared in Dutch in 1948), with an appendix by Lauwers, remains a brief classic. There is an enormous work, 27 volumes long, by Louis de Jong in Dutch about the German occupation of the Netherlands, but it has not been translated nor was the author able to produce the abbreviation that he once contemplated. His brief lectures on *The Netherlands and Nazi Germany* have to stand in instead, for English readers. On the Dutch background, Herman Friedhoff's *Requiem for the Resistance* is evocative, and Anna Simoni's bibliography of secret literature is telling; while Henri van der Zee's *Hunger Winter* reminds us of the 16,000 who died of starvation in one of the most fertile spots in Europe. But these are some way away from SOE.

On the Belgian secret front there is nothing recommendable in English except Doneux's vivid autobiography. In French, the summary by Henri Bernard in *La Résistance 1940–1945* is excellent, and he has also edited a valuable work in French on *L'Armée Secrète*, the most important indigenous underground movement, which worked closely with SOE. There are also two volumes of the *Revue du Nord*, edited by Etienne Dejonghe, which cover the occupation system of Nazi Germany in Belgium and the two French *départements* which came under the same military headquarters in Brussels: reconstituted from that body which became world-infamous in 1915 for shooting Edith Cavell.[7] I make no apology for ending with a reminder of what passed in early twentieth-century Germany for justice.

Notes

1   J. C. Masterman, *The Double-Cross System in the War of 1939 to 1945*, New Haven: Yale University Press 1972, *passim*.
2   See Pieter Dourlein (tr. F. G. Renier and Anne Cliff), *Inside North Pole*, London: Kimber, 1953.

3 Georges de Lovinfosse, *Au Service de Leurs Majestés*, Strombeek-Bever: Byblos, 1974, 2 edn, p. 188.
4 Conversation with Mijnheer Deuss, who ran it, in Paris, 5 June 1984.
5 See Callum Macdonald, 'The Venlo Incident', in *European Studies Review*, viii, pp. 445–64 (October 1978) for how deep the War Cabinet sank in this pool of German deception.
6 Cp Christopher Andrew, *Secret Service* London: Heinemann 1985, *passim*. The rest of this article depends on SOE's operational and personal files for the Low Countries; the former of which have now been released to The National Archives, under the call sign HS. Detailed references appear in my official history of the subject, M. R. D. Foot, *SOE in the Low Countries*, London: St Ermin's Press, 2001.
7 Philip Johns, *Within Two Cloaks*, London: Kimber, 1979; H. J. Giskes, *London Calling North Pole*, London: Kimber, 1953; Louis de Jong, *Het Koninkrijk der Nederlanden in de tweede Wereldoorlog*, The Hague: SdU, 1969–96, (14 vols in 27 parts); the same, *The Netherlands and Nazi Germany*, Cambridge, MA: Harvard University Press, 1990; Herman Friedhoff, *Requiem for the Resistance*, London: Bloomsbury, 1988; Anna Simoni, *Publish and be Free*, London: British Museum, 1975; Henri van der Zee, *The Hunger Winter*, London: Jill Norman & Hobhouse 1982; Jacques Doneux, *They came by Moonlight*, London: Odhams, 1956; Henri Bernard, *La Résistance 1940–1945*, Brussels: La Renaissance du Livre, 1968; Etienne Dejonghe (ed.), *L'occupation en France et en Belgique 1940–1944* (2 vols), Lille: Revue du Nord, 1987–88, conference proceedings reprinted.

8

SOE IN ITALY

Christopher Woods

Consider the history of SOE's activity towards Italy as a drama in two Acts linked by a short, but significant, Entr'acte. Act I is long and slow, much of the action is inconclusive, but some important characters are introduced, whose roles develop more strongly in Act II. In this second act – the time-scale is only half that of Act I, just 20 as against the 40-odd months of the first Act – the action becomes more intensive and builds up to a fine climax at the end. The brief Entr'acte, which spans no more than a few weeks, not only carries some action forward from Act I to Act II but also introduces important new themes.

This chapter is designed not so much to tell the story of SOE's activity in or towards Italy as to identify the distinguishing features of this activity compared with other geographical areas of its work. But since this story itself is less well known than that of SOE's work in other countries, some outline at least will need to be sketched in as a background.[1]

Act I (June 1940–September 1943)

When SOE was formally constituted in July 1940, Britain had been at war with Italy for one month. As an enemy country, Italy was thus for SOE in a similar category to that of Germany. But there were differences. Most importantly, SOE was starting from scratch in Italy, whereas SOE's predecessor organizations, Section D and MI(R), had been set up two or three years earlier, specifically to plan and prepare for the eventuality of war with Germany. SOE did not inherit the benefit of similar preparations for action against Italy. Indeed, the Foreign Office had since war with Germany began prohibited any covert action towards Italy, for fear of jeopardizing the policy of appeasement, which was sustained right up until the last moment in the vain hope of keeping Italy out of the war.

Therefore, SOE had to improvise from the start. The new organization was given a strong, personal stimulus from the top by the minister, Dr. Dalton, fired in part by his experiences in the First World War as a gunner officer in Italy in the winter of 1917/18. His first lieutenant, the Chief Executive Officer, Gladwyn Jebb, also had personal experience of service in Italy, in the pre-war British Embassy in Rome. Dalton, in particular in the first year of his responsibility for SOE, kept spurring it on to urgent action against what was commonly regarded as the weaker Axis partner.

However, Italy was to prove more impervious to subversive action than Dalton, and probably most others, expected. But first there were domestic problems to solve. An organizational framework for action had to be devised and men found to run it; neither was easily or rapidly achieved.

Whereas there already existed in cadre form the makings of a Country Section (X) for work against Germany (with Austria), there was no such Italian cadre latent in Section D or MI(R). It was not until December that SOE managed to recruit and appoint its first official head of the Italian Section (J), and he only lasted a few months before another organization made good a priority claim to his services. Under his successor, Italy was temporarily linked with Greece. It was not until October 1941 that a new Head of Section J was brought in who was to provide continuity through to the end of the war. Under him, Italy was now linked with Switzerland (and for a while Corsica), yet not the whole of Italy, only the northern half, deemed vulnerable to attack from Switzerland. The other half of Italy was judged more accessible for attack from the south.

Thus Italy did not immediately, nor indeed for a long time, become the sole responsibility of one Country Section – unlike, for instance, the Low Countries (Sections N for Holland and T for Belgium) or Scandinavia (S). (France was peculiar in having two main country sections (F and RF) with two more (DF and EU/P) overlapping.) The cause of this dispersal of effort lay in Italy's particular geographical position and configuration (another difference here from Germany), which seemed to lend itself to a bi-polar approach, with attack from the south mounted from SOE bases in the Mediterranean: Cairo, Malta and, later, Algiers. There was an organizational difficulty here in that these bases came under the control at SOE Headquarters of other sections, through which the Italian Section could only exert indirect influence on their work into Italy. This limitation applied especially to the Cairo Mission which, apart from having other more immediate country targets, particularly in South-East Europe, had from the outset cultivated a strong measure of independence from London. In the event, Cairo did not turn out to be a successful launching point for operations into Italy. Nor did Malta.

As the fate of the first Head of J Section has already shown, SOE in its search for personnel with knowledge of Italy and the Italian language had to contend with many competitors: SIS, Bletchley Park, the propaganda department and the BBC and the Services Intelligence Directorates among others. The field of available talent proved limited, nor had SOE in the summer of 1940 first access to it. By October 1941 it had largely been worked out. The new J then recruited, Cecil Roseberry, had no Italian background. But by that time there was in the Section an assistant (JA) who spoke Italian and had lived and worked in Italy for some years. These two were to remain the only members of the Section until summer 1943.

JA was not the only British subject with specialist Italian qualifications whom SOE managed to recruit in its early days. Amongst a few others recruited then, two were to occupy posts in the coming years of particular importance for work into Italy. Jock McCaffery, who joined in August 1940, was a Roman Catholic who had been British Council representative in Genoa, following earlier study for the priesthood in Rome. In February 1941, SOE sent him to Switzerland to be their representative in Berne. There from the start, and indeed up to the end, among his wider responsibilities for work into all the surrounding countries, he devoted most of his abundant enthusiasm and energy to Italy.

The other was Count Julian Dobrski (better known in SOE by the name of Dolbey). Born in Italy of mixed parentage, he had spent most of his early life there and elsewhere on the Continent, doing two years service in the Italian Army, before coming to England in 1928 and taking British nationality shortly before the war. Dolbey was sent to Malta in October 1941 and then on to Cairo, where in June 1942, he was put in charge of the Italian Section in the SOE mission. In September 1943, in the wake of the Italian armistice, he was to be parachuted into Rhodes with George Jellicoe in an attempt to rally the Italian forces there against the Germans. (He, as did Roseberry, ended the war as a Lieutenant-Colonel in SOE; McCaffery, on the other hand, remained a civilian.)

But perhaps in the long run, SOE's most important recruit to its Italian ranks in these early days was Max (Massimo) Salvadori. This anti-Fascist exile, who came from an aristocratic Italian family with British connections (he had a cousin then serving in the Foreign Office in London), held British nationality by virtue of his birth in London. At the outbreak of war with Germany he crossed the Atlantic from America, where he held an academic post, for the purpose of joining the British Army. Rejected by the War Office as too old (31), through contact with Colonel Grand of Section D arising out of earlier work he had done in the anti-Nazi propaganda field, he was taken on by SOE, but after the fall of France he chose to return to the USA until his desire to see active service on the Allied side could be met. In the meantime he continued in the USA and Mexico the work he had already begun briefly in France as a link with politically active Italian anti-Fascist exiles, backing in particular their efforts to counter Fascist subversive activities and to influence the large Italian community in America towards support for the Allied cause. It was through him that the most effective members of this group were later brought into direct contact with SOE and helped to return via the United Kingdom to Italy around the time of the Armistice, there to play important roles in, or in support of, Italian resistance. Salvadori's personal wish to join the British Army was eventually granted in 1943 and he was to serve with SOE (No. 1 Special Force) through the whole of the Italian campaign, ending up as a Lieutenant-Colonel DSO MC.

If these were SOE's major recruitment successes in the early days in building a directing cadre for work on the Italian target, it was much less successful in finding collaborators willing to extend SOE's work into Italy itself. Here, the Italian Section might have expected to enjoy some advantage over the German Section in terms at least of the size of the potential recruitment pool. Yet efforts at recruitment among the large expatriate Italian communities in the United Kingdom and elsewhere, and amongst the many thousands of Italian prisoners of war captured early on in the Libyan and East African campaigns, yielded only meagre results.

However resistant to Fascist indoctrination or even sympathetic to the Allied cause many may have been, few could be found willing to hazard their lives, or those of relatives still in Italy, by playing an active role with SOE in the overthrow of Fascism. An initial trawl, conducted by SOE in the winter of 1940/44, through the thousands of Italian internees in the Isle of Man netted no more than five recruits for training (known as the 'Quins'). Of these only one, a former employee of the Savoy Hotel, went into action, as an interpreter on loan from SOE, on the first British airborne operation of the war, 'Colossus', an attack on an aqueduct in southern Italy. The whole party was captured before they could reach their submarine rendezvous – the Italian was shot. Reported in the British press in April 1941, this was no help to SOE's recruitment campaign.

In the prisoner of war camps the Fascist organization proved strikingly efficient. Later on, with prompting from SOE Cairo, a system of early segregation was introduced, but by then it was too late for most practical purposes. Successive recruitment drives in East Africa, amongst internees as well as prisoners of war, organized by SOE Cairo, yielded a number of recruits for training. But most turned out to be of insufficient calibre for active use, even if SOE Cairo had been able to organize operational employment for them. Not all were failures: three survived, morale intact, to play active parts in Act II.

A perhaps unexpected difficulty often encountered with potential Italian recruits was their sensitivity to the likelihood of being labelled as traitors by their compatriots. A surprising incident which illustrates the grounds for this sensitivity occurred later, in the summer of 1944, when Max Salvadori, wearing the uniform of a British captain, entered his parental home in the Marche to be met by his father with the words 'foreign agent'.

Sensitivities of a similar nature inhibited even active anti-Fascist political exiles. Perhaps the most promising, certainly the most ambitious, project engaged in by J Section in this period, one in which SOE invested much effort at all levels was 'Postbox'. The protagonist was Emilio Lussu, one of the leading political figures in the anti-Fascist movement Giustizia e Liberta, a Sardinian former deputy and First World War military hero (and incidentally married to Max Salvadori's sister). Having made his way with his wife from France across Spain to Portugal, he contacted the SOE mission in Lisbon, with the purpose in the first instance of seeking help to enable other Italian anti-Fascists, who had escaped from France to North Africa, to gain asylum across the Atlantic, assistance which SOE was in a position to offer. While in Lisbon, Lussu put forward an idea to raise, with SOE support, the standard of anti-Fascist revolt in his native Sardinia. SOE arranged for him to visit first Malta and then the United Kingdom for discussion on the feasibility and modalities of SOE support for such a scheme. A trip to the USA was also facilitated to allow him to consult with other leading anti-Fascists there. Meanwhile in the United Kingdom his wife was given a course of training as a radio operator. But in the end, despite persistent SOE efforts, and advocacy at a higher level, the project foundered on Lussu's unshakeable condition that he would only agree to act with SOE support (without which, as indeed it proved, the scheme's prospects were poor) provided the Allies would guarantee the integrity at the conclusion of hostilities of Italy's existing territorial boundaries, an undertaking which could not be given, if only on account of conflicting British undertakings to Greece and Yugoslavia.

In Switzerland contacts with emissaries from Italy also ran into rather similar difficulties. Opponents of Fascism inside Italy were said to be unwilling to take decisive action except under the cover of public Allied support for some prominent Italian political leaders in exile. The name most frequently cited was that of Count Sforza, *persona non grata* with the Foreign Office, which in any case showed reluctance to support any leader who did not emerge spontaneously from within Italy. This seriously restricted McCaffery in his dealings with representatives of the Italian internal political opposition.

Possibly the most promising lead to come his way from this quarter met with similar political objections. The proposal was for a retired Italian general to fly to North Africa, there to organize with British military commanders the raising from among Italian prisoners of war of an Italian Legion to fight, with Allied equipment, on the Allied side. Arrangements were made through the Air Ministry for the reception of the Italian plane but, in the absence at the Casablanca conference of the Prime Minister, for whom such a Garibaldian gesture would surely have had historical and romantic appeal, political approval was withheld on the grounds that no prior undertaking of any sort could be given to the general or his political backers, but he might make the attempt at his own personal risk. Though the case was reopened at the Prime Minister's request on his return to London, by then it was too late because the link to Italy had been severed in the meantime.

The reason that this contact had been lost did not emerge until later on, some way indeed into Act II, when it was revealed that most of SOE's lines into Italy from Switzerland had been under Italian control, some from the start, others as in this case because, in the anxiety to speed up difficult communications, lines had deliberately (but unfortunately) been crossed. The Italian military counter-intelligence service run by the Servizio Informazione Militare (SIM) was shown to have been an efficient and imaginative opponent and to have effectively won its contest with SOE, even while the Italian Army itself was losing on the field of battle. Interestingly, it was found also that SIM had acted throughout without disclosure to their German allies.

By the end of Act I SOE, in terms of actual penetration of Italy, and leaving aside the long-term value of certain contacts made, had, besides a few deliveries of sabotage stores by air and sea (all, as it turned out, known to and mostly recovered by SIM) managed to infiltrate only two 'agents'. The first was a young Italian trained by SOE as a radio operator, a Jew and with parents still in Italy, the most promising of the few recruits found by SOE among Italians in the United Kingdom. After being smuggled into Switzerland at the end of November 1942

95

following a sea landing on the French Mediterranean coast, he was sent on by McCaffrey to Milan, where he was received and accommodated under the auspices of SIM, though without his knowledge, still less that of SOE. Radio contact was established but only a few messages were received from him – and those carefully prepared by SIM. He survived to do some good work in Act II.

The second agent infiltrated by SOE into Italy before the Armistice was also a radio operator, this time an Englishman. He was dropped in August 1943 and what happened to him forms the theme of the Entr'acte, which now follows.

Entr'acte (August–September 1943)

That SOE played an important ancillary role ('Monkey') in the military contacts with the Italians which led to the proclamation of the Armistice on 8 September 1943 is well enough known, and it is not necessary to retell the story here. It will, however, be useful to record, first (by way of rounding off Act I) how SOE came to be in a position to meet the requirement, suddenly placed on it by Allied Forces Headquarters (AFHQ) Algiers at the end of August, to provide a system of clandestine communications between Rome and Algiers; and secondly (as an introduction to Act II) the effects this was to have on SOE's conduct of future operations.

As already seen in Act I, the second agent to be infiltrated into Italy by SOE was an English radio operator, Lieutenant Richard Mallaby. He was parachuted into Lake Como from North Africa on the night of 13/14 August 1943, briefed to make his way to an address near the lake, there to place himself at the disposal of a group of supposed Italian resisters and saboteurs, whom McCaffery had been directing from Berne – unaware that in fact SIM was calling the shots. SOE's intention had been to promote timely action, using stores already supplied to this group, against enemy lines of communications in northern Italy in support of the impending Allied landings in the south.

Account had evidently not been taken in Algiers of the fact that the RAF had bombed Milan on the previous night, as a result of which the area around the lake was more frequented and more brightly illuminated than usual on account of refugees from the city. Mallaby was picked up even before he had had time to row ashore in his inflatable rubber boat. News of the capture of a British parachutist was publicized and reached SOE in London, fortuitously just when Roseberry was leaving for Lisbon to provide the Italian peace emissaries with a clandestine radio link with Algiers for use on their return to Rome. He was thus able to offer them, not only the means, but also the man, even implying that with its legendary foresight, wily, British Intelligence had infiltrated Mallaby with precisely this end in view. Thus a failed operation was transformed into an uncovenanted success.

The ongoing importance of this for SOE was, in the first place, that it raised SOE's profile and stock in the eyes of military commanders both in AFHQ and 15th Army Group, thereby boosting SOE's prospects of more fruitful collaboration in the impending military campaign in Italy. SOE's assistance included also the attachment to the British team, in the role of interpreter for the meetings in Sicily, of an SOE officer, the head of the Italian Section in the SOE mission in Algiers ('Massingham'). This afforded him, but also Roseberry who came out from London, an opportunity for direct contact and preliminary discussions on a professional plane, not only with General Castellano, but also with an officer of SIM who accompanied Castellano on his second visit to Italy. As this Italian officer was included with Mallaby in the Italian government party which escaped from Rome to Brindisi, this made for an easy, early and auspicious start to post-armistice collaboration with SIM, which is an important theme in Act II.

Act II (September 1943–May 1945)

In the changed circumstances – with Italy (at least that part of it not still held by the Germans and nominally restored to Mussolini) no longer to be treated as an enemy (yet not as an ally but merely a co-belligerent) – the prospects for action by SOE and the achievement of results in Act II greatly improves.

In Act I we saw SOE starting from scratch and by the end it has to be conceded that its contribution towards the Allied defeat of Italy had been minimal. Yet the experience gained, particularly in dealing with representatives of the Italian anti-Fascist opposition, both inside and outside Italy, would surely help some of the key players, notably McCaffery in Berne (despite early errors of judgement) and Roseberry (now a Lieutenant-Colonel) in charge of J Section to perform with greater assurance their continuing roles in Act II. Again Max Salvadori, after playing a subsidiary, though valuable, part in Act I, was now, at last a captain in the British Army and in action with a forward unit of SOE at Salerno, in place to perform a key role in Italy for which his experience and dual national allegiance so well fitted him. Likewise, the group of influential anti-Fascist Italian exiles from America and Mexico, contacted through Salvadori, and now brought back to Italy, were on hand to help SOE in their various individual ways to develop contacts with Italian resistance in the German-occupied area. In short, much of the action in Act I would pay off in Act II, at the opening of which, unlike in Act I, SOE was already well positioned to meet its future commitments.

How it organized itself to deal with them needs to be explained briefly. 'Massingham' had already secured the attachment of a small SOE unit to the Eighth Army for the preliminary campaign in Sicily. Although its contribution to the success of military operations was minimal, the episode had proved a useful small-scale exercise in cooperation with military forces in the field. Now for the major landing on the mainland of Italy ('Avalanche') an expanded 'Special Force' unit ('Vigilant') was attached to the American Fifth Army. This was one prong of SOE's two-pronged approach to Italy from the south.

The other, as foreshadowed in the Entr'acte, was to be an SOE unit on the opposite Adriatic coast of Italy, in touch with the rump of the Italian government which established itself in Brindisi on 10 September. With the backing of AFHQ a small advance SOE party was despatched from 'Massingham' within days to make the first contact with the Italians there and to reinforce radio communications. This small party was to be built up as quickly as possible into a full-scale SOE unit equipped to exploit the opportunities of a secure base in southern Italy for mounting operations by land, sea and air. At first it was unclear, in view of the as yet uncertain course of the Italian campaign, whether this was to be an independent unit or a preliminary stage in the transfer of the whole 'Massingham' HQ, along with AFHQ, onto Italian soil. Since Brindisi offered scope for trans-Adriatic operations into the Balkans, there was also some initial uncertainty as to how SOE's responsibilities in this direction were to be handled. In the event 'Massingham' remained in North Africa along with AFHQ until the following summer, while responsibility for SOE's trans-Adriatic operations into the Balkans was met by the establishment by SOE Cairo of their own separate advance unit in Bari.

Thus the Mission in Brindisi, soon to move its HQ a few miles up the coast to Monopoli, developed as an independent unit, having its own direct signals link to SOE HQ in London and exclusive responsibility for operations into enemy-occupied Italy, with the title of No. 1 Special Force (also known as 'Maryland', a personal tribute to the wife of its commanding officer, Gerry Holdsworth, about to be promoted to the rank of Commander RNVR). Early in the New Year 'Vigilant' was closed down and No. 1 Special Force (1 SF) in Monopoli assumed full control of all operations mounted from southern Italy into enemy-occupied territory.

This was brought about not without internal difficulties which required the personal intervention of the new CD, Major-General Colin Gubbins, who took over from Sir Charles Hambro just at the time of the Armistice and made it one of his first priorities to pay an extended visit to all SOE missions in the Mediterranean. His main purpose was to sort out a number of problems of organization and command, both actual and impending in view of anticipated changes in the military command structure in the Mediterranean theatre. One of the problems to be resolved in relation to Italian operations was the role of Roseberry who, at the bidding of 'Massingham', had been in Brindisi since early October, leaving his deputy in charge of J Section in London. CD's decision was for Roseberry to return to London at the end of the year to resume his place in J Section with the particular task of coordinating the activities of 1 SF with those of the Berne Mission. A radio link between Berne and Monopoli was considered but deferred as unlikely yet to be acceptable to the Swiss. (It was eventually introduced but not until late the following year.)

Throughout the Italian campaign the primary aim of 1 SF was to lend support to Allied military plans and operations. In this, 1 SF was following the doctrine long promoted by Gubbins, and which had had its first limited experiment during the North African campaign, where the 'Brandon' mission worked in direct support of the British First Army. At 'Massingham' in North Africa Colonel Douglas Dodds-Parker had taken pains to establish good working relations with AFHQ. In the planning stages of 'Husky' and 'Avalanche' SOE officers had discussed with 15th Army Group their requirements for SOE support, and had negotiated the inclusion of SOE units in the invasion forces. SOE's performance in 'Monkey' had greatly improved its standing with AFHQ and 15th Army Group, so that when the latter set up its advance HQ in Italy near Bari, 1 SF was at hand to pick up contact.

At first 15th Army Group, having as yet little knowledge of Italian resistance or appreciation of its possible military effectiveness, for the most part left 1 SF with a free hand in developing operations, apart from direction on the planning of some sabotage schemes. It was only with the approach of summer, and the launching of the May offensive 'Diadem', that 15th Army Group/Allied Armies in Italy (AAI) started to take a closer interest in the military potential of Italian partisan forces. It was then at their urging that 1 SF began in June to reinforce their missions to the partisans with British Liaison Officers (BLOs). 1 SF also improved their mechanism for liaison by placing a special detachment alongside Advance HQ AAI in Siena with its own radio link back to 1 SF HQ in Monopoli.

Once seized of the potential advantage to be gained from irregular warfare behind the lines in Italy – his awareness no doubt stimulated by the depletion of his own regular troops – General Sir Harold Alexander took to treating the Italian partisans as an integral part of the forces under his command. Periodic exhortations and instructions of a mostly general nature were now conveyed to them in his name by broadcast and through the medium of Allied Liaison Missions.

One such Alexander message broadcast in mid-November 1944 provoked some adverse reactions and has since become notorious in Italian historiography of the resistance. The general burden of this message to the partisans – to lie low during the winter – was sound enough and showed some care for their welfare in the coming months. But its phrasing fell short of conveying awareness of all the circumstances of their predicament, thus lending itself to misinterpretation, particularly by certain communist commanders alert for opportunities to denigrate the actions of the Anglo-Americans. This line was followed by most Italian historians of the resistance who came predominantly from the post-war Italian Left. The fact that this message was drafted without reference to 1 SF provides an indication of the limits still applying to coordination between SOE and the military in Italy.

By the time of the final spring offensive a much wider network of Allied Liaison Missions, by then attached to most of the main partisan formations, allowed more detailed instructions to be disseminated from Lieutenant-General Mark Clark, Alexander's successor in command of 15th Army Group. These were intended to coordinate the actions of particular partisan formations as closely as possible tactically with those of the advancing Allied forces. By then, however, Italian resistance had its own plans ready, and was hardly to be restrained, in the heat of the long anticipated moment of final liberation, from carrying them out. Though some arguments arose (and once again the Allies were made a target for criticism both then and in Italian post-war, politically motivated historiography), the overall results were highly satisfactory, both in helping the Allies to polish off and round up the defeated enemy forces in northern Italy and in preserving important industrial installations from destruction.

There had been fears that things might not have gone so well; and here we come to another particular aspect of SOE activity in Italy. Already in the summer of 1944, in planning for the next Allied offensive, designed to drive the enemy up into the north-east corner of Italy, attention had focused on a potential vacuum in the north-west corner which there would be no available Allied troops to fill. In these circumstances 1 SF was led to prepare a 'Rankin' plan or the deployment in the area outside the path of the Allied line of advance of a wide network of British liaison missions (the US Office of Strategic Services – OSS – was invited to participate but declined), briefed to arrange with local Italian political and partisan leaders for the maintenance of law and order in the interregnum, which might last a matter of weeks, before the arrival of Allied forces and Allied Military Government (AMG). The original timing for the execution of this plan was disrupted, first by bad weather and shortage of aircraft (priority being given to support of the Warsaw rising), and then by a temporary ban by 15th Army Group on body-dropping sorties to north-west Italy in favour of reinforcing missions in the north-east to support the, by then faltering, military offensive. Most of the 'Rankin' missions for north-west Italy could not be delivered until the early months of the following year.

Meanwhile in the winter, events in Greece exacerbated fears for the situation with which Allied forces might be faced on the final liberation of Italy. That these fears eventually proved exaggerated, indeed fundamentally misplaced, was due to the political cohesion of the Italian resistance movement. Here we find another feature of the Italian scene, if not quite unique, at least most distinctive: the overriding spirit of unity maintained within the movement, despite the differing political aims of its various components, right up to the day of liberation and, briefly at least, into the immediately following period of Allied Military Government. The existence of this force of cohesion was well appreciated in 1 SF from early days and strongly supported and promoted by it as a matter of policy. It may not perhaps be coincidence that, in two instances in the last days of April where disagreement arose over the interpretation and execution of Allied instructions between partisan leaders and BLOs, the latter in both cases were late arrivals in 1 SF, having previously served with SOE in Greece.

The next distinctive feature to be mentioned of special operations in Italy is the relationship between SOE and OSS. In all other European countries hitherto the American organization had been willing, as the late arrival, to integrate its special operations with those of SOE. In Italy, however, OSS chose to go its own way in special operations without reference to SOE. It was a deliberate policy decision by General Donovan (on the spot in person at the start of the Italian campaign) to exploit this first opening in Europe to act independently of SOE, in a country where, as he saw it, both organizations would be starting more or less from scratch (and perhaps with a potential advantage for OSS with a large pool of Italo-American talent to draw on). His long-term aim was to produce independent results to back up his post-war case in Washington for the permanent establishment of a national American secret intelligence organization.

This stand off on the part of OSS left the task of coordinating the operational work of SOE and OSS to be carried out at HQ 15th Army Group/AAI, specifically by the G3 Special Operations Section, where an American Army colonel was in charge with a British Army major as his assistant from the summer of 1944. While this arrangement seems to have given no cause for complaint, there is little to suggest that G3 Special Operations Section exercised its role in much more than a reactive sense.

Such working contacts as there were between 1 SF and OSS at HQ level were apparently found generally satisfactory by 1 SF. There are instances of useful cooperation in the field. However, there was one not infrequent cause for complaint from BLOs who found OSS missions obtaining a disproportionate number of supply drops for what the BLOs regarded as less deserving partisan formations in a given area, especially where this seemed to conflict with Allied policy of maintaining a balance. A complicating factor here was that some OSS/SI (Secret Intelligence) missions also engaged in the business of procuring supplies for partisan formations. There were indeed three separate branches of OSS involved in the support of military resistance: SO, SI and OG (Operational Groups – roughly the American counterpart of the Special Air Service (SAS)). There is some evidence that relations between them were governed as much by rivalry as by the need for coordination.

On the British domestic side (and this may be another distinction for SOE in Italy) cooperation and mutual support generally governed 1 SF's relations with the other clandestine services and special forces operating alongside them. The first Italian missions sent into the field by 1 SF in the early days from Brindisi were in fact mounted and briefed jointly with the Inter-Services Liaison Department (ISLD – the Mediterranean theatre cover name for SIS) and, incidentally, in association also with SIM. One of these first missions was later transferred by 1 SF to ISLD control. Conversely an Italian sent into the field early on with an ISLD mission was subsequently, by agreement, taken over by 1 SF – and became their star Italian operative in northern Italy. 1 SF lent practical support from the beginning to A Force (later IS9) in their work of recovery of escaped Allied prisoners of war and evading airmen. Close relations were established with the Political Warfare Executive with particular reference to a jointly promoted broadcast programme specially directed at Italian resistance. The services of 1 SF's parachute school near Brindisi were made available to other organizations including OSS and PPA ('Popski's Private Army').

Collaboration with SAS merits special mention. A squadron of 2 SAS was sent to Italy in late December 1944 specifically to work with Italian partisans in close association with 1 SF. It set up its HQ alongside 1 SF's forward Tactical (TAC) HQ in Florence and all its operations were planned and executed, with greater or less success, in liaison with 1 SF both at HQ and in the field.

The matter of air supply, a common problem for SOE wherever it operated, presented particular difficulties for 1 SF in Italy. Apart from meteorological conditions, over which there could be no control, and the generally inadequate overall availability of aircraft (a central problem for SOE), there was an awkward issue of priorities to be negotiated. With the unification of the Mediterranean theatre command the pool of Allied Special Duty (SD) aircraft in Italy had to meet the needs of all the various British and American clandestine organizations and special forces operating in Italy – and not just for operations within Italy but also for operations to other countries accessible by air from Italy, whether within the actual theatre command (e.g. the Balkans) or outside it (e.g. Poland and Czechoslovakia). Up to the final months of the war (when the reduction of other commitments in Europe released more aircraft for Italian operations) 1 SF was engaged in a perpetual struggle, pursued at one point right up to the Prime Minister, to obtain even what it considered the minimum allocations needed to meet its requirements. Even then, securing monthly allocations at AFHQ/Mediterranean Allied Air Forces (MAAF) level was only the first stage in a complex procedure in which competition for priority still had to be pursued at lower command levels, and final decisions were only taken 'on the night'. Though the general problem was not peculiar to SOE in Italy, to 1 SF it presented particular difficulties due to the many competing demands and the complexities of the command structure.

To give even a simplified account of these complexities, involving an overloaded Services hierarchy of HQs and the evolution of an SOE structure adapted to it, would take us beyond the bounds of this paper. Although certainly peculiar to SOE in Italy, the organizational developments relate as much to operations into the Balkans and Central Europe as to operations in Italy itself. Some idea of the difficulties caused to those who had to work within such a complex and, worse, shifting structure, may be had from the fact that an SOE staff officer who at the end of the war wrote an account of the organizational background to SOE work in Italy headed it 'HQ SOM: History and Problems' and needed 13 pages (not including charts and appendices) to deal with the subject. Furthermore, he prefaced his account with the hope that it might serve as a warning against the creation of a similar set-up in any future war.

Within this complicated set-up, 1 SF succeeded somehow in maintaining a largely autonomous existence, with its own radio communications and range of training schools – but dependent on Special Operations Mediterranean (SOM) for the provision and packing of supplies for the field. For mainly administrative convenience it accommodated within its HQ in Monopoli an Austrian Section and a Central European Section, both subordinate operationally to the relevant Country Sections in London. The work of these Sections spilled over occasionally into 1 SF's own Italian field: in the case of the Austrian Section over missions sent into northern Italy to operate across the border into Austria; and in the case of the Central European Section over missions sent into the field to suborn satellite troops in the German Army in Italy.

In a final act of administrative amalgamation of all SOE units still operating in Italy carried out in March 1945, 1 SF, which had just moved its HQ up from Monopoli to Siena the previous month, was subsumed in a reorganized SOM in Siena. This change, however, had only marginal immediate impact in practice on the continuing autonomy of 1 SF. By then anyway the war was almost over.

Note

1 The surviving SOE files on Italy have been released into the National Archives under references HS 6/775 to HS 6/908. Other references can be found in related SOE papers.

9

RESISTANCE FROM ABROAD

Anglo-Soviet efforts to coordinate Yugoslav resistance, 1941–42

Mark Wheeler

This chapter must be prefaced by what amounts to an academic health warning. In the first place, it was written in 1990 as a report on work in progress. It was apparent to me then that there were still many loose ends, open questions, unfollowed leads and unseen documents. Little has changed in the intervening years, save that I no longer have access to many of the files on which this article is based.

Secondly, the terms under which I then worked as an 'official historian' of the Special Operations Executive (SOE) precluded me from providing either exact references to or many quotations from SOE documents. The release in the meantime to the Public Record Office of some SOE files – including the main group relating to Yugoslavia – means that citations might now be provided for a portion of what appears below. But the bulk of the documents used to prepare this chapter came from other record groups, which have not yet been cleared for release. In these circumstances, it seems sensible to leave the chapter largely as it was.

A third disclaimer is also required. Although most of the present text is based on British records which remain unavailable to the public, that does not mean that the Soviet side of the story is any more complete than it ever is. Although this perennial gap may soon be filled, my chapter reveals no startling secrets from the inner sanctum of the wartime Kremlin. The British and Yugoslav agents and officials who endeavoured to forge collaborative links with those whom they assumed to be their Soviet opposite numbers were themselves usually mystified by the workings of these authorities and uncertain about the real status of the men with whom they sought to co-operate. They presumed, for example, that they would find their counterparts in the defunct OGPU (Unified State Political Directorate). SOE, too, and perhaps just because it was a new and insecure weapon of war, also made a fetish of impenetrable secrecy, refusing to reveal anything to the Soviets about its own structure and successively passing off two imposters as its executive head in meetings with senior NKVD (People's Commisariat for Internal Affairs) liaison officers in London.

Very few details of SOE-NKVD relations in the Second World War have come to light. Despite Sir Harry Hinsley's many volumes, even less that is reliable is known about links between the Secret Intelligence Service (SIS) and the NKVD, though it can be assumed that Britain's senior secret service also sought at least tactical alliances. A history of SOE's Russian Section may one day be written, but for the present only snippets have emerged. The most important of these relate to Operation 'Pickaxe', by which SOE undertook to infiltrate 30-odd Soviet agents into France, Belgium, Holland, Austria, Germany and Italy between 1942 and 1944. Far from cementing close and mutually beneficial relations – as the British intended the operation should – the difficulties, delays and disputes which attended the delivery of 'Pickaxe' missions became, instead, a principal measure (if not a cause) of the ultimate failure of SOE to collaborate effectively with the NKVD in subversive warfare on anything like the scale – or with anything like the quarrelsome intimacy – which characterized its cooperation with the American Office of Strategic Services (OSS).

Something more has been known (and for a longer period) about SOE's efforts to coordinate with the Soviets their response to the 1941 Yugoslav uprisings. And more still, of course, has been written about Foreign Office attempts (often initiated at SOE's behest) to get the Soviets to cooperate over Yugoslavia: that is, to order the communist-led Partisans to rally to Mihailović in late 1941 and throughout 1942 and, then, in 1943, when such hopes had proved vain, to bless and assist the British themselves in entering into contact with Tito. The emphasis here, however, will be on SOE's own relations with the Soviets during the period when it seemed possible that a common policy towards Yugoslav resistance might be agreed.

The first published account of the abortive plan in the summer of 1941 to send a joint Yugoslav-British-Soviet mission to Mihailović from the USSR was Jovan Đonović (in an article in a Serb émigré journal in America) as long ago as 1958.[1] Đonović, who had been a trusted contact of SOE in Belgrade before the 27 March 1941 coup d'état and consequent Axis invasion, was appointed delegate of the exile government in the Middle East when King Peter and his ministers left Palestine for London in June. As such he was notionally in charge of his government's efforts both to restore communications with the occupied homeland and to maintain liaison with SOE. It was Đonović who established the first links with the NKVD later that summer in Istanbul.

An account from the British point of view of what has since become known as 'the Russian project' was added by Julian Amery in his war memoirs, *Approach March*, published in 1973.[2] Amery, who as a young SOE agent in Belgrade in 1940 and 1941 had worked with Đonović on Albanian projects and claimed to have known Mihailović, was involved in helping prepare from Jerusalem and Cairo the Anglo-Yugoslav components of both the air mission proposed by the Soviets – which did not go – and the submarine mission, codenamed 'Bullseye' – which did, landing Captain D. T. (Bill) Hudson and three Yugoslavs on the Montenegrin coast on 20 September.

Latterly, Milan Deroc, a Serb-Australian, was enabled – by the assistance of the SOE Adviser at the Foreign Office – to provide the fullest account to date of the Russian project in his 1988 book, *British Special Operations Explored*.[3] What his version lacks, aside from innumerable details which this chapter can ignore, is the SOE context in which the Russian project was born, developed and died. It is this context which I intend to explore.

A good deal has also emerged in recent years (albeit in partial, garbled or sensationalized form) about the second case of Anglo-Soviet cooperation over Yugoslavia which I propose to explicate. This was the operation, carried out under the auspices of the legendary Sir William Stephenson's British Security Coordination (BSC) office in New York (which represented all of Britain's wartime secret services), and which enlisted the help of the American and Canadian communist parties in recruiting Yugoslav immigrants for training as organizers of guerrilla warfare for eventual despatch to their homeland. These recruits have usually – and inaccurately – been identified as Canadian-Croats. In fact, they were residents of the United States as well as of Canada and included Serbs, Montenegrins and Slovenes in addition to Croats. Nor were they all communist party members, though the earliest recruits certainly did 'volunteer' under party orders.

A longer-lived and, from SOE's point of view, a vastly more successful enterprise than the ill-fated Russian project, 40-odd men were enlisted, trained and sent off to Cairo between late 1941 and early 1943. They comprised the first missions dropped 'blind' to the Partisans in Croatia and Bosnia in spring 1943, and usually served later as interpreters for the British Liaison Officers who succeeded them with Tito's forces.

This secret North American recruiting drive can be regarded as a continuation in a new venue of SOE's efforts to work with the Soviets on Yugoslav resistance or as a distinct and a very different exercise. My own inclination is to view it as the effective successor to the Russian project. For one thing, it followed directly upon the abandonment of the tripartite mission plan. For another, both operations were controlled by the same man, Colonel S. W. (Bill) Bailey. (A victim of the first annual SOE Mid-East purges, Bailey left Cairo for London in the autumn, and then proceeded to New York. Later still, on Christmas Day 1942, he parachuted into Yugoslavia as senior liaison officer to Mihailović). Moreover, both operations were inspired by the same assumption: that cooperation with the Soviets in propagating, guiding and supplying anti-Axis resistance was natural, necessary and feasible. Because SOE tended to oscillate between deprecating 'premature' revolts and wanting to foment them, it did not seem to worry about the possibility that the Soviets might view their strategic requirements rather differently. In any case, given the fact that the discharge by SOE of its charter to stimulate sabotage and raise rebellions behind German lines was, at that stage of the war, one of the few means by which Britain could attempt to meet Stalin's insistent pleas for a Second Front, SOE's expectation of loyal Soviet collaboration was not unreasonable.

105

Cooperation with the NKVD was not, of course, necessarily the same thing as working with foreign sections of the Comintern. The British naturally disbelieved NKVD assurances that it had no influence over the Comintern or foreign communists. But that does not mean that Stalin's right hand always knew or controlled what his left hand was doing. He, presumably, preferred it that way. In any case, it is probably safe to assume that SOE's plan to recruit communists in North America was more congenial to the Soviets than their own earlier suggestion of a combined mission to the then virtually unknown Colonel Draža Mihailović had turned out to be. Not only might the Soviets have been expected to rub their hands with glee at the thought that the British proposed to employ and deploy men whose first loyalty could be assumed to be to the USSR (though their *second* thought might well have been that it was too good to be true), but the North American scheme also had the significant virtues of indirectness, deniability and reversibility.

A full-fledged Yugoslav-SOE-NKVD mission to Mihailović in August–September 1941 just might – as Julian Amery later lamented – have had the effect of committing Moscow to back a Serb royalist whose aims and claims were, once they had been understood, unlikely to commend themselves to Stalin. Although Tito's relations with *Djeda* ('Grandfather', that is, the Comintern) were at this stage fraught with mutual distrust and incomprehension, it is also unlikely that the Soviets could have imagined for very long that they stood to secure better information about what was going on in Yugoslavia by joining forces with the British and the Yugoslav exiles than they were already getting from Tito and their Sofia legation. It is possible, of course, that a joint mission to Mihailović might have been conceived by the Soviets as a means of disciplining or supplanting Tito: an objective which the Comintern seems to have been pursuing half-heartedly at this time through its radio operator in Zagreb, Josip Kopinič. The scrapping of the mission project could, therefore, have been a sign that Moscow had reconciled itself to Tito's continued leadership of the Yugoslav party and its nascent army. It is also possible that the Soviets were, for simple reasons of logistics, unable to deliver the mission they had proposed.

Be all that as it may, it turned out that SOE and the Yugoslav government were themselves to provide the Soviets with more than sufficient cause to abandon the joint mission project. But we must now return to the beginning.

The re-orientation of the SOE attitude towards the Soviet Union from one of suspicious hostility to sceptical friendship, like that of the British government generally, followed swiftly upon Hitler's invasion of Russia. The British Ambassador in Moscow, Sir Stafford Cripps, apparently suggested in late June that SOE should seek to establish links with the OGPU, mobilizing for the purpose the Czechoslovak intelligence service's well-established contacts. London, although willing to consider using Czech channels elsewhere, insisted that it should have its own British representative in the Soviet capital. In the meantime, two SOE agents were despatched to the USSR with embassy and military mission covers in July. They were meant to be on hand should it prove necessary either to raise a rebellion in the Caucasus or to assist the Soviets in destroying the oil installations in that region in anticipation of a German occupation. Since it was deemed politic to avoid suggesting that the Red Army might not prove capable of withstanding the German onslaught, the possibility of collaboration to forestall a German descent into Persia was made the subject of Cripps's first formal overture to the Kremlin on behalf of SOE. He reported in late July that not only had Stalin blessed personally the idea of cooperation in Persia, but had proposed that the British and Soviet subversive warfare organizations should work together in Germany, the Balkans and other areas as well.

London seems to have been taken aback by Stalin's far-reaching and enthusiastic response. Cripps was urged to secure Soviet agreement to a formal, five-point agenda for discussions. The Ambassador regarded such pussyfooting as otiose, and pressed instead for the immediate despatch of a senior SOE representative to enter into direct negotiations with the NKVD. The officer eventually selected for the task, Lieutenant-Colonel D. R. Guinness, flew to Moscow in mid-August. He was put in touch with General Vladimir Nicolaev, reputedly the head of NKVD subversive operations. Together they negotiated what amounted to a draft treaty providing for a worldwide common policy in strategic sabotage, subversion and propaganda. It was to be applicable everywhere outside the USSR, the British Commonwealth and those territories occupied militarily by either side. Liaison missions were to be exchanged, agents of one party were to be assisted by the other in infiltrating enemy-occupied countries and cooperation in communications and technical matters was envisaged. Spheres of responsibility were also agreed. Western Europe and Greece were to fall into the British; while Romania, Bulgaria and Finland were allotted to the Soviets. The question of existing or potential guerrilla forces in Czechoslovakia, Poland and Yugoslavia was reserved for subsequent discussion between the Soviets and those countries' governments-in-exile, but the implication was that they should expect help primarily from the Soviets. Claiming, however, to have no organization whatsoever in the Americas, the NKVD agreed that they should be a British zone. Finally, each side pledged not to seek to raise revolt in the other's spheres without its prior consent.

Guinness returned to London in early September to secure his chiefs' and Foreign Office sanction for the two documents which embodied this agreement. He then flew back to Moscow where he signed them with Nikolaev on 30 September. This was indeed the comprehensive and far-reaching agreement that Stalin had offered to Cripps. The trouble was that very little was to come of it: a result which neither side appeared to mourn very much as the war progressed. That, however, is another story.

The sequence of events leading to the SOE-NKVD treaty proved important to the fate of the Russian project, which had been emerging simultaneously in Istanbul. Fearful of getting at cross purposes with the talks proceeding in Moscow, London had ordered its representatives in Turkey to hang fire in their discussions with their local Soviet colleague. Đonović, however, should maintain contact. SOE was influenced also by Foreign Office alarm that the Turks might get wind of any

Anglo-Soviet talks and conclude that some deal inimical to their precarious neutrality was in the making. Although the SOE-NKVD agreement as signed did provide for discreet cooperation between the two organizations in Istanbul with the object of restoring their links with the Balkan states, this came too late to save the projected joint mission to Mihailović.

In London, meantime, SIS and SOE had been examining the opportunities which might now be expected to arise for using international communist organizations for their respective purposes. The stance of the Comintern parties with regard to the anti-Nazi war still seemed obscure in early July, but the possibility of enlisting the support of dissident communist factions – and particularly of Trotskyites – appeared promising. SIS and SOE resolved to tread warily in making approaches.

With so much of Europe inaccessible since the summer of 1940, the immigrant communities of North and South America had already struck SOE as being likely to offer an almost inexhaustible pool for recruitment. Given the ethos of revolutionary resistance which pervaded SOE under its first minister, Hugh Dalton, it was natural, too, that SOE representatives in the Americas should have focused especially on the Left once the Soviets had entered the war. Not only were the Trotskyites thought to be well-represented and amenable, but experienced and disciplined veterans of the International Brigades which had fought for the Spanish Republic were also numerous. Interestingly enough, however, the first group which appears to have been targeted, in July 1941, was Irish-American communists. In their case the idea seems to have been to use them to counter the anti-British sentiments of the bulk of Irish-Americans rather than to mount an insurgency against de Valera's republic.

A political and minorities section of BSC was established by Stephenson in September. Also in that month, plans were laid for the opening by year's end of a training school on the north shore of Lake Ontario, 30 miles east of Toronto. STS 103 (otherwise known as Camp X) was designed primarily to instruct recruits to Colonel William Donovan's nascent OSS in British methods of subversive warfare; but it was also intended to help meet SOE Cairo's already insistent demands for Balkan guerrilla organizers, fifth columnists and wireless operators. It was through the intimate relationship established between Donovan and Stephenson that SOE won its principal American communist helpmate, Milton Wolff, former commander of the Abraham Lincoln Brigade in Spain. Wolff, who went on to become an OSS officer and source of some embarrassment to Donovan in Italy in 1944, seems simply to have been lent by Donovan to Stephenson during the period before the USA entered the war and OSS became operational. It was Wolff, in any case, who assembled the first party of 11 Yugoslavs and three Greeks (mostly fellow communist veterans of the war in Spain who resided in America illegally) for whom Bill Bailey was to assume responsibility when he arrived in New York at the end of the year.

With this background, it should now be possible to provide fairly brief and comprehensible accounts of both the Russian and the communist recruiting projects.

Bailey, who had been put it charge of all SOE efforts to work back into South-eastern Europe, was authorized by London in early July to make his headquarters in Istanbul. His headquarters also agreed that he should try to mobilize Soviet channels for this purpose and to seek the cooperation of Comintern agents as well, so long as the Russians were denied all knowledge of the SOE organization. There is, however, no evidence that any approaches to the Soviets or to Balkan communists were in fact made at this time. Bailey, in any case, remained based in Jerusalem.

By August, travellers reaching Istanbul and Axis press reports spoke of wide-spread revolts in Yugoslavia. Hope had by now evaporated that any of the several radio sets left behind by SOE with putative leaders of Yugoslav resistance would come on the air. The re-establishment and maintenance of secure communications by means of couriers was realized to be impossible. It thus seemed urgent to get agents capable of offering guidance to the rebels and supplying them with funds and radio sets into the country before the onset of winter. SOE had plenty of money, but it possessed neither suitable men nor wireless sets in adequate number. Even worse, it had no established claim on the services of the RAF or Royal Navy to provide the requisite transport.

Đonović suggested to Bailey's deputy, John Bennett, in early August that he [Đonović] should approach the Russians to see if they could provide an aircraft. Bennett, aware of London's earlier instructions, concurred, and Đonović made contact with a certain Nikolaev (*sic*), ostensibly the Soviet press attaché in Istanbul. At the same time, however, Đonović proposed mounting a mission by air to be led by a former Yugoslav air force colonel, Dušan Radović, who was working for him. The plan was for Radović to pilot a French plane, which they hoped to acquire in Syria, and to take with him another of Đonović's agents, the elderly Balkan War Četnik Vasilje Trbić, and a W/T set. Radović was highly esteemed by both Bennett and Bailey, and Bailey was already thinking of employing him to lead a mission which he hoped to send from Cairo.

At the beginning of September, then, it looked as if two missions might be mounted: one to travel by air from Cairo to Malta, and thence by submarine to the Yugoslav Adriatic coast; while the second might fly either from Syria or – if the Russians provided the means – from Soviet territory to western Serbia. The existence of Mihailović, the location of his headquarters on Mount Suvobor and his desperate need of assistance had meanwhile been revealed by couriers reaching Istanbul from Belgrade.

The emergence of a specific objective no doubt redoubled SOE's sense of urgency. Unfortunately, the mission that appeared more important was also the mission that seemed less likely to come off. Nor was it clear who might go on which mission. Radović and Trbić were summoned to Jerusalem by Bailey in mid-August to stand by for the Cairo option, only to be recalled to Istanbul by Đonović at the end of the month when he received word from Nikolaev that Moscow's approval of a mission was expected any day. Whether or not British officers would accompany either or both missions was still undecided.

On 5–6 September both Amery and his superiors in Cairo and Bennett, Bailey and Đonović in Istanbul learned that their respective ships had come in: the British service chiefs now promised to mount an operation via Malta the following week; while Nikolaev announced that an aircraft, W/T sets and operators were standing by in Armenia to fly to Mihailović's landing ground in western Serbia.

Disregarding London's intervening injunction against direct talks, Bailey and Bennett agreed with Nikolaev that Radović should proceed immediately to Moscow, accompanied by three or four officers from the Yugoslav air force camp at Amman. At this Cairo protested, demanding that Radović and Trbić must be reserved for its mission. It was absolutely essential, Bailey was told, that this first venture should be a success; otherwise SOE might forfeit the future assistance of the services in realizing its aims. Radović was indispensable because only the presence of an experienced air staff officer on the ground in Yugoslavia could persuade the RAF to undertake regular sorties to the country. Moreover – and more immediately relevant – Cairo now revealed that its relations in Egypt with the Yugoslav war minister, General Bogoljub Ilić, had so far deteriorated that he was refusing to provide any suitable substitutes from the small pool of escaped Yugoslav airmen in the Middle East. SOE's Cairo staff denied responsibility for this breach, but they were necessarily mixed up in the tortuous intrigues, personal animosities and party rivalries which beset the Yugoslav emigration. The most important of these at the moment was the antipathy which prevailed between Ilić and the Yugoslav premier, General Dušan Simović, on the one hand, and SOE's chosen favourites, Đonović and Radović, on the other.

Bailey, who had himself been sacked in August as a side-effect of an SOE scandal of nearly Yugoslav intricacy, and who was now merely 'serving out his notice' pending the arrival of a replacement, was in a position to resist Cairo's orders. He offered to send Trbić to Cairo, but refused to relinquish Radović. The Russian project was vital, he reported, 'to secure the adherence of pro-Russian elements [in Yugoslavia], to demonstrate Anglo-Russian cooperation and as a check on Russian intentions'. Bailey suggested that Simović's hostility to Radović might be overcome if a British officer were to be attached to both his and Cairo's missions. In any case, he had no more authority to order Radović to proceed to Cairo than did Ilić; while Radović was unwilling to scupper his chances of returning to Yugoslavia by showing his face in Cairo.

Although Terence Maxwell, the new SOE chief in Cairo, continued to press Bailey for Radović, he also endorsed to London Bailey's objective of nobbling the Soviets and their Yugoslav communist followers. As far as he was concerned, however, the Russian mission should serve as a back-up to Cairo's operation. He asked London on 9 September to appeal to Simović to order Ilić to provide the men required for both missions. Simović refused, but not it seems (and contrary to previous accounts) because he took fright at the implications of the Russian project. Rather, he and Ilić were fed up with receiving requests for personnel from several British secret organizations whose identity and purposes they did not understand, but who all seemed intent on carrying out operations about which the Yugoslav government was permitted no knowledge.

Maxwell informed London that, if Simović and Ilić refused to cooperate, he might be forced either to invoke the authority of the minister of state or to suborn the airmen he needed from Amman. To make matters worse, when Trbić and a colleague turned up in Cairo on 12 September they declared themselves unfit to endure the long cross-country trek from the coast such as the submarine mission would necessitate. Ilić, however, was now prevailed upon to nominate two Montenegrin air force officers for what had become 'Bullseye', to which Bill Hudson was an equally last-minute addition. (Their Yugoslav W/T operator was provided by SIS.) They left Cairo for Malta and Montenegro on 13 September, Amery going along for the ride.

Radović, for his part, departed Istanbul for Moscow on the same day, Bailey having agreed with Nikolaev that the other Yugoslavs who would complete the party should follow via Persia. Bailey hoped that he would be allowed to follow.

This confusing concatenation of events continued when Bailey's successor, Colonel Tom Masterson, arrived in Cairo on 15 September determined to mend SOE's frayed relations with the Yugoslav authorities. His intention was reinforced by news from London that Simović now alleged Radović to be an enemy agent. It is just as likely, however, that Simović's imprecations against Radović stemmed both from the long-standing feud between them (Radović having been cashiered by Simović in 1938 when the latter was chief of staff) and Radović's membership of the Serbian Agrarian Party. The Agrarians were at this time claiming all Yugoslav resistance as their own and inveighing against Simović's inept leadership of the April War. The Yugoslav premier's animus could only have been deepened by his knowledge of the close links that had been forged between the Agrarians and the agents of SOE in Serbia before the 27 March coup.

Masterson ordered Bailey to stop Radović before he got to Moscow. He also instructed Bailey to inform Nikolaev that Radović must not be included in any mission. Despite expressing some more misgivings at this point, Ilić agreed to appoint replacements. Masterson, for his part, promised that all SOE work into Yugoslavia would take place in full accord with Ilić. Bailey, however, was unable either to stop Radović or to confer with Nikolaev (who had vanished) about new arrangements.

London cabled Guinness in Moscow on 22 September to explain the mess. Since the maintenance of good relations with the Yugoslav government was now deemed 'more important than the object of Radović's journey,' the Soviets must be prevailed upon to exclude Radović from their mission and to detain him in the USSR. The Soviets were also to be requested to confirm that Nikolaev remained their accredited agent in Istanbul.

A few days later London asked Masterson for proofs of Radović's treachery such as would warrant pressing the Russians to keep him on ice. Masterson replied that the Yugoslavs' (and his) objection to Radović was, in fact, that he was likely to seek to undermine the authority of the Simović government were he to return home. Meanwhile, Nikolaev had resurfaced in Istanbul and told Hugh Seton-Watson (whom Bailey had left in charge of the NKVD connection when he departed on 24 September) that all questions relating to the infiltration of agents would in future have to be handled in Moscow. Seton-Watson and Đonović reported Nikolaev to be as well-disposed as ever, but depressed by the misunderstanding over Radović and the loss of valuable time.

Oblivious as yet to the unravelling of the Russian project, Dalton reported on SOE's progress to Churchill on 24 September. The landing of agents in Montenegro and the efforts 'to get in touch with the revolutionary Četniks' through Istanbul were proceeding, he wrote, 'in strict agreement with the Russians'. In fact, 'the extreme willingness of the Russians to co-operate with us on subversive matters' had been one of the most remarkable features of the previous six weeks. Then, in a passage which cannot have struck the Prime Minister as short of ludicrous, Dalton confided:

> Our negotiations with the OGPU in Moscow are necessarily so secret that I would prefer to talk to you about them and not to put anything on paper. (In Moscow the two Soviet negotiators do their own typing and, apart from them, only Stalin, Molotoff and Beria apparently know of our conversations.) But I can assure you that they have already borne fruit and are likely in the future to be very important indeed. But it is essential that no wind of the fact that we are negotiating with the OGPU should get out here.

Churchill replied the following day to thank Dalton for his paper and to express his appreciation for the minister's 'difficult and delicate' work. But, as usual, he neglected to invite Dalton to report in person.

London passed on to Moscow on 29 September Simović's allegation that Radović had been in the pay of French-Jewish aircraft interests in the thirties, but admitted two days later that there was no evidence against him. Nor did SOE wish any longer that he should be detained or interrogated. The new SOE representative in Moscow, Lieutenant-Colonel G. A. Hill, reported at length about the problem of disposing of Radović on 3 October. He also lamented that SOE's first exercise in cooperation with the NKVD should have come to such a sorry end. The Soviets were angry, considering that they had been made to look like fools, first in taking on Radović, then in being told he was a suspected enemy agent and, finally, in discovering there was no evidence against him.[4]

Although SOE Cairo continued for a time to consider the Russian project merely in abeyance, the highly unforthcoming attitude of Nikolaev's successor in Istanbul, a certain Bakhlanov, indicated otherwise. In London in late October Dalton's deputy, Gladwyn Jebb, was still able to cite SOE's cooperation with 'OGPU' as a reason why the Foreign Secretary, Anthony Eden, should deny Soviet Ambassador Ivan Maisky full details of Britain's proposed assistance to the Yugoslav rebels: '... since the OGPU chiefs live in terror any whisper getting out to the effect that they are negotiating with us'.

Both then and for nearly a year thereafter, SOE and the Foreign Office would fight shy of recognizing that Britain's deepening commitment to Mihailović rendered active Soviet collaboration in Yugoslavia impossible.

SOE's successful recruitment of communists in North America was – if the expression means anything – the exception that proved the rule. For one thing, these men were always intended for employment in areas where Mihailović's writ did not run. For another, they were initially thought of as 'guerrilla organizers', that is, as leaders who might help weld an inchoate, amorphous and semi-criminal rabble – which is what the British then considered the Partisans to be – into an instrument that might be of some use. Moreover, during the period when Bailey was in charge (from late December 1941 to early August 1942) Britain's commitment to Mihailović was *not* exclusive. Since the Soviets would not themselves publicly denounce Mihailović as an Axis collaborator until the late summer of 1942, Bailey's work with the North American communists was largely untroubled by political complications on that score. These came, rather, from the American authorities and, to a lesser extent, from the Royal Canadian Mounted Police.

The surviving SOE files relating to North American recruitment are both more and less informative than those dealing with the first missions to Yugoslavia. They provide copious details about the 'tradecraft' of recruitment, about the backgrounds of the recruits themselves and about the arrangements made for their engagement, payment, training and onward travel. They are less enlightening as regards the origins of the communist contacts that made the operation possible or, indeed, about the aims and assumptions that underlay the project.

It is plain that the many difficulties Bailey encountered with the Wolff party that awaited him in New York at the end of 1941 inclined him to look to Canada for future recruitment. Aside from the fact that the quality of the American group was not particularly high, he found himself embroiled in bureaucratic battles over payments and pensions with his head office (which wanted Donovan's organization to foot these bills), as well as with the Americans over the men's release from the draft, the discharge of their income tax obligations, the provision of travel documents and their secure holding and training away from the prying eyes of the Federal Bureau of Investigation and the Immigration Service until such time as transport to England or the Middle East could be arranged.

The entry of the United States into the war seems to have made things more complicated rather than less. Donovan came to Bailey's rescue in spring 1942 (when arrangements for the men's transport had fallen through once more) by accepting them at the OSS training camp in Maryland. But their experience there of 'red baiting' reinforced Bailey's decision to transfer recruitment operations to Canada. The first (American) party, led by a Croatian Serb veteran of the Spanish Civil War, Djordje Diklić, finally left New York for England and further training at the end of June 1942. This group did not reach Cairo until February 1943: just in time, as it turned out, for the first missions to the Partisans in Bosnia and Croatia.

BSC's link with the Communist Party of the United States seems to have been quite informal, the result of Donovan's introduction of Wolff to Stephenson. In

May 1942 Bailey entered into a more formal arrangement with the Communist Party of Canada (CPC). He was put in touch with Paul Phillips (a Ukrainian described as the treasurer of the semi-legal party), with a Croat called Joseph Yardas (*sic*) and with a Montenegrin known as Marko Šikić (who was, in fact, the prominent Yugoslav Communist Party organizer and Comintern agent, Nikola Kovačević) by the self-confessed Bulgarian 'firebrand' and SOE collaborator Kosta Todorov. They agreed to provide recruits in return for expenses and such good reports of their patriotic war work as SOE could pass on to the Canadian authorities.

As far as Bailey and BSC were concerned, their relationship with the CPC was especially advantageous in that it freed them from OSS supervision and control. As far as SOE in London was concerned (although Bailey found it difficult to get explicit sanction for the deal), the financial advantages were at least equally significant. SOE Cairo, on whose behalf the operation was carried out, was for its part fulsome in its praise of Bailey's Canadian recruits when it saw them.

Milton Wolff continued to offer help and advice about what Bailey always referred to as 'radical groups'. The SOE/SIS resident in Toronto, Tommy Drew-Brook, was extremely helpful, as were several officials of the Canadian Department of External Affairs. The latter were not only able to cut through myriad bureaucratic knots, but they could also call off the RCMP when Phillips and others were travelling across Canada setting up interviews with likely prospects for Bailey. Surprisingly, Bailey appears to have kept the Yugoslav consul general in Montreal apprised of what he was doing.

Kovačević assembled the first party of seven men and joined it as their leader. They passed through STS 103 in July 1942 and embarked on a Greek tramp steamer for Cairo in the autumn. This ship was torpedoed and sunk by a German submarine off the Brazilian coast in early November. Two of the eight were killed and Kovačević was badly wounded. He was sent back to Canada to recuperate, but the five survivors proceeded to Cairo. Like the American party, they arrived in February 1943 and joined the early missions to the Partisans.[5]

A second group of Yugoslav-Canadian communists was recruited by Bailey and a third by his successor, Robert Lethbridge, in the summer and autumn of 1942. They, too, were trained at STS 103 and shipped to Cairo. Mate Siaus (*sic*), a Dalmatian Croat, had meanwhile succeeded Kovačević as BSC's chief Yugoslav recruiter. Subsequent recruitment in Canada by Lethbridge (of two parties of so-called 'paramilitary' Yugoslavs and of Italians), as well as by other SOE officers of Hungarians, Bulgarians, French Canadians, Chinese and Japanese, was carried out among serving members of the Canadian army. Leftists or communists were not, therefore, any longer the objects of special attention.

Two observations about the recruitment campaign can be made in conclusion. First of all – as has been implied already – the men enlisted as 'guerrilla organizers' were not in the event destined to play that role. Aside from the half dozen agents who performed the crucial task of opening up relations with the Partisans, the others served mainly as interpreters for later British missions. (A good many did, however, defect to the Partisans, fight with them and stay on in Yugoslavia after the war.) Their relegation to this subordinate role happened because Tito's army turned out to be a vastly more organized, competent and cohesive force than SOE had envisaged when recruitment commenced. As far as the Partisan leadership was concerned, the British missions were welcomed in order to provide material and logistical support, to coordinate strategic plans and to help win international recognition for the Partisans' war effort. They were not in Yugoslavia to reorganize, take over or otherwise subvert the KPJ's (Yugoslav Communist Party) revolutionary struggle.

Secondly and finally, the fact that Tito's was a revolutionary war had already involved him in acrimonious arguments by wireless with the Comintern, which regularly queried his tactics and challenged his truthfulness. But Tito, too, had cause for complaint. While it is virtually inconceivable that the American and Canadian communist parties should have cooperated with SOE without Moscow's knowledge and approval, it does seem that Tito was kept in the dark. He thus regarded the sudden descent from the skies in British uniform of several well-known comrades from the KPJ's faction-ridden 1930s with alarm and suspicion. He asked *Djeda* to explain, but it appears that no satisfactory answers were forthcoming. Tito was thus left to make up his own mind about the potential usefulness of British contacts. That was not an insignificant side-effect of SOE's efforts to work with the Russians.

Notes

1 Jovan Đonović, 'Veze sa Dražom Mihailovićem sa srednjeg I bliskog istoka I severne Afrike', Glanik srpskog istorisko-kulturnog društva 'Njegoš' (Chicago), No. 1 (July 1958), pp. 41–65.

2 Julian Amery, *Approach March: A Venture in Autobiography*, London: Hutchinson, 1973.

3 M. Deroc, *British Special Operations Explored: Yugoslavia in Turmoil, 1941–1943, and the British Response*, Boulder, CO: East European Monographs/New York: Columbia University Press, 1988.

4 Radović's subsequent career was very strange. He reappeared in Turkey in February 1942. By summer 1943, Bailey was suggesting that he should replace Mihailović as the Četnik leader following the 'palace revolution' Bailey then advocated. Meanwhile, Radović had been taken on by OSS in North Africa and the Middle East, though SOE in Cairo had come to regard him as an NKVD agent. In 1948–49, Radović was in Trieste and reputedly broadcasting anti-Tito propaganda into Yugoslavia on behalf of the Comintern. In the early 1950s, however, he emigrated via South Africa to the USA. He died in America in the early 1970s.

5 Kovačević returned to Yugoslavia after the war and became Tito's first Ambassador to Bulgaria and, later, a party leader in his native Montenegro.

Three of SOE's founding fathers on a visit to Czechoslovak forces in the United Kingdom, March 1941. Dr Hugh Dalton, Minister of Economic Warfare, (right) Brigadier Colin Gubbins, SOE Director of Operations, (centre) and Gladwyn Jebb, Chief Executive Officer. (IWM H8185)

One of SOE's most deadly inventions, the sleeve gun. Designed towards the end of the war by SOE technical staff, there is no record of this assassination weapon being deployed. (IWM HU56777)

Commander Gerard Holdsworth, an early member of SOE's clandestine sea communications operations and, later, the head of SOE's No 1 Special Force in Italy. (IWM HU66772)

Winston Churchill tries out a Sten submachine-gun in June 1941. Both the Prime Minister
and the weapon were to prove essential elements in SOE's successes. (IWM H10688)

Dr Hugh Dalton, the Minister of Economic Warfare, admires an artillery shell. As an artillery officer during the First World War, Dalton possessed frontline experience of conflict but nevertheless maintained a profound faith in the potency of unconventional warfare. (IWM H8191)

The scene of one of SOE's most celebrated *coup de main* operations. The Norsk Hydro 'heavy water' production plant at Vemork, Norway, was attacked by the Norwegian Section's 'Gunnerside' team on 27/28 February 1943. (IWM HU47400)

British soldiers packing supply containers with weapons destined for the Italian resistance. In the last year of the war Mediterranean-based Special Duty aircraft dropped over 2,500 tons of stores to resistance groups behind enemy lines. (IWM NA25369)

The difficulties of clandestine communications. An SOE wireless operator in Yugoslavia ruefully contemplates the remains of his damaged transceiver. (IWM HU45139)

British Liaison Officers in Albania, October 1943. Left to right: Brigadier 'Trotsky' Davies, Captain Alan Hare, Lieutenant-Colonel Arthur Nicholls, Major Billy McLean, Captain David Smiley and (partially obscured, far left) Captain Frank Smythe. (IWM HU65047)

Irregular and regular forces link up. A French maquisard armed with an SOE-supplied Sten gun meets a Canadian paratrooper. (IWM AP268469)

An SOE 'spectacular'. The remains of the limousine of SS-Obergruppenführer Reinhard Heydrich after the assassination attempt made by SOE-trained Czechoslovak agents, Prague, 27 May 1942. (IWM HU47379)

A reception committee in southern France collects a supply drop, July 1944. Although most RAF operations in support of the resistance took place at night, after D-Day many mass drops took place in daylight. (IWM HU41895)

Sabotage of the French railways. A de-railed train on the Bussy-Varache viaduct on the Limoges-Ussel line, 13 March 1943. In the three weeks following D-Day SOE was able to claim responsibility for some two thousand cuts in French railway traffic. (IWM MH1164)

10

SOE IN ROMANIA

Maurice Pearton

The analysis of SOE's activities in Romania divides into two episodes – the first, from 1938/39 to January/February 1941, when British nationals were forced to quit the country, and the second from December 1943 onwards, when a mission was sent to establish personal connection with the Romanian opposition. Ivor Porter's admirable narrative of his experiences in *Operation Autonomous* obviates the necessity to cover that mission in this chapter and allows me to concentrate on the first, more inchoate, period.[1] Also, cooperation with French agencies – a complex story in itself – is omitted, for reasons of space.

Formally, SOE was in being only from July 1940. Until then, the activities which it undertook were carried out by MI(R) and Section D, which had its own forward Balkan headquarters in Belgrade. Their roles, unlike SOE's in 1940, were well defined, mutually agreed and uncontested. Nevertheless, they did not have the field to themselves. From December 1939, the Inter-Service Balkan Intelligence Centre, in Ankara, took Romania into its purview. In London, Naval Intelligence largely devised its own plans, on the incontrovertible grounds that the Danube was a river. And the Foreign Office was determined to maintain its influence by setting limits to plans and operations which it did not, in some sense, control. Those were only the domestic opponents. On the German side, the head of the Abwehr, Admiral Canaris, took a personal interest in his agency's Romanian operations and established close working relationships with his counterpart in Bucharest, Michael Moruzov, head of the Serviciul Special de Informatii (SSI), in a series of meetings beginning in Venice in September 1939. The SSI was a military counter-intelligence service, but also was adopted by King Carol as his personal secret service. (Moruzov was a versatile professional; in March 1940, he managed successively to visit Berlin, Paris and London.)

Romania offered a volatile political environment in which to operate. The King had abolished the existing parties and exercised a royal dictatorship, assisted by a Cabinet of personalities drawn from the old leaderships. Foreign affairs remained very much in his hands. He nominated ministers and – to the Romania watcher – his choices indicated the tendencies of state policy. Under a Cabinet presided over by Armand Calinescu, policy tended towards Britain and France; one under Ion Gigurtu could safely reckoned to be pro-German. But, in Romanian thinking, not only in government but among the scattered and mutually hostile opposition groups, relations with both Germany and the western Allies turned on the country's relations with Russia. It was axiomatic that Germany was less of a threat to Romanian interests than the Soviet Union, with the corollary that, even if the western Allies defeated Germany, the Russian danger would still exist for Romania. That is fundamental to any analysis of Romania's politics at this period.

The domestic scene was equally problematic. The King might dictate policy but could only do so by striking bargains with various interests surviving from the old political and economic structure. Communism, which was irretrievably associated with Russian policies and particularly with the Comintern's demand for the return of Bessarabia, was represented by a small, illegal fraction, most of whose leaders were in Russia or in jail. (That did mean that SOE, at this stage, did not have to worry about pro-communist leanings among the local people on whom it relied.) Romania's indigenous fascist party – the Iron Guard – posed a more immediate threat to internal stability. Carol's crackdown on its leadership in November 1938 left it sullenly meditating revenge. The existence of a Hungarian minority acquired in 1919 but as yet unreconciled to Romanian rule and of an ethnic German minority, which although enjoying better relations with Romanian authority, was proving susceptible to *'Grossdeutschland'* propaganda – especially its younger members – were both sources of manipulation from outside. Additionally, there were Jews in Moldavia, Bukovina and Bessarabia who, deeply Orthodox and speaking Yiddish or Russian, were regarded by Romanians as 'Russian' and, as such, a stalking horse for the Soviet Union.

On paper, Romania's international position was favourable. Its frontiers had been guaranteed against German aggression by Britain and France on 13 April 1939. It had allies in the Balkans. But the Romanians were also looking for a guarantor against Russia, regarded as irremediably hostile and bent on annexing – in the Russian view, recovering – Bessarabia, acquired in contentious circumstances by Romania in 1919. In that context, the only viable candidate was Germany, but, even before the war, Romania's quandary was how to engage Germany without surrendering to its dominance. In September 1939, the Romanian Government adopted a policy of neutrality. This is a precarious option, since its maintenance depends not only on the neutral state's behaviour but on the rights conferred on belligerents in their relations with it. 'Unneutral behaviour' carries penalties and, hence, provides openings for varieties of suasion by belligerents in pursuit of their own objectives. In this regard, 'neutrality' raised for the British a crucial dilemma: did it warrant any action short of giving the Romanian Government reasons for accepting the blandishments or succumbing to the threats of the Germans, or, contrariwise, did it mean that British agencies should just act as they wished and damn the consequences? This dilemma was never solved; it was only superseded by events. The German government had no need of any such inhibitions; its policy was to tie up the Romanian government through its ability to supply – or withhold – the armaments and training necessary for the defence of Romania against the threat from Russia. It succeeded.

In the late 1930s, after two decades of public theorizing about 'economic warfare', no one, in Britain or Germany, needed to be told about the importance of Romanian oil. The main British objective, of course, was to cripple supply to Germany. The problem was that Germany was perfectly capable of collecting its requirements from Ploesti itself, if so minded, *and* long before British forces could get there. This consideration governed government pre-war planning, which, initially, considered Romania only as a source to make up shortfalls in India, during a British war with Japan. Subsequently, as war with Germany became more likely, the possibility that Romania threw in its lot with the Axis, or was invaded and occupied by a German army, required measures to deny Germany the oilfields for as long as possible. In 1916, an Anglo-French military mission, in a hastily arranged operation, had successfully damaged fields and installations so as to deprive the German war machine of oil supplies for about five months. Just how effective that was, in the context of the war, was debatable but enough was done to suggest in 1938/39 that, with careful planning, more lasting damage might be inflicted. This was the more urgent, as the mechanization of armed forces, and in particular, aircraft with far higher performance and therefore higher fuel consumption, had vastly increased the demand. The Romanian Government had an additional rationale of its own – fully accepted by the British – that an adequately advertised readiness to destroy the fields and installations might act to *deter* an invasion, from either Germany or Russia, or both. The concern of the German Government was to maximize the supply of oil from a source which covered about a fifth of its total requirements, pre-war, and when the Allied blockade ruled out its main peacetime supply line by sea from Constanta to Hamburg. 'Maximizing supply' meant not only increasing deliveries, as such, but also persuading the Romanian government to control, if not take over, concerns with a predominantly Allied shareholding. So, with Romania neutral, oil was to be the central objective for both belligerents.

The British considered the 'oil problem' under two rubrics – destruction of fields and installations and interdiction of supply routes by the Danube and the rail system. D Section and MI(R) both began to busy themselves with the first of these in 1938. Lieutenant-Colonel Gubbins, MI(R), visited Romania secretly and talked with selected personnel of companies with a British shareholding, whose expertise was vital to any attempt on the oilfields and installations. Final plans were agreed with the Chief of the Romanian General Staff in August 1939. In Bucharest, the direction of the scheme was entrusted to Colonel Leonida of the General Staff and Lieutenant-Colonel Macnab, the Military Attaché. Operational liaison devolved on Major Radulescu and Major Davidson-Houston – a Sapper officer who had served in China and Russia, and who arrived in Bucharest in July 1939. Their task was to destroy or put out of action the main fields centred on Ploesti. That, in the absence of a Romanian engineering branch, required the assistance of a company of Royal Engineers, to be despatched from Egypt. Additional personnel were to be sent to the Shell associate company, Astra Romana, in Ploesti as 'oilfield trainees'.

Plans to destroy the oilfields necessarily relied on the companies with a British shareholding for personnel and their detailed knowledge of installations and field operations. The companies' full cooperation was secured in a series of meetings with their directors at the Petroleum Division (Board of Trade). It was popularly assumed that the position their respective associate companies had gained in Romania conferred on them 'control' of the oil industry. This was erroneous. The local companies were all registered under Romanian law, in virtue of which the Romanian government had a lien on them, if it cared to exercise one. (The companies, therefore, aimed to avoid giving government the opportunity.) Additionally, the state-owned transport system, which included the export pipelines, conferred on the government leverage over the companies' operations. 'Control' optimistically overstated the position. On the Danube, local business enterprises, notably Watson and Youell, ship-chandlers long-established at Galati, provided expertise and, when necessary, cover for D Section or Naval Intelligence officers. It was supplemented from January 1940 by the Goeland Transport and Trading Company, an enterprise set up by the British government specifically to concentrate under one management measures of economic warfare involving Danube shipping.

From the outset, the British recognized that success depended on the working-out of three conditions which they could not control. The whole scheme was designedly a *response* to a German initiative – which put a premium on timely and accurate intelligence; it depended on the cooperation of the Romanian government – which was assured if Calinescu was in charge but could be problem-atic if he were not; it required a helpful attitude from the Turkish Government, also neutral but one, also, which was bound by – or could shelter behind – the restrictions of the Montreux Convention governing wartime access to the Straits and which, moreover, like the Romanian Government, regarded Russia as a far greater threat than Germany to its national interests.

In Romania itself, the crucial problem was timing. Initially, the British had calculated that German troops could overrun Romania in between 10 and 14 days. Colonel Macnab's report on the state of the Romanian army in April 1939, drastically shortened this period. Having reported favourably on the qualities of Romanian infantry, Macnab singled out the virtual absence of defence works in depth, the lack of armoured fighting vehicles and air cover, and all the associated training, especially between different arms, and concluded:

> In about 18 months, the Army may well become a force to be reckoned with seriously. At present, it has every hope of success if asked to fight any of its neighbours, but in conflict with a western power, its chances of protracted resistance are not worth betting on.

This judgement meant that the Field Company had to be in Romania and ready to move, *before* the Reichswehr moved. But that raised for the Romanian Government the prospect that the Germans would regard any such military presence at that juncture as an opportunity to 'protect' Romania from the Allies.

The scope of the envisaged task required a Field Company to be of eight officers and 204 other ranks. The problem, then, was how to transport them and their equipment and maintain security so that they might not give the Germans an excuse to invade. The advance party of four RAF officers and radio operators – to receive and transmit intelligence – could travel in civilian clothes by train, through Palestine, Lebanon and Turkey, to Istanbul – which, eventually, it did. Moving over 200 personnel and their equipments posed problems of a different order. Effectively, they could go by air or sea; or a combination of both. Three routes were possible – the first, by sea to Istanbul, with transfer to airfields in Thrace from which RAF Bristol Bombay troop carriers would fly to Ploesti; the Field Company would then arrive three days after leaving Alexandria. Alternatively, the troops could be ferried by air, with stop-overs, possibly, in Greece or preferably, in Turkey – effectively two days in each case. The third route was by ship from Alexandria to Constanta or Galati, and thence by motor transport to Ploesti. Greece excepted, all the other routes required the acquiescence, if not the positive cooperation, of the Turkish Government. Aircraft would need to land and refuel; a ship would have to go through the Straits, or at least get into the Sea of Mamara. Both courses of action had to comply with international treaties, interpreting which gave Turkish negotiators ample room for manoeuvre.

The Turkish Government proved to be willing to turn a blind eye to flights in Turkish air space, provided they looked suitably civilian, and was prepared to allow refuelling on Turkish soil, but maintained that the number of trips required to move the company in the machines available would be impossible to conceal and would allow the Germans to attack or to claim political compensation for the breach of neutrality. By reason of these objections, the aircraft proposal was dropped in favour of the sea route. But there again, the need to avoid the overtly military impelled Middle East HQ in Cairo to charter ships – in the event, the SS *Deebank*, for the troops, and the SS *Fouadieh*, for the equipment, which included two tons of explosive and two Morris trucks. The choice of Field Company lighted on No. 54 RE, under Captain G. A. D. Young – at the time in the Western Desert. Additional personnel were to be sent to the Shell associate company, working in Ploesti as 'oilfield trainees'. Local overall command of the operation was vested in Commander R. D. Watson, RN.

Plans for Danube operations revolved around blocking the Iron Gates, either by blockships or by detonating the cliffs on the Yugoslav side. Additionally, pre-emptive chartering of all available river tonnage and creating a shortage of pilots at the Iron Gates by offering them extended paid holidays in the Near East – undertaken by Goeland – were courses to which the Germans might well object but which they could not attribute to the Romanians. Blocking and sabotage operations on the river were devised by D Section and Naval Intelligence, acting through the Attaché in Bucharest, Captain Max Despard. After the failure of the attempt to dynamite the cliffs at the Iron Gates, it was decided to try to achieve the same result from the river. The scheme was, therefore, to some extent an improvisation and was tacked on to the increasingly evident need to arm Allied ships trading on the Danube and stiffen their complement with RN officers and ratings.

Canaris did not have to contend with third parties or with complicated logistics. Once the Romanian Government was brought into line, the rest would be comparatively easy. In October 1939, he sent Lieutenant-Colonel Erich Pruck to Bucharest to conclude an agreement with Moruzov whereby the Abwehr looked after supply routes to Germany. In short order, the Brandenburg Division – an Abwehr unit – moved in to police transport and port facilities, in the guise of employees of the Danube Shipping Co. Soldiers in mufti acted as sentries on every train routed through Hungary. The main detachment set up camp near the Iron Gates. Two hundred and fifty Brandenburgers, disguised as a Reichsbund Sports Group, were moved to the Bulgarian port of Russe, opposite the main river oil terminal at Giurgiu, and could be observed happily improving their boating skills along the Danube. Canaris himself spent four days in Bucharest in November, getting Moruzov's agreement to a stricter surveillance of refineries and power installations in the oil fields and at river terminals, notably Giurgiu and Turnu Severin. Further, Moruzov undertook to report all foreigners' movements to the Abwehr and to remove 'undesirable elements' from oil companies, especially the Shell subsidiary. Canaris installed Major Dr. Wagner as his Bucharest link with Moruzov. He also infiltrated an agent into the security section of the Romanian General Staff, and recruited nine officers in the upper echelons of the Siguranta, the secret police (whose job was not counter-espionage, but, at the time, surveillance of Communists, Jew and Hungarians). These officers were *Vertrauensmaenner* – native Romanians, i.e. specifically *not* ethnic Germans, on which the Abwehr relied for much of its 'illegal' operations, as distinct from those concerted formally with Moruzov. Additionally, German agencies in Romania were backed up by the *Alarmbereitschaft* – an organization of ethnic Germans and of *Reichsdeutsche* employed in Romanian industry, covering the whole country. Its duties included providing information and assistance to German officials about political developments in their localities and keeping a register of political, military or economic enemies of the Reich. In the oil fields, its activities were coordinated by the German Consul in Ploesti, who was an officer of the Gestapo. (The British had no consular posts at all in the oil area.) German or German-controlled surveillance structures were well in place before the end of 1939.

By that time, too, the Romanian Government had also improved its own surveillance of the industry. In December, a number of accidental fires in refineries at Ploesti gave it the opportunity to station two infantry divisions in the fields, commanding a total area about 40 miles by 20. From the British point of view, that in itself would not be a problem if the official, Romanian-endorsed, plan were to be put through. If, however, the Romanian Government were to be more favourable to Germany, then the presence of Romanian troops could inhibit or negate British action.

In September, 1939, after the official plans had been agreed, King Carol told the German Air Attaché, Colonel Gerstenberg, that the British had submitted a plan to sabotage the oil fields but that he had rejected it. (Gerstenberg, with access to Goering dating from their former service in Richthofen's squadron, was in Bucharest as important a figure as Fabricius, the German Minister, or his successor von Killinger.) The arrival of the 'trainees' in September was duly observed by the deputy consul in Ploesti, whose cover was a technical consultancy bureau. His information was duly received by Colonel Wahle, the German Military Attaché.

At the beginning of October, *Fouadieh* tied up at Galati. Its cargo was moved to a mountain artillery depot between Ploesti and Brasov. Davidson-Houston records in his memoirs, *Armed Pilgrimage*, that, en route, the trucks had stood for a day, unattended by their Romanian drivers, in the market-place of Ploesti – so he was 'uncertain how much secrecy still surrounded the consignment'.[2] On 10 October, he, with Romanian colleagues, supervised the unloading. They found a number of bizarre items – an Army Bible, a darts board (which Davidson-Houston adroitly explained was used for target practice), three hockey sticks, some Arabic grammars, and packets of toilet paper – which, he records, were 'greatly admired and immediately taken into use as office stationery'. The more orthodox supplies were used by him for training both Romanian officers and selected oil company employees. This proceeded throughout the winter and into the next spring.

The despatch of the Field Company awaited an assessment of German intentions, but experience proved that, into that calculation, had also to be built Romanian responses. During his service in Romania, Colonel Macnab found that the General Staff's attitudes were far more closely aligned to government than was the case in Britain. At this time, the Romanian government had concluded that the Ribbentrop/ Molotov pact of 23 August 1939 presaged an attack on Romania by the Red Army; after September, the fate of Poland raised the spectre of the country's being similarly partitioned between the two allies. Calinescu was murdered by the Iron Guard on 21 September 1939, and, in him, disappeared the last determined proponent of the 'western' orientation. His successors increasingly viewed Germany as the only external guarantor against Russia – a view reinforced by Allied military failures. In that situation, the British position was particularly vulnerable in that, for security reasons, the oilfield project had not been disclosed to the General Staff as a whole. To Macnab, his opposite number, Major Radulescu, appeared to have been sidelined by his superiors. With the support of the Romanian military no longer unqualified, the right to initiate the move of the Field Company was given by the War Cabinet to Sir Rex Hoare, the British Minister, in March 1940. By then, the local training programme had been completed and the detailed instructions for the different teams, with targets, methods and rendezvous for the destruction of three main fields and the Ploesti area installations were ready in the Legation. Hoare himself, sensing the slide towards Germany, argued fiercely for reinstating the air route, and as soon as possible.

On 10 May, the German invasion of the Low Countries and France changed the context in which British decisions had to be taken. An immediate German attack on Romania was now unlikely. At the same time, deprivation of oil supplies became even more crucial to the outcome in the west. The 54th Field Company embarked at Alexandria on 25 May and arrived off Kilia, on the west side of the southern entrance to the Straits, three days later. It was then found that the charter party obliged the ship to go to Chanak, on the opposite shore, to unload the general cargo carried on Turkish Government insistence. The master and the local Turkish authorities at Kilia were prevailed upon to allow the troops to disembark – which at least made slightly more plausible the cover story that they were intended to build roads in Thrace. The question then was whether to wait until *Deebank* would be available, or find another craft for the onward journey. Above all, the Turks were adamant that the ship should not remain in the Marmara too long. At the same time, Romanian officials, seeing the final disintegration of any hopes from 'the West' and looking to Germany for the future security of their country, were increasingly disinclined to join in the destruction of the one asset, apart from geography, they could offer. Military failure is dissuasive. Colonel Macnab found doors closed to him; Davidson-Houston found himself of great interest to the police. While no one formally cancelled Romanian participation in the scheme, no one was willing to promote it, either. It was rumoured that 54 Field Company would be forbidden to land. A ban was never necessary. The Company's mere presence in Turkey was causing severe problems with the Turkish administration, particularly in that the nominally civilian RE company did not have individual passports and had to be handled *en bloc*. The trend of events in France only increased official anxiety. The solution was unexpectedly provided by Italy's entry into the war, on 10 June. Then an attack on Egypt could be expected and the security of the Eastern Mediterranean was put at risk. Middle East HQ, Cairo, unwilling to see its engineers on the wrong side of the Aegean and possibly interned, ordered their recall on 22 June. They left Turkish waters on 28 June, the day Russian troops entered Bessarabia, northern Bukovina and districts of Moldavia.

Macnab only learned of the withdrawal three days later and that from his fellow attaché in Ankara. He protested that any advance by the Russians further south might easily create a situation in which the destruction plans could be carried out. Hoare, who, equally, had not been advised of the withdrawal, argued vigorously that a nucleus should be kept ready to be flown in, regardless of Turkish and Romanian sensibilities, as a coup against the oilfields would inhibit the Wehrmacht and, by compelling the Germans to intervene, possibly embroil Germany with the Soviet Union. Romania, in his view, 'seems the best field in which to sow seeds of early German/Soviet antagonism'. He was perceptive but his plea was not acted upon. In France, the Reichswehr had reached Saumur on the Loire and in Whitehall immediate action in Romania was not the most pressing of priorities.

There was, however, an alternative scheme – not disclosed to the Romanian Government – which Hoare fully supported. It was devised by Leslie Forster, Chief Engineer of Astra Romana, who, after Munich, had begun to consider political circumstances which might make the destruction of the oil-fields necessary. In his expectation, the Nazi-organized Saxon minority – among them some of his own colleagues – would provide a ready-made local force to police the installations, or provide intelligence of any operations. It was essential, therefore, to ensure that significant damage could be inflicted quickly, within a night, if possible. In turn, this would mean abandoning wholesale destruction, as planned, and concentrating on very precise targets. The numbers required to effect this would be minimal and could be recruited easily from among company staff with a detailed knowledge of oilfield working. By 1939, the Tintea and Boldesti fields offered a combination of structures and gas pressures which could sustain extensive fires for years, especially as their flow had been restricted for reasons of conservation. The technique was to burn or explode the 'Christmas trees' at the well-heads, so that the heat generated would set the escaping gas on fire, which would not die down until the structure was near exhausted. Such fires, in the given state of the art, could not be put out until the subsurface gas pressure was sufficiently reduced. Experience showed that that could take years. Furthermore, eliminating these fields, virtually all Astra property, required blowing only 65 wells and would cut out over 50 per cent of Romania's immediately ascertainable production.

Forster's scheme was approved by the General Manager of Astra Romana and the British Petroleum Attaché, Eric Berthoud, who alerted Rex Hoare. He recruited and trained his team in the use of thermite. On the eve of the action, the company guards in the fields were replaced by the Romanian army – two private soldiers to each well – and the entire oil area was put under restriction. As very few were privy to the scheme, betrayal was, obviously, suspected, though its origin cannot be established. Circumstantially, a M. Lazarescu, manager of a British insurance company in Bucharest, who had contacts with the Abwehr, is identified as the most likely link, but his source of information, either deliberate or accidental, is unknown. The Romanian government responded by decreeing that foreigners required special permits to be employed in the oilfields and used the consequent registration procedure to get rid of the technical staff of British-capital companies. This category included Forster and the 'trainees'. In France, the Germans got hold of documentary evidence about the original oilfield scheme and the names of the British oil participants, which had been given to the Romanian General Staff. The Abwehr demanded their expulsion from the country, which was formally ordered by the new pro-Axis government under Argetoianu on the day it took office (4 July). Of the 17 expellees, 11 were involved in the oilfield destruction scheme. The Legation learned that the Romanian government had offered the Germans the oilfields *en bloc*, in return for a guarantee of Romania's frontiers. Romania was the only piece of Europe which Britain had actually *planned* to 'set ablaze' but both attempts had failed.

Action on the Danube suffered a like fate. On 29 March 1940, SS *Mardinian*, out of Liverpool, berthed at Sulina with 68 officers and ratings and a cargo of 95 cases in bond and invoiced as Chrysler spares to the Chrysler agent in Budapest. The RN personnel were transferred directly to river craft – in contravention of Romanian regulations – and disappeared to their Danube protection assignments. The cases passed customs' inspection – Despard having been thoughtfully supplied with £1,500 'to ensure the cooperation of Romanian personnel' – and were handed over to his men. Some 30 tons of arms and ammunition, including three Vickers machine guns, limpet mines and 600 lbs. of high explosives were stowed aboard a lighter, *Termonde*. A number of other lighter, self-propelled barges and tugs, all secured by Goeland and flying the Red Ensign, imparted a commercial appearance to the enterprise. The crews comprised personnel from the Royal and Royal Australian navies, and Greeks, Hungarians and Romanians normally engaged in Danube traffic. The expedition was led by Commander A. P. Gibson, RN.

His immediate problem was that from the Black Sea to Braila, the Danube was juridically Romanian. He had, therefore, to get through the first 110 miles of waterway without raising the suspicions of Romanian officials or causing them to wilt under German pressure. Above Braila, the river was under the international regime of the International Danube Commission on which British and French representatives continued to sit, offering a degree of protection. The flotilla left Sulina on 1st April, shadowed by a river steamer hastily chartered by the Abwehr. Giurgiu, where the tugs had to refuel, was reached in the afternoon of the 3rd. Unexpectedly, the vessels were promptly searched, at the instigation of the Port Captain. In Romanian maritime administration, Port Captains were key officials whose power to interpret the regulations, not only of the Port Administration and of Customs authorities but also of the National Bank, effectively controlled all shipping operations in port. They were political nominees – disinterested bureaucracy was unknown in the Balkans – and were not well paid, but, within broad limits, were in a position to set their own agenda. The agenda of the official at Giurgiu, Drencianu, was pro-German. By April 1940 there was already a considerable German military and security presence in the port, including the German Naval Attaché who appears to have been the link in this particular instance.

Drencianu (who was related to the Minister of Marine, Admiral Pais) dragged out giving permission for the British tugs to go to the oiling berth, about four miles from the port, for 36 hours, during which time Major Dr. Wagner urged a strict examination of the cargo on the grounds that it had not been cleared through Customs. The Giurgiu officers duly searched the main tug and found uniforms, arms and about £500 in lei. The last two were impounded. British representations to Bucharest brought an order to desist and a return of the pistols and money. With this, the incident was thought to be closed, but on 5 April another sudden inspection revealed the cargo on *Termonde*. One of the cases still bore the official label, 'demolition explosives'. It did not help. There then ensued a complex struggle between officials in Bucharest and between them and their subordinate officers in Giurgiu which ended when Fabricius overcame the obstinacy of Gafencu, the Foreign Minister, by threatening a cessation of arms' deliveries, if the flotilla were allowed to proceed. This argument, it appears, was referred to the King, and was accepted. The ships were ordered to return to Braila, their cargo to remain in Giurgiu – though with a promise that – Romania being neutral – the British could have access to their property, later. No legal charges were preferred. The flotilla arrived at Braila on 10 and 11 April, and then was directed to Sulina, for repairs and strengthening for a sea voyage to Istanbul. That process was protracted by bureaucratic delays and the need for ministerial permission (Pais's) to sail – which had to be negotiated separately for each vessel. The flotilla, therefore, though still unprepared for a sea voyage, left by individual units between the end of May and 20 June. By that time, the Romanian and Yugoslav delegates, at German prompting, had persuaded the International Danube Commission to rule that the only armed vessels allowed on the Danube were to be those of the riparian states in their own sectors of the river and that its permission was required for every transit of arms and explosives. Additionally, the Romanian authorities blocked the Danube at Sulina to control entrance and exit and German forces took over Constanta. The Danube was shut.

As the war developed, after 1940, Romania, instead of becoming a way station for oil from the Caucasus and a secondary source of supply – which was the German intention – came to provide about 40 per cent of German requirements, mostly for fuel oils and motor gasoline. In the short term, Romanian supplies allowed the Reichswehr to carry the attack on France to the Loire and beyond. The failures of spring and summer 1940 have, accordingly, been severely censured. As regards the local conduct of the agencies involved, censure is justified, particularly in the Danube expedition (though it also provided the Foreign Office with the satisfactions of 'Schadenfreude'). Even if you are improvising such an operation, it is as well to ensure that the foreign crews, of unmistakably local origin, do not have shiny new passports, innocent of stamps and visas, issued in Malta. It is even more important to ensure that one of your officers, having found himself in a brothel without the means to pay for services rendered, does not assault the police who are called by the madam to deal with him. It is also necessary to bribe the right people. Anecdotal evidence implies that Admiral Pais thought himself left out. But whether the scheme, even if perfectly prepared, would have succeeded in the face of the Abwehr network or the Brandenburg troops at the Iron Gates, seems doubtful, on the available evidence. Canaris was there first.

In response to defeat on the Continent, MI(R) and D Section were transmogrified into SOE, with additions of hitherto civilian personnel. The process in Romania was so haphazard that the actual strength of the new organization there remains unclear. (Perhaps it was to SOE.) Individuals are known to the record – Hugh Seton-Watson emerged from temporary civil service in Bloomsbury, but, although he was enrolled in the new organization, he continued to be paid by the Ministry of Information for another six months. William Harris Burland had arrived with the mission from Warsaw and joined Goeland. He 'played' the black market for currencies so successfully that he cut the costs of SOE operations in Hungary and Turkey, as well as Romania, to the delight of the Treasury. Geoffrey Household has left a vivid account of his recruitment and subsequent arrival in Romania as an 'Insurance Agent'.[3] Ivor Porter joined as a civilian from his British Council academic job in Bucharest. By 1941, there are neat lists of personnel, but for the previous summer and autumn, assessing those who were on the strength, in contrast to those who claimed they were or would like to have been, is a task which awaits research.

SOE began to operate during the last weeks of King Carol's regime, when, on the day after German forces reached Calais, the King installed a pro-German government which, in quick succession, repudiated the Anglo-French Guarantee, left the League of Nations and invited German help in re-equipping and training the Romanian Army and Air Force. Germans began to arrive in July 1940 to supervise the repatriation of 60,000 '*Volksdeutsche*' from Bessarabia and the other districts occupied by Russia, in larger numbers than the British observed the operation warranted. It appeared to them, also, that the assembly-point, the port of Galati, was being taken over de facto to establish day-to-day military control over the Danube. Luftwaffe units appeared in September. (A squadron of Me 109s fighters was detailed to protect Ploesti and one of Me 110s was based in Bulgaria). German army units arrived in October – again, on a scale far larger than its nominal training mission required and with the specific assignment of protecting the oilfields. The premise of all British planning was neatly negated; the Germans did not invade Romania, they arrived by invitation.

The 'oil' plans having failed, SOE's task now was essentially to build a coherent opposition for anti-German activities, i.e. to take the role which Romanian governments, for their own reasons, had failed to sustain. This took SOE into politics. The central figure was Iuliu Maniu, former leader of the National Peasant party; a man who, by reason of his personal integrity, was a somewhat isolated figure in Romanian political life. Unfortunately, his moral qualities were in no way matched by his record for action. Hugh Seton-Watson turned his family connection with Maniu to good use. Maniu was given funds and a radio transmitter. In December 1940, SOE schemed to create a local pro-Ally organization comprising the residue of Maniu's party, the Ploughman's Front, dissident Iron Guardists, university groups opposing the Iron Guard and 'other suitable elements'. This organization was to promote the 'major upheaval' which SOE intended to produce, in March 1941. It would have the task of impeding the transport of oil to the Reich and destroying German facilities if the Reichswehr moved south – though whether that was 'the major upheaval' or was a separate exercise is not clear. Plans for sabotage in the oilfields had to be abandoned, as the RAF pleaded it had no aircraft available to stage the bombing raid necessary to provide cover. The group's composition suggests either sheer desperation or an over-estimate of Maniu's capacity to hold such a disparate collection together. Operationally, it was to be under the command of the SOE officer in the Legation, but by March, of course, there was no Legation. It had been withdrawn the previous month and SOE personnel left also, variously to Belgrade, Istanbul or Cairo. 'For the time being' wrote Hoare 'the game is up'. It was, and for nearly three years, any contact with Romania relied principally on radio communication.

The German success and British failure both hung on a factor which neither state could control, *viz* Romania's deep-rooted fear of Russia, but which the Germans could exploit and the British could not. The supply of weapons and help with modernizing Romania's armed forces allowed Germany to gain benefits in other aspects of policy – among them, continuity in the supply of oil. As Romania was neutral, the task of ensuring that continuity fell to the Abwehr. Admiral Canaris personally took charge of the operations, using the considerable assets represented by members of the ethnic German community and those Romanians who were pro-German, either from conviction or from tactical sensitivity. Additionally, the Brandenburg Division, in suitably civil guise was put in place to counter threats to the oilfields and transport systems. By October 1940, the stationing of German troops and air units and firefighters from the Hamburg brigade, finally extinguished any probability of a successful British coup against the Ploesti area.

By contrast, the British had pinned their hopes on an inter-governmental arrangement which crumbled with the slide of opinion in the Romanian Cabinet towards Germany. Soviet menaces provided the Romanian government with solid reasons for maintaining intact the major asset it could offer the Germans for their support. It was, perhaps, natural for the British to think of destroying the oilfields as a re-run of 1916, relying on Allied personnel in the oil industry and specialist troops, all to be protected by the Romanian army and with the Romanian government taking care of pro-German elements. But the scheme was administratively cumbersome, it lacked unity of command and it relied on too many imponderables. Forster's scheme took greater account of technological possibilities and the realities of ethnic or political allegiance, and, by concentrating on precise targets, was more economical. The official destruction scheme faded away, and the unofficial i.e. Forsters', alternative was brought to naught.

The Danube operations failed through faulty preparation, indiscipline and the flouting of security but also through changes in Romanian attitudes induced by German success in the west. For the Romanians, Norway was *the* test case of Allied resolve to save a small country from aggression. In the event, Allied forces were pitched out of central Norway within three weeks of their arrival in April and the Norwegian Army forced to surrender. The Allies had failed in a campaign they themselves had initiated. Hoare reported the 'great shock to Romanian public opinion'. Thereafter, one can correlate shifts in Romanian policies with German successes. In consequence, even those Romanians who had hitherto favoured the Allies began to switch to the more practical problem of limiting the degree of influence the Germans would inevitably exercise. The catastrophe in the Low Countries and France in May and June, merely galvanized the trend, at the same time as the Soviet take over of the Baltic States (14/15 June) underlined Romania's imperative need of a guarantor. During these weeks, the effective or tacit support of Romanian officials, essential to carrying out any of the planned operations, faded away. By the time the more subtle schemes, *viz* of sinking barges loaded with unexceptionable materials, such as cement and scrap iron and wrecking the towing railway at the Iron Gates, were evolved, the Danube was under German control.

Thereafter, Romania was, from the British standpoint, unique in that it was occupied territory in which, however, Britain still enjoyed diplomatic representation. But, after May 1940, Romania was also entering on a period of political turmoil from which it emerged four months later as a military dictatorship firmly aligned with Germany, an unfavourable context in which to establish pro-Ally forces among the scattered and fragmented opposition. All SOE could do in Romania, before its operatives were withdrawn in February 1941, was to locate and stimulate opposition groups, ensure radio and, to a lesser extent, courier com-munication with the outside world, and thereby begin to create the assets which, in December 1943, helped to make the 'Autonomous' mission a credible venture.

Notes

1 Ivor Porter, *Operation Autonomous*, London: Chatto & Windus, 1989.
2 J. V. Davidson-Houston, *Armed Pilgrimage*, London: Hale, 1949.
3 Geoffrey Household, *Against the Wind*, London: Michael Joseph, 1958.

11

SOE IN AFGHANISTAN DURING THE SECOND WORLD WAR

Bradley F. Smith

Among the many anomalies which affected intelligence and special operational organizations during the Second World War were a series of reversals of alliances which abruptly turned old friends into new enemies, and old enemies into new friends. Japan had a four-decades long alliance with Britain in the twentieth century, and had marched with the Western Powers during the First World War, but turned toward Germany during the 1930s, and on the eve of the Second World War aligned herself with the Axis Pact of Nazi Germany and Fascist Italy. Japan's new Fascist partner, Italy, had also been on the Allied side during the First World War. Then, after beginning the Second World War with Germany, and having experienced many failures and disappointments including the loss of much of her empire, and ultimately an Allied invasion and the destruction of the Fascist regime, again changed sides to become a quite junior member of the Anglo-American team during 1943.

The Soviet Union was also an enthusiastic participant in the Second World War game of alliance hopping. After energetically championing united front opposition to Nazi-Fascist expansionism in the early and mid-1930s, Moscow switched to the role of being Hitler's ally via the Nazi-Soviet Pact in August 1939, as the Soviet Union tried to save its skin and pick up valuable territorial booty in Poland and the Baltic States through this dance with the Nazis. But Russia's turn to experience the new military-political-racist horror came in June 1941 when the USSR became the target of Hitler's Operation 'Barbarossa'. Three huge German Army Groups smashed into western Russia and the Nazis massacred more Soviet citizens, especially Jews, Gypsies and Communist Party members, than even Stalin had managed to kill in the 1930s.

Understandably, those regions of the Soviet Union which were able to escape the nightmare of Nazi occupation fought back furiously against Hitler's forces, and were soon perceived in the West as among the bravest and most effective of the United Nations. The popular image of the Soviet Union temporarily brightened, and even Stalin was reshaped into a world leader, perhaps even a soldier of freedom,

137

whose heroic and able efforts had done so much to save the West, as well as to preserve, and increase the power, of the Soviet system.

Given the scale of these military, psycho-political, and geo-political changes occurring between 1940 and 1941, the traditional system of balance of power appeared to be on its way toward 'the scrap heap of history', or at least to be undergoing unusually far-reaching changes. The creation of the United Nations Organization near the end of hostilities also seemed to testify to the popular belief and hope that the old system had been damaged beyond repair and that a new, and hopefully better, one was about to be born. In many regions of the world, including China and southern Asia, revolutionary history actually was on the march, while at the same time the first stages of the great consumer revolution (which would outlast many dramatic political changes) were beginning to appear in North America, and would fundamentally change the way of life of much of the whole world's population.

But while these forces of change were rising in some areas of the world during the 1940s, it is also true that in many regions stretching from Central Africa to much of Central America, the changes which had actually taken place in the political systems and manner of life, by 1940 or 1945, were modest indeed. Many peoples were barely aware of the new technologies, or the existence of such things as mass consumption. Within these 'backward' regions, however, lay the homes of 50 per cent or more of the world's population, and for these people there was no likelihood of fundamental change in the foreseeable future. The majority of the world's people still experienced a life within traditional ways and mores, and the 'Four Freedoms' and the 'United Nations' had very little immediate meaning for them.

During the 1930s, and on into the 1940s, the landlocked ancient Kingdom of Afghanistan, in Central Asia, might well have served as the embodiment of those countries which had long struggled and endured to be sure, but had not moved beyond the starting point of pre-industrialization. Afghanistan had been shielded from many of the buffetings of modernism by its customary ways and a deep societal devotion to Islam. Large numbers of its people were committed to the monastic life, a fact which when combined with the country's remote location (protected by some of the highest mountains in the world) and an extremely primitive communication and transport system, made isolation a fundamental reality of life. Although containing handfuls of individuals who had been trained in Western universities, which helped build some bridges to the developed world, the great bulk of the often illiterate population of Afghanistan laboured on in traditional ways, while nearly all aspects of the country's social and political power remained in the hands of its theological-aristocratic elite.

Despite its remoteness, backwardness and the exotic mysteries it seemed to exude, Afghanistan had long been at the centre of one of the classic power struggles of the nineteenth and the early twentieth centuries. Throughout that era, the British government had feared that Tsarist Russia was about to pounce on its Indian Empire either by storming through mile-high Afghanistan, or by persuading the Afghans to give free passage to the Russian Army so that it might smite the British 'oppressors' of Afghanistan's Moslem cousins in India. 'The Great Game' played out by British adventurers in Afghanistan during the late nineteenth and early twentieth centuries had therefore often been intended to thwart such Russian expansionism and 'intrigue'.

Due to the major diplomatic reshuffle of 1907, however, Britain and Russia (along with France) had suddenly become partners (in a stand off with the Central Powers of Germany, Austria-Hungary and Italy), and, consequently, some of the traditional 'Great Game' activity ceased. Instead, during the run up to the First World War the British and Russians gingerly linked arms to counter alleged Central Power political activities in Afghanistan, and continued to do so during the First World War when Germany, Austria and Turkey carried out political warfare against the Allies in this region.

Two additional elements were added to the wartime 'Great Game' in 1917, when the USA entered the war on the Allied side and the Bolshevik revolution knocked Moscow out of the war. Although the US government did not promote democracy or Wilsonian self-determination very vigorously in Afghanistan, US representatives were frequently quite free with their money and promises of aid, occasionally coupling these with promotion of heretical doctrines such as political and social equality. Russian communist representatives were even more disturbing to Afghan traditionalists because the new Moscow openly promoted universal political rights and social equality, along with attacks on religion and a litany of calls for the overthrow of capitalist and 'feudal' institutions.

By the 1920s and early 1930s the USA had largely anchored itself in home waters, which made it possible for the French, Italians, Germans and Japanese to hold on to some influence in such marginal areas as Afghanistan. The Soviet Union also dabbled energetically in Afghan affairs, carrying on the tried-and-true principle of Russian nineteenth-century policy which held that Afghanistan might at some point hold the key to the defence of southern Russia (now apparently threatened by 'capitalist encirclement') and could provide an easily opened door to what were now perceived in Moscow to be the oppressed and struggling masses of the Indian subcontinent.

Nonetheless, Britain continued to be the most significant foreign power concerned with Afghanistan, and it was in the interwar period when the British introduced to the Afghan scene the use of air power as a magic means to terrify and tame potential threats to India by the Afghan border tribes (a practice continued by the British even in the wartime and post Second World War eras, and at this writing it is still being used in Kashmir by Pakistan).[1]

Yet during the middle and late 1930s, when the intensity of international rivalry had increased worldwide and conflicts erupted first in China and Ethiopia and then in Europe itself, Britain remained surprisingly sanguine about the Afghan situation. In early 1938, Sir P. J. Grigg, later a Secretary of State for War, dismissed the possibility of a Soviet threat to India by way of Afghanistan as nothing more than 'a bogey', and in early 1939, the Committee on the Defence of India concluded that the Russian danger to Afghanistan was only 'latent' and did not constitute a 'serious current threat'.[2]

But the Afghans themselves tended to be much more uneasy about the situation and were keenly aware of their vulnerability. Kabul bought weapons from a number of foreign suppliers in the mid-1930s, and as MI5 knew in 1940, the Afghans had continued to purchase some weaponry from Skoda, even though by that time this company was located well within Hitler's Third Reich.[3]

When the Nazi-Soviet Pact was signed in August 1939, and war began in the following September, the Afghans suffered a serious panic attack. At this time London was also concerned about the vulnerability of Afghanistan to German-Soviet pressure and was eager to secure intelligence on the Afghan situation from everyone, including the Polish government-in-exile.[4] British officials also made extensive use of their cryptanalytic assets in an effort to gauge Axis-Soviet intentions in Afghanistan, and broke into at least one Japanese agent key used on this area well before the USA provided the British with a 'Magic' machine to assist the British in breaking into the main Japanese diplomatic cipher. Britain's Afghanistan worries were also somewhat eased by the fact that the Government Code and Cypher School had broken into, and regularly read, the traffic of the Vichy French Minister in Kabul from at least as early as October 1940.[5]

But down in the day-to-day world of international power and force, Britain lacked the men and machines necessary to stop a possible German-Russian attack on India via Afghanistan, and the situation therefore continued to seem serious. By May 1940, official Whitehall policy consisted of a British promise to protect Afghanistan from attack both by the Russians and Germans, but when the Indian Government informed London in mid-1940 that it did not have sufficient men and material to carry through such a policy, Whitehall seems to have ignored this unpleasant fact, and settled into a position of determined wobble and bluff. General Auchinleck declared at a meeting of the planning staff in London on 20 December 1940, that 'it was desirable that our policy ... in Afghanistan should be clearly defined and agreed with the Government of India', but in fact no practical defensive measures seem to have been taken.[6]

Consequently, British officials in Kabul and Delhi were left yet again to make most of their own swords out of ploughshares in order to protect their domains from the Axis-Soviet colossus looming in the north. A perfect environment had thereby been created for rumour, intrigue and a festival of belief in the power of intelligence and covert operations. Coming on the heels of the great shock engendered by the fall of France, and the wave of belief that clandestine warfare had played a major role in producing that débâcle, such fears and fantasies seemed especially close to reality along the remote border area of India and Afghanistan.

By early 1941, although some old British security measures remained intact, including the usual air attacks on the Faqir of Ipi in January, a new phase in the Afghan security drama opened when the Indian pro-Nazi, Chandra Bose, slipped over the border into Afghanistan thinly disguised by the cover name 'Zia-Ud-Din'. He was guided on this journey by a young communist sympathizer named

Bhagat Ram who, for security reasons was using the cover name 'Rahmat Khan' in Afghanistan, and 'Harbans Lal' in India. Unlike Chandra Bose, who frequently tried to hide his Nazi sympathies by falsely portraying himself as a supporter of the hard Left, Bhagat was simultaneously a devout Hindu and a sincere communist revolutionary whose brother had been executed by the British. Bhagat Ram had, in fact, only assisted in Bose's escape because he had been deceived into believing that once Bose got beyond British controlled territory he would set off for Moscow.

After arriving in Kabul with Bose in tow, Bhagat Ram joined up with one of his communist friends and colleagues, a young man named Uttam Chand, and they then tried to deposit Bose with the Soviet diplomatic mission. But the Soviet officials in Afghanistan refused to touch Bose (after 22 June the Indian Communist Party would call Bose a 'traitor, hangman, and a puppet of the Axis powers'), so Bhagat Ram and Chand did the next best thing and handed him on to the Italian Embassy in Kabul, at a time when Italy was still an important pillar in the Axis pact, and Italian officials were cultivating contacts with anti-British Indian leaders such as the Faqir of Ipi (against whom the British were still launching RAF attacks during May).

The Italians were so eager to secure intelligence sources regarding British India that without further security checks on Bhagat Ram they arranged for him to be the communications link to Bose's Nazi and Fascist associates. Three months later (22 June 1941), however, when Hitler and Mussolini attacked the USSR and a number of international partnerships were rearranged, Bhagat Ram (still following Moscow's orders) handed over all the details he had acquired on these Indian Fascist-Nazi sympathizers to the British Indian Police who promptly arrested the members of these groups or rolled them over so they worked for Allied intelligence organizations.[7] Other significant changes in Anglo-Soviet relations regarding subversive activity in India and Afghanistan also occurred in the aftermath of the German attack on the USSR as these old enemies in Central Asia now locked arms in order to prevent Axis subversive activity in Afghanistan. On 17 July 1941 they strongly protested the Afghan decision permitting the Germans to post a Minister (Herr von Herti) in Kabul.[8] The British were especially worried that the Afghans might throw in their lot with the Axis because, as the Joint Intelligence Committee (JIC) declared on 30 July with serious understatement, 'much trouble' might result in India if they did.[9]

Therefore, the British decision to establish an SOE unit in India in June/July 1941 under Colin Mackenzie was primarily an expression of Delhi's worries about Axis subversive activities, not a product of expansionism from within SOE. The decision was actually made by the Viceroy in response to Axis subversive activities in Central Asia. It was simply a cry for help by an administration in Delhi which faced a possible threat from the sea if Tokyo so chose, and had now discovered that the Nazis were actually at the back door carrying out dirty tricks in Afghanistan, and might soon be tempted to employ some of them to try to pick the defensive locks on India's northern frontier.[10]

SOE India had an especially difficult time establishing, and defending, itself in 1941/42, not only because it was a new and small organization in India with a peculiar, unorthodox and complex mission, but also because it was separated by thousands of miles from its superiors in London. Supplies and directives for SOE India were frequently shipped via interminably slow surface transport, yet no intermediate SOE station seems to have been able to exercise any helpful authority over SOE India until 30 Mission Moscow was established in September 1941 and, on occasion, they came to SOE India's aid. Not until three months after Japan entered the war (March 1942) was SOE India given its first serious, if contingent, operational assignment of carrying out sabotage and countering 'existing enemy agents' in Afghanistan whenever the Axis or Japan carried the war into that country. In the meantime, the Chiefs of Staff (COS) ordered in March 1942 that SOE propaganda, political work and 'post occupational' preparations should continue in Persia, Afghanistan and India, which seemed to mean that SOE's work in the region should be keyed primarily for an operational life after conquest by Germany.[11]

By June 1942, SOE India had made arrangements with the Indian Communist Party for that organization to cooperate with SOE in its training programme for saboteurs, an arrangement which must have left many doubts in the minds of old Indian hands.[12] SOE was on more secure and acceptable ground when it established an operational office in Kabul and began 'effective intelligence' collaboration in Afghanistan, although all of its initial covert operational schemes seem to have failed or been aborted. SOE's intelligence efforts were also frequently over-shadowed by the dramatic successes of British codebreakers, because Japanese coded traffic from Kabul to Tokyo continued to be read by the British at least in 1941–42. Included in this decoded Japanese material was an October 1941 message from Kabul to Japan which contained detailed information on Italian subversive operations in Afghanistan. The Japanese Mission had secured this material by decoding the traffic of their Italian ally, only then to have the British double the operation and break the coded Japanese transmitted message to Tokyo, thereby scooping up the Italian information on subversive activities as well![13]

By late 1941, the British JIC continued to foresee 'much trouble' for British India if the Afghans gave significant assistance to the Germans,[14] and in early September, Prime Minister Churchill, as well as the new British Minister to Kabul, Sir S. Wylie, pressed for action to get the Italians and Germans expelled from Afghanistan. Their apprehensions about the Axis representatives were based on the most solid foundations because throughout this period the British continued to read considerable Italian coded traffic, including an October 1941 message to Rome in which the Italian Mission in Kabul asserted that in regard to Axis activities in Afghanistan, 'as you know it is we rather than the Germans who control these activities'. Similarly, a mid-October Italian message (also broken by the British) spelled out the details of Axis efforts to avoid having their personnel expelled by Afghanistan, thereby providing British officials with more data to help the Afghans to do just that.[15] Many Axis officials actually were expelled after the application of additional Anglo-Soviet pressure in November.[16] Also in November, the new

Japanese Minister to Afghanistan suddenly died (of natural causes) but no replacement could reach Kabul in the post Pearl Harbor era, so Japan was weakly represented in Kabul throughout the rest of the wartime period.[17] Nonetheless, immediately following the Western disaster at Pearl Harbor, some Afghan officials again tried to ingratiate themselves with the Italians and the Japanese, only soon thereafter to fall into a panic in the face of the possibility that Japan herself might actually overrun all of India and then come knocking on Kabul's door.[18]

Given this muddle of political and ideological groups, as well as national vagaries, military threats and confusing alliance systems, clear and reliable information on what was actually going on in Afghanistan, and between the powers involved there, was very difficult to come by, yet remained an eagerly sought commodity by many. In addition to code and cipher breaking, in which the British held most of the high cards, every government in the region, as well as many local authorities, and even some religious leaders, acquired and used intelligence agents to gather secret data from other governments, religious organizations, and a wide range of political factions and special interest groups. Overall, in the secret agent realm, the Soviets were probably paramount because of their long experience, skill and the permanent attraction of the communist messianic message for some members of the small, mobile, educated population in the swath of territory stretching out from Afghanistan to India. In the person of a young man named Bhagat Ram, first the Germans (who had pushed the Italians aside), and then the British, but always primarily the Soviets, had one especially well-placed agent, who by 1941/42 had an established pattern of movement which took him back and forth between India and Afghanistan along routes where his numerous acquaintances, and his convenient stopping places, provided shelter, cover, and on occasion also useful supplemental intelligence information. In the second half of 1941, for example, Bhagat Ram passed back and forth between Kabul and India at least three times, and made another such round trip in early 1942. On each of these journeys he hooked up with old friends and associates, observing how the great changes unleashed by the Second World War were actually playing out in daily life and which political and ideological positions were gaining popular support.[19]

During his journeys, Bhagat Ram was also able to pick up bits of counter-intelligence information useful to the Allies, including the identity of three Uzbeks carrying on espionage activity for the Germans in February 1942, whom he immediately turned in to the Allied authorities, and another German agent whom he denounced to the Afghans in April 1942.[20]

But Bhagat Ram was never inclined to come completely clean with his immediate associates or any of the governments which he served, except, perhaps, the USSR. For example, in April 1942 he was careful to deny to the Afghan authorities that he was working for Soviet intelligence, even though he had just met with a Soviet representative in Kabul, and that Soviet official had come especially to Afghanistan to obtain every scrap of information he could regarding possible German offensive plans for the summer of 1942. As he later admitted to his British interrogators, Bhagat Ram had also chosen to keep his partner, Uttam Chand, in the dark about many aspects of his secret activities. But he appears to have been more candid with the British and the Russians after March 1942 regarding the information which had been entrusted to him by the Germans, including an April 1942 German directive instructing Bhagat Ram to begin assembling an irregular operational staff to aid in the forthcoming German invasion of India.[21]

Bhagat Ram, the Germans, and the Russians, had good reasons to worry about one of the key players in their operations because, in the course of spring 1942, real suspicions were being aroused in many quarters regarding Uttam Chand. The British Military Attaché in Kabul (who, apparently, was not privy to the British-Soviet secret arrangement regarding Bhagat Ram) reported on 4 April 1942 that from 'a Jewish source' he had learned that Uttam Chand had been working for German interests for a year and a half. This may well have been a garbled version of Chand's role in the Baghat Ram operation, but the Attaché also thought that Chand ran that operation, with Bhagat Ram as his deputy, when in fact the relationship was the other way around. Nonetheless, such rumours about Bhagat Ram and his associates had come so uncomfortably close to the truth about the Anglo-Soviet double-cross game in Afghanistan that the Allies must have uttered a sigh of relief in late May or early June when only Chand was arrested by the Afghans, while Bhagat Ram, who had been very quiet while all of this was going on, was allowed to remain free.[22]

The NKVD seems to have realized that this was too close for comfort and that it was time to come clean with the British on the Bhagat Ram affair. On 27 June 1942, the NKVD presented Mason Macfarlane's 30 Mission in Moscow with the instructions which the NKVD had given to Bhagat Ram. The NKVD then explained to the British that both Bhagat Ram and Uttam Chand worked for them and that these two men were disinformation agents who Moscow now wished to run jointly with the British. Once that was established, the NKVD wanted to arrange a more general deal on Afghanistan with the British which they wanted worked out between themselves and George Hill's SOE 'Sam' Mission in Moscow. The only price that NKVD placed on its Afghanistan proposal was that the British should supply them with whatever useful intelligence they possessed regarding the Chinese-Russian border areas, evidently an especially sensitive matter for Moscow in 1942 because of the Japanese control of much of northern China.[23]

For SOE India this initially probably looked like a golden opportunity to strengthen its operations in Afghanistan, and possibly a chance to improve its general standing with the British government. The organization's officials in India realized though that SOE was too small a player in India to make such an important arrangement on its own, and begged the Soviets to give them time to consult with both the London authorities and the Indian administration. However, the Soviets were not tolerant of delay and continued to push SOE India very hard to go ahead and act quickly on the offer as it stood. SOE India therefore immediately took up the matter with SOE London which then passed the Soviet offer to 'C' and the SIS staff. In the course of this journey the proposal, acquired some of the standard features of farce. This occurred initially because, although many of the major participants in the process found it difficult to believe, the whole Soviet file of documents which accompanied the proposal were lost in transit from one high level British intelligence office to another, and though no British officials could bring themselves to admit to the Soviets that this had happened, the documents were never recovered and the authorities in London and Delhi were compelled to play out the discussion with the Russians in complete ignorance of what the Soviets had proposed.

As if this was not enough of a problem, 'C' then maintained that SIS did not possess a single secret document regarding the Russian/Chinese border area and therefore was completely unable to assist SOE India, or the Soviets. In consequence, no general deal on subversive activities regarding Afghanistan could be cut between SOE and the NKVD, and the two organizations, and indeed the two governments, functioned in the region henceforth in something approximating watertight compartments which certainly did nothing for Allied efficiency or effectiveness. Nor did it enhance SOE's reputation, or help to open bright prospects for East-West cooperation in the post-war world.[24]

Nonetheless, in the summer of 1942 SOE India turned much of its attention to another sensitive project – 'post-occupation' training for Indian communists to help enable them to carry out covert operations in India if the Japanese (or the Germans) succeeded in overrunning the country. After SOE assured the India Government that it would not contact the Indian Communist Party immediately on these matters, the Indian Police actually approved use of communists in a 'stay behind force'. SOE actually succeeded in training 150 such Communist Party members in seven months, but understandably, the Madras Police Force, and probably other police organizations in the subcontinent, were not overjoyed by these forays onto collaboration with the communists, and SOE was compelled to walk as softly as possible in regard to them.[25]

In contrast to the Indian Police, the Afghan authorities seem to have seriously misjudged the war situation and therefore tried to move closer to Germany in the summer of 1942, just as the Soviet and German forces rushed toward the Stalingrad confrontation. On 28 July 1942, a senior Afghan Minister told the Germans that the Afghan government would supply them with intelligence on both India and Russia, and even though British intelligence later decided that the quality and importance of the Afghan information was not very high, the incident itself was not helpful to Afghanistan's relations with the British and Soviet governments. In September 1942, the Afghan prime minister even confidentially declared that he believed that the Soviets were now truly finished, just two months before the Red Army's Stalingrad offensive which was the operation that would soon unequivocally decide that not Hitler's Germany, but the Soviet Union and the Western Powers would triumph decisively in the Second World War.[26]

Although the India Office remained nervous about indications that the Afghans were continuing to snuggle up with the Axis powers in September/October 1942, Soviet and British officials managed to sort out some of their difficulties, and Bhagat Ram continued to carry out his deception relations with German officials.

In October 1942, he again set off for India to explain and defend his activities to the Indian authorities after the Soviets had done their best to smooth his way with the British. In India, Bhagat Ram was initially simply arrested by the Indian police, but ultimately stood up well to police interrogation and then convinced the British that he had not failed them and that he was eager to go on with the game. By November 1942 the Indian Police had released him, and he went off once more to Afghanistan to take up his double-cross game with German officials there. But on 28/29 November he was again apprehended by the Indian Police, this time in Lahore, and was forced to go through the whole investigation process again before he was cleared to resume his double agent game.[27]

Players in real spy dramas seldom have long and happy lives though, and two weeks later (15 January 1943), a British intelligence summary declared in the spirit of that fact that Bhagat Ram had returned to Afghanistan, only then to have died in jail.[28] But Bhagat Ram would report to the Indian authorities on 7 May 1943, and resume his espionage activities in support of the Allies. Five months later on 2 October 1943, the three British organizations currently controlling Bhagat Ram's operations MI5, MI6 and SOE, together with the Indian government, expressed their appreciation of his performance and the value of the information he was netting from the Axis. Even the Afghan Government fell in with part of the Allied line by June 1943 and at last carried out token arrests and deportations of some of the individuals carrying out pro-Axis intelligence operations on Afghan territory.

The Baghat Ram operation was therefore a real success for the Allied cause and for SOE. But one must be somewhat cautious about drawing too glowing conclusions about the British organizations which turned former 'bad boys' into good secret agents during the Second World War. SOE India was not always a model of effectiveness and efficiency even though it strongly contended that it carefully vetted all its agent candidates. In late July 1944, SOE's India Office desperately tried to locate one of its newly recruited agents with a dubious pedigree who had not only gotten away from his SOE handlers but had managed to escape from the Indian Police as well. Presumably he had simply returned to his communist underworld from which SOE had recruited him, which does make the historian ask whether despite serious research, any explanation can hope accurately to extend from the most complex of Afghan conspiracies to the darkest corners of Delhi's underworld.

Notes

1 16 January, 9 and 24 April, 29 May 1941, RAF border attacks on Waziristan and the Faqir of Ipi WP (R) 41, 4, TNA CAB 68/9. For other such attacks see February 1939, TNA PREM 4/45/7, 21 March 1942, WP (R) (42), 17, TNA CAB 65/9 and October 1942, WP (R) 42, TNA CAB 68/8.
2 16 January 1938, TNA PREM 1/339.
3 1935/36 and 1940/41, TNA WO 208/22.
4 On Poland see 19 December 1939. TNA FO 371/23632/N7717.

5 29 March and October 1940, TNA WO 208/6.

6 8 May 1940, WP (40) 179, TNA CAB 66/8; 20 December 1940, TNA CAB 84/2.

7 L. A. Gordon, *Brothers Against the Raj*, New York: Princeton University Press, 1990, pp. 418–23 and N.G. Jog, *In Freedom's Quest*, Bombay: Orient Longmans, 1969, p. 179; March 1941 return date is from TNA WO 208/761B, and see also statement by Ram in November 1942 in TNA WO 208/773.

8 17 July 1941, JIC (41) 2, TNA CAB 65/19.

9 30 July 1941, JIC (41) 291, TNA CAB 81/103.

10 June/July 1941, TNA HS 1/346.

11 31 March 1942, COS (42) 82 (0), TNA CAB 121/317.

12 June 1942, TNA HS 1/203.

13 13 October 1941, TNA WO 208/6.

14 30 July 1941, JIC (41) 291, TNA CAB 81/103.

15 6 September 1941, TNA CAB120/572; October 1941, TNA WO 208/6, and 17 October 1941, TNA WO 208/26.

16 October 1941, TNA WO 208/26 and Milan Hauner, 'Afghanistan Between the Great Powers 1938–1945', *International Journal of Middle East Studies*, 14, no. 4 (November 1982).

17 21 November 1941, WP (R) 41, 69, TNA CAB 68/8.

18 Early 1942, TNA WO 208/30.

19 For Bhagat Ram's journeys in this period see TNA WO 208/773.

20 TNA WO 208/773, and Hauner, p. 514.

21 TNA WO 208/773.

22 4 April 1942, TNA FO 371/31322 and 25 May 1942, TNA FO 371/31323/E 3890, Hauner, p. 513.

23 27 June 1942, TNA HS 1/190.

24 7 July and 24 July 1942, TNA HS 1/190, and 23 July 1942, TNA HS 1/203. That the documents were apparently lost is shown by the telegram routing list in TNA HS 1/190 under the entry for 17 October 1942.

25 26 July 1942, TNA HS 1/212. The legalization of the Communist Party, and the Indian Authorities' indication that they wanted their own link with the NKVD come from TNA HS 1/190.

26 28 July 1942, Mohamed Maim Khan to the German Minister in 17 October 1942 report, TNA FO 371/31324. See also September 1942, TNA CAB 68/8, WR (R) 42.

27 TNA FO 371/34918/E1557.

28 20 July 1944, TNA HS 1/190.

12

'NEGOTIATIONS OF A COMPLICATED CHARACTER'

Don Stott's 'adventures' in Athens,
October–November 1943

Richard Clogg

Rather than present what would necessarily be a summary overview of SOE's role in Greece during the occupation, I intend to concentrate on a more detailed analysis of one of the most controversial episodes in SOE's extensive involvement in that country, namely Captain D. J. (Don) Stott's contacts with high ranking German officials in Athens during October/November 1943. These contacts were made in highly unusual circumstances and, given their nature, they have inevitably, both at the time and subsequently, been the subject of much fevered discussion and, no less inevitably, of much misunderstanding and misinterpretation as to the mainsprings of British policy in wartime Greece.[1]

Stott, a New Zealander, had demonstrated courage and physical endurance of a quite unusual order in the destruction of the Asopos railway viaduct in June 1943, one of the most extraordinary feats of sabotage carried out by SOE not only in Greece but anywhere. He had subsequently been smuggled into Athens for treatment for an abscess on his ear, evacuated to the Middle East for further treatment and then parachuted back into Greece on 30 September of the same year. In the autumn of 1943 he was charged with a new mission. This was to destroy aircraft on airfields in the Athens region; to investigate the possibility of blowing up the Asopos viaduct for a second time; to organize sabotage and counter-sabotage in Athens and Piraeus; and to take steps to prevent any attempt to demolish the Marathon dam, the source of the Athens water supply, should the Germans evacuate the city, as was widely but erroneously expected at the time to be imminent.

Stott, accompanied by Captain H. N. (Harry) McIntyre, made for Athens there to meet up with Lieutenant R. M. (Bob) Morton. Morton had already managed to smuggle a quantity of explosives, anti-aircraft bombs and limpet mines concealed in baskets of grapes past seven roadblocks into the city. Stott and Morton had both fought during the battle for Crete in May 1941. Following their capture by

German airborne forces, they had escaped together, eventually making their way to Alexandria. Stott's extraordinary athletic prowess had been demonstrated during the Asopos operation. It was apparently shared by Morton for the two New Zealanders had pole-vaulted their way to freedom over the wire.[2] En route to Athens, Stott and McIntyre encountered a truck driver who demanded ten gold sovereigns to carry them, although he did not persist in his demand when Stott drew his pistol. On 5 October, the two were able to drive into Athens in a car belonging to the mayor of Athens, although without the mayor's knowledge, and make their way to an SOE flat.

Stott's earlier experiences in Greece had disposed him to be very hostile to ELAS, the military arm of the communist-controlled National Liberation Front (EAM), which was much the largest resistance organization in occupied Greece. In the summer of 1943, at the time of the operations code-named 'Animals', of which the Asopos sabotage had formed a part, and which were intended to deceive Hitler into expecting Allied landings in Greece rather than Sicily, ELAS, so he reported, had not 'helped at all, but put every obstacle in my way, and hindered me as much as they could'. He categorized an ELAS officer whom he had encountered on the journey to Athens as amongst the most uncooperative even of ELAS officers, being 'violently Bolshevistic and anti-British'. I quote these remarks as they indicate Stott's political views, and, in particular, his pronounced anti-communism, which was to lead to his consorting with some highly dubious company in Athens.

Once in Athens, Stott rapidly came to the conclusion that the proposed attack on German aircraft based at airfields within the Athens area was a hopeless undertaking. This was after Morton, dressed as a Greek workman, carrying papers and passes issued by the Germans and accompanied by, and riding in the official car of, the assistant chief of the Athens police, had reconnoitred Khasani airfield. Stott and McIntyre had not gone on this reconnaissance as they were 'too British looking'. Over six feet tall, wiry and with red hair, Stott was indeed scarcely an inconspicuous figure in the Greek capital.

Stott now plunged into the treacherous shoals of Greek occupation politics and was soon to find himself seriously out of his depth, although he was blissfully unaware of this. In the course of laying the groundwork for the proposed airfield raids, Stott had engaged in discussion with members of a number of right-wing resistance groups or more accurately groupuscules, some of which emerged as having dubious links with the occupation authorities. In early November, acting without any kind of authorization either on the part of SOE Cairo or of Colonel C. M. Woodhouse, the commander of the Allied Military Mission, Stott met with the leaders of a number of *ethnikophron* (literally 'nationally-minded', an expression with strong overtones of both hyper-nationalism and anti-communism) organizations, many of them led by former army officers. Stott's interlocutors included beside Colonel Giorgios Grivas, the leader of the right-wing *Khi* organization and, in the 1950s, the military leader of the EOKA struggle against the British in Cyprus, a functionary of the quisling Rallis government.

Stott's activities during October/November 1943 were to reveal grave deficiencies in his political judgement. Nonetheless, he clearly possessed considerable powers of persuasion for he was able to negotiate an agreement with the eight *ethnikophrones* by which they agreed to place their (albeit exiguous) resources under the authority of General Headquarters in the Middle East and pledged them to assistance in the maintenance of order (i.e. to thwart any prospective bid for power by EAM/ELAS) on the withdrawal of the Germans, which, as has been noted, was widely rumoured to be in prospect. By early November, Yannis Peltekis, one of the most remarkable of SOE's Greek collaborators, was clearly aware of these contacts with dubious right-wing elements, contacts of which, understandably, he thoroughly disapproved. For, on 1 November, he radioed SOE's Cairo Headquarters that he considered it imperative that an 'English political observer' be sent to Athens instead of Stott and Morton who are 'guided by exploiters of the English'. He elaborated in a later message, sent on 14 November, to the effect that, at a meeting with the right-wing leaders, Stott, in uniform, had 'co-allied them for the purpose of seizing power and keeping order'. He warned that as a consequence 'it should not appear surprising if the left-wing organizations take all measures of armed defence and attack'.

Moreover, it was one thing for Stott to engage in heady discussions with right-wing elements (some of them of ambiguous loyalties). It was quite another to engage in wholly unauthorized contacts with senior German officials with responsibility for Balkan affairs. According to Stott, this particular initiative got under way when he was approached by what he termed one of his 'agents', with the news that the (German-appointed) mayor of Athens, Angelos Georgatos, wanted urgently to contact a British officer to obtain advice as to how he might reach Cairo bearing a German peace offer. Stott's initial reaction was to have nothing to do with the mayor. But, on reflection, he thought that by listening to him he might glean for the Middle East 'some idea of the position the Germans were in'. He therefore decided to send Pavlos Bakouros, one of his best 'agents', to contact the mayor and get some idea of the peace proposals. Bakouros reported back that he thought such a meeting was worthwhile, for the mayor had some 'quite startling' statements to make.

Stott consequently arranged to meet the mayor on the night of Sunday 17 October although, owing to a German security crackdown, he was unable to make the rendezvous. This was attended by McIntyre instead. McIntyre found Georgatos, the mayor, to be verbose in the extreme, continually stressing his devotion to the Allied cause and his freedom from German taint. The mayor claimed that he had been approached by certain German officers in Athens with the proposal that he should take to Cairo terms (not yet clearly specified) for an armistice between the Germans and the British.

The proposal that he visit Cairo, according to the mayor, had originated with Captain Karl Schurmann, who was married to a Greek and whose family had long been established in Greece. Schurmann was adjutant to Colonel Roman Loos, whom Stott believed to be the Gestapo chief in the Balkans but who was, in fact, chief of the Secret Field Police (Geheime Feldpolizei) in south-eastern Europe. In Schurmann's estimation, the grim news from the Russian Front made it apparent that the Germans could not fight both the Russians and the British. On the assumption that the Americans were not really interested in the European theatre, the Germans were proposing an armistice or secret treaty so as to destroy the Russian menace. The price 'stated roughly' of such a deal was 'a good bit of the Ukraine and a slice of White Russia' for Germany. Moreover, if the British would destroy EAM in Greece then the Germans would cease to harry the Allied Military Mission in the country.

Given that Loos was soon expected in Athens, the mayor, at this preliminary meeting, was concerned to find out whether Cairo would be interested in the German proposals and whether he should continue with the contacts. McIntyre replied that he did not know how the British government would react, although in his report to Stott, written on the same evening as this initial encounter with the mayor, he wrote that, privately, he had no doubt that the German proposals would be refused and derided. He told the mayor to find out the definitive German terms and the approximate date they wanted to send him to Cairo. McIntyre concluded his report to Stott by saying that the mayor was reported to be 'completely untrustworthy and a rat, Mark I'. Nonetheless, McIntyre believed that it would be worth finding out what the Germans were thinking, while Cairo would certainly be interested.

Stott subsequently reported that, after this initial contact, he tried very hard to get in touch with Cairo for instructions as to whether or not to proceed but had been unable to do so. It should be emphasized that Stott was out of direct radio contact with Cairo throughout his October/November escapade, a fact which strongly militated against SOE Cairo's efforts to rein him in once they became aware of the insalubrious nature of his contacts. About 24 or 25 October, Stott learned that Schurmann and his chief, Loos, were themselves anxious to meet a British representative. With the situation 'fast becoming complicated', Stott, now proposed to take the mayor's place as the emissary to Cairo. He therefore agreed to meet with Loos on 4 November.

The preliminaries to the meeting arranged for 4 November took place on a piece of wasteland off Patissia Avenue, a central area of Athens. Twenty heavily-armed men, presumably drawn from the right-wing groups with whom Stott had been in contact, had previously staked out the area after taking elaborate precautions to ensure that they were not being followed. McIntyre himself was carrying a tommy-gun concealed in a bag. Schurmann, who offered himself as a hostage for the duration of the meeting, invited Stott to meet with Loos and Rudi Stärker, who represented Dr. Hermann Neubacher, Hitler's Plenipotentiary for South-Eastern Europe, and was thought by the British security authorities to be a Gestapo agent.

Stott now had to make up his mind on the spot whether to accept the proposed arrangement, for, as he subsequently reported, he had nobody to turn to for advice. He decided to go ahead, arguing, as he later told his de-briefers in Cairo, that this afforded a unique opportunity to learn the German position 'right from the horse's mouth'. What was more, and most important, it might provide him with a means of reaching Cairo. Stott discounted the notion that an attempt might be made to liquidate him as Schurmann had agreed to act as a hostage and could easily be given his 'one way ticket' should this prove necessary. As to the possibility that efforts that might be made to extract information from him under torture about the Allied Military Mission, Stott believed that he would be able to take it 'without blabbing'.

For his meeting with Loos and Stärker, Stott had changed into British uniform. In this he walked for a quarter of a mile along Patissa Avenue, one of the busiest in Athens, to the mayor's flat without arousing the least interest. Stott, indeed, appears to have delighted in tempting fate in such a blatant fashion. He put the wind up his Greek collaborators by insisting on frequenting Zonars, the fashionable café in the centre of Athens, wearing only an old mac over his uniform.[3] Once he was inside the flat, after much hand shaking all round, a bottle of whisky was produced and one of the oddest encounters to take place in occupied Europe during the Second World War got under way. Stärker started the ball rolling by welcoming the opportunity of discussing their 'personal' opinions about political and military affairs in Europe.

To this Stott replied to the effect that he was a soldier and not a diplomat and that he could not give personal opinions, answer questions or make decisions. Stärker then spoke of the gigantic war that Germany was waging against communism, a war of which Britain was as much a beneficiary as Germany but a struggle which Germany was no longer willing to wage alone. He asked how contact could be made with a British diplomat in a neutral country. Stott replied that, if it could be arranged for him to go to Cairo, he would see whether such a meeting could be set up. Meanwhile, by his own account, he resolutely refused to be drawn on any political questions. Stärker then asked for an hour and a half's adjournment so that he could consult his superior, who turned out to be Neubacher. On returning, Stärker stated that Neubacher had shown great interest in the link that had been established but that, before making any decision, contact would have to be made with Berlin. On the understanding that the results of such discussions would be known within the week, Stott volunteered to remain in the mayor's flat until the party returned from Berlin. The meeting then broke up with Loos in a distinctly cheerful frame of mind.

Loos declared the mayor's flat pro tem to be neutral territory and granted Stott parole, with the result that, during his stay of over two weeks with the mayor, he was apparently able not only to take walks around Athens, but also to visit his mission headquarters at Kyriaki in Mount Helicon, hoping thereby to inspect the defences of the Corinth canal, a possible sabotage target, and to get a message through to Cairo on the mission W/T. This was clearly an extremely risky undertaking.

On 7 November, SOE Cairo received a message from Stott to the effect that seven German generals (most of them apparently fictitious), accompanied by a hundred staff officers, had arrived in Athens on 27 October in connection with Balkan problems of great concern to the Germans. One of these generals 'Linkenbach', he recorded:

> is meeting Colonel Loss [*sic*], Gestapo Chief of the Balkans, who has expressed an urgent wish to make proposals to be submitted to Cairo on this problem. Loss is now with Hitler but is flying to Athens in a few days expressly for this meeting. I have met and had feelers put forward to me by a representative of Loss.

Although an inkling that something was seriously amiss had already been contained in a signal, dated 2 November, from the Central Committee of EAM, the National Liberation Front, the 7 November telegram seems to have been the first direct intelligence that Cairo had received on Stott's compromising contacts with Germans, as opposed to Greek ultra-nationalists. It met with an immediate and unequivocal reply in the form of a telegram despatched by SOE Cairo on the following day, 8 November. Expressing grave concern at Stott's apparent irresponsibility, it instructed him to return to Cairo immediately. Under no circumstances were any members of the Allied Military Mission to have any contact 'with any Axis authority or officer or any person suspected of collaboration with the enemy'. It is not clear, however, when, or indeed if at all, this message reached Stott.

Although the German party was supposed to be away only for a week, it was delayed and Stott received a message stating that it was very important that he remain where he was, i.e. in the mayor's flat, while Loos informed him (apparently on 19 November) that Stärker and Neubacher had gone to talk to Hitler himself, while, he, Loos, had got no further than Belgrade. During this period of waiting Stott had somehow managed to make contact with Peltekis (again one might have thought this to be a very hazardous undertaking in the circumstances), and the two messages that Peltekis transmitted on his behalf on 15 and 16 November appear to have been the next that Cairo heard of the affair.

On 16 November, Peltekis himself weighed in with his own note of warning not merely about Stott's contacts in far-right circles but about his dealings with German officials. Despite the fact that he had known for some time that Stott had been in contact with the Germans, he had not passed the information on to Cairo for fear of being accused of transmitting fantastic information. People in Athens, he reported, were greatly confused by Stott's behaviour and Peltekis himself feared that he might be under Gestapo control and being used in an attempt to entrap British agents in Athens. On 17 November, Cairo sent a signal, which was repeated on 19 and 20 November, instructing Peltekis not to get involved in Stott's negotiations and asking whether Stott and Morton were free agents. He was told to inform Stott that the Gestapo made a practice of killing their contacts once they had served their purpose. Nonetheless, the question of his immediate return was left to Stott's discretion, while he was instructed to signal as soon as possible the results of his talks with the Gestapo.

Stott, in his own account of these events, records that Cairo's reply to the messages he had passed through Peltekis ordered him to break off all contact but it had reached him only in the late afternoon of 21 November. This was too late, in his view, to break off the meeting that had been arranged for the same day with Stärker. Stott subsequently reported that Stärker's manner at this meeting was radically different from that manifested in their first encounter. Whereas before he had been very willing to please and had not been very sure of himself, now he was cocksure and arrogant. He insisted on meeting Stott in another flat in the same building as the mayor's and, with only interpreters present, declared that their conversation was 'merely one between the respective Intelligence Services'. When asked whether he had contacted Cairo, Stott replied that he had informed SOE of the contacts but did not reveal that he had received instructions that very afternoon to break them off. He said instead that, due to poor atmospheric conditions, he had only been able to get an acknowledgement that his message had been received before losing contact. This apparent absence of instructions from Cairo seemed to disconcert Stärker who now put three questions to Stott before asking the interpreters to leave the room. These sought to establish what high British personalities were interested in the talks; what guarantees could be given as to British sincerity in the matter; and whether Stott was able to give a rough outline of any British agreement, for the Germans could only continue the discussions when they had formed a clear idea of the basis of such a deal. When Stott insisted that, as a soldier and not a diplomat, he had no authority to answer such questions and could only act as a courier to convey the 'agreement feelers' to Cairo, Stärker appeared to be exasperated. After discussing the matter with Loos and, apparently, by phone with Neubacher, Stärker informed Stott that he was free to go to Cairo if he wished. Loos subsequently informed Bakouros that Stärker, very much the diplomat, was afraid of being trapped into saying something that he should not have, which would have meant losing his head, and that there could be little hope of agreement. The whole episode therefore fizzled out inconclusively, with Stott rebuffing an approach from the Romanian ambassador likewise made through the mayor of Athens. Meanwhile Peltekis had been continuing to do whatever he could to alert Cairo as to the seriousness of the situation. Ever more alarmed, Cairo, at the behest of Major-General Colin Gubbins, the executive head of SOE, ordered Stott to proceed to the Middle East by the fastest possible means and to discuss nothing with anyone until he had arrived.

In an odd postscript to an odd affair, Stärker facilitated Stott's departure on 23 November for Chios in a caique that Stott had himself acquired and which had a concealed compartment capable of holding five people. At Lavrion, Stott was seen off by two of his 'agents' and on Chios the local German commander, under the impression that Stott and his party were German agents, tipped them off as to the best method of landing in Turkey, where they arrived at midday on 25 November.

Rex Leeper, the British ambassador to the Greek government-in-exile based in Cairo, a bitter foe of SOE and at that time savouring his victory in 'the Great War against SOE' in the Middle East, on learning of his activities had demanded Stott's immediate withdrawal, warning that EAM would be bound to exploit the issue. In fact, although the Stott affair, and the wild rumours to which it inevitably gave rise as the news of his contacts leaked out, represented a heaven-sent propaganda opportunity, the EAM leadership chose not to exploit it. Indeed, one of the first hints that Woodhouse, the commander of the Allied Military Mission, received that EAM might be prepared to contemplate a negotiated end to the civil war between communist and non-communist resistance groups in Greece that had broken out in the autumn of 1943, came in the form of a warning on 11 December, given more in sorrow than in anger, from Kostas Despotopoulos, the political adviser to ELAS GHQ, about the deplorable impression that had been created by Stott's 'strange and perilous interchange of communications with the German High Command'.

Alarm bells had also been sounding in SOE London, which had to consider the possibility that Stott was acting under some kind of duress, and two lengthy memoranda were drawn up on 24 November and 1 December piecing together what was known of Stott's activities in Athens. Their author, Colonel J. S. A. Pearson, argued that, in the light of Stott's behaviour, there was now a strong case for the Commander-in-Chief in the Middle East to accede to EAM's request that he send a secret mission of inquiry to investigate the situation in Greece.

Stott, meanwhile, was making his way from Cheshme, on the Turkish coast opposite Chios, to Cairo. His report on the whole extraordinary affair, written in Cairo on 22 December 1943, demonstrated that, to the end, he remained blithely unaware of the implications of what he had done, and naively concluded that he had gained more from the encounters than had the Germans. He had, he maintained, gained 'a fair insight into the current thoughts of the Germans and the German war situation'. He had, moreover, been able to view Corinth and other strategically important target areas which would otherwise have been impossible to reconnoitre and had gained a free passage to Turkey to boot, bringing with him an 80-ton caique. He rejected the fears that had been expressed in diplomatic quarters in the Middle East that his meetings might be exploited in EAM propaganda. He attributed such fears to an agent whom he regarded as having 'EAM leanings which may even go beyond just "leanings"'. This was clearly a reference to Peltekis, who in the summer of 1944 was to be subjected to a Court of Inquiry, convened by the British military authorities in the Middle East, arising out of his allegedly pro-EAM sympathies. Peltekis was to be completely exonerated by the Court of Inquiry but Stott appears to have been among the first to arouse suspicions in Cairo as to his ultimate political loyalties.

When the news of Stott's activities first reached London, an SOE official, J. G. Beevor, had minuted that it was a fantastic story and that 'Stott sounds mental'. But when Stott's final report of the episode arrived, however, Beevor took a different line, minuting 'I think S[tott] did rather well'. Stott himself never seems to have appreciated why his conduct had been viewed with such alarm. On his return to Cairo, indeed, he blithely composed a plan for his return to Greece to sabotage the airfields around the capital, which had of course been his original mission before he was sidetracked into his contacts with the Germans. He complained, uncomprehendingly, that the diplomats had taken a dim view of his recent 'adventures' (Stott's own expression) in Athens: 'apparently we cannot step on the toes of the diplomats, yet attack we must and we cannot expect the diplomats to attack our aerodromes for us'. He also concluded that since the Greeks were 'hopelessly uncooperative' with one another there was 'need for a "firm" hand at the "top"'. Although he was awarded, while in the Middle East, a bar to the DSO he had received for his role in the Asopos operation, he was never allowed to return to Greece, and subsequently served with SOE in the Far East. In March 1945, this 'brave, impulsive man, a real-life Don Quixote', as Woodhouse characterized him,[4] was reported missing and was believed to have been caught and shot by the Japanese after landing by submarine at the mouth of the Mahakam river in Borneo. Brigadier E. C. W. Myers, the first commander of the British (subsequently Allied) Military Mission to the Greek Resistance, wrote of Stott that he was 'one of the bravest men I have ever met and his powers of endurance are terrific'. The same cannot be said of his political judgement. Lord Selborne, who, as Minister of Economic Warfare, bore ministerial responsibility for SOE, had the measure of Stott when he characterized him as 'a brave but simple man'.

Notes

1 This strange affair is the subject of Hagen Fleischer's careful and balanced study, 'The Don Stott affair: overtures for an Anglo-German local peace in Greece' in Marion Sarafis, (ed.) *Greece: from Resistance to Civil War*, Nottingham: Spokesman, 1980, pp. 91–107. The present study is based largely on the surviving SOE records, principally in TNA HS 5/636 and HS 5/426.

2 Fleischer, 'The Don Stott Affair: overtures for an Anglo-German local peace in Greece', p. 91; Arthur Edmonds, *With Greek Guerrillas*, Putaruru, NZ: (privately published), 1998, p. 93.

3 Hagen Fleischer, *Stemma kai Swastika: I Ellada tis Katokhis kai tis Antistasis, 1941–1944*, ii (Athens: Ekdoseis Papazhsh, 1995) p. 371.

4 C. M. Woodhouse, *Something Ventured*, London: Granada, 1982, p. 75. The phrase 'negotiations of a complicated character' in the title derives from C. M. Woodhouse, *Apple of Discord: A Survey of Recent Greek Politics in their International Setting*, London: Hutchinson, 1948, p. 39.

13

SOE AND THE NEUTRALS

Neville Wylie

Amongst the burgeoning corpus of literature on the Special Operations Executive, only rarely does one find explicit mention of the exploits of its stations based in neutral Europe. Writing SOE's 'in-house' history in 1948, William Mackenzie saw fit to confine his comments to SOE's neutral work with an outline of its exploits in the Balkans and Scandinavia before the spring of 1941. Subsequent historians, even those with privileged access to the SOE archive, have unwittingly followed Mackenzie's lead.[1] Memoir literature is equally silent on this aspect of SOE's war. Only a handful of SOE staff who worked in or out of neutral countries committed their recollections to print. Most, one suspects, shared the view of one long-serving 'neutral' station officer who felt that, in comparison with the dramatic exploits of his colleagues in occupied Europe, his station was 'a small and second rate lot [who] were mainly a channel of communication, rather than action lads'.[2] The 'no bangs' policy that governed SOE's 'neutral' work for most of the war has had the effect of all but eliminating the neutrals from SOE's history. Fortunately, the recent release of the SOE archive has allowed historians to see what SOE was up to in these countries. While the picture that emerges is necessarily far from complete, we can, with the aid of oral testimonies, begin to piece together some of the outlines of this neglected area of the SOE story. Given the number and diversity of neutral states in Europe – a dozen at the moment of SOE's birth in July 1940 – it is clearly impossible to do justice to the range of SOE activities in these countries. Instead, this chapter will examine how SOE policy towards the neutrals evolved over the war, and investigate some of the particular characteristics of this aspect of SOE's war.[3]

SOE's reputation is largely founded on the contribution it made to the Allied victory in western Europe during the last years of the war. This success did not come easily.[4] SOE's high hopes of mobilizing popular resistance against German rule quickly faded over the autumn of 1940, as officials took a dispassionate view of the possibilities – more often the impossibilities – of covert operations on the continent. Far from being goaded into action by German occupation the vast majority of Europe's population turned their backs on the war and set about getting on with their lives as best they could. European society was not a 'powder keg' awaiting detonation. In Britain meanwhile, SOE's chronic lack of resources, information, transportation, men and materiel inevitably limited the range of options open to the fledgling organization, irrespective of the imaginative creativity of its planning staff. It was in these distinctly inauspicious circumstances that the neutrals emerged as a central feature in SOE's discussions. As a group, they offered London the easiest, most accessible and, potentially at least, the most receptive environment for special operations on the continent. In the summer of 1940, there were still a good many neutrals to choose from, and in some of them SOE's predecessors, the War Office's MI(R) and Section D of the Secret Intelligence Service (SIS), had already developed a certain amount of expertise upon which SOE's new cadres could draw.[5] In these early months, the neutrals became SOE's primary battlefield almost by default. It was in these countries that SOE felt it could notch up some early triumphs and begin to contest German power on the continent on something like an equal footing.

SOE's own thoughts conveniently coincided with Britain's reading of its broader strategic priorities after the fall of France. It was to the neutrals that London looked to shore up its position and demonstrate its determination to continue the struggle. The Balkan and south-east European neutrals seemed particularly appropriate for this purpose, possessing important economic and political prizes that could, potentially, be exploited for Britain's benefit. Although British prestige in the region had plummeted after the collapse of France in June 1940, Italy's disastrous attack on Greece four months later rekindled London's interest in the region, and revived pro-British sentiment amongst its traditional supporters in Romania, Greece and Yugoslavia. In other parts of Europe, neutrals continued to play an important part in British planning. The task of hampering German access to Sweden's ore fields remained on the agenda in the Ministry of Economic Warfare (MEW), despite Britain's earlier abysmal efforts in this direction. Meanwhile in the south-west, as Denis Smyth observes, 'Spain's strategic location astride maritime, imperial and inter-continental lines of communication made its attitude towards the war crucial for the British fight to survive'. The same might equally be said of Portugal once German troops arrived at the Pyrenees in June 1940.[6] Obstructing, or at least delaying, the spread of German influence over neutral Europe was thus a key strategic objective for Britain's military planners in the 18 months after the collapse of France.

The extent to which SOE's interest in the neutrals converged with Britain's core strategic objectives in late 1940 can be seen in the Chiefs of Staff's first strategic directive on 'subversive activities in relation to strategy', composed at the end of November 1940. The neutrals' prominence in this document is unmistakable. Of the nine tasks, (a) to (i), given 'first priority', six related directly to neutral states:

(b) Interference with communications across the Italian northern frontiers, so long as this does not endanger Swiss neutrality.

    …

(d) Interference with communications by rail and river from Romania to Germany and Italy, particularly of oil.

...

(f) Preparation for destruction of communications in Yugoslavia and Bulgaria.

(g) Preparations for destruction of communications in Spain and Portugal, particularly of Franco-Spanish frontier and for guerrilla warfare in event of a German advance.

(h) Preparation of organisations for co-operation with our own forces should we require to operate in the Azores, Madeira, Cape Verdes, Tangier, the Balearics, Spanish Morocco and southern Spain.

(i) Action against enemy shipping in neutral ports.[7]

SOE's official historian sounded a note of caution about the Chiefs' confident pronouncement, remarking that, 'it bore no relation to [SOE's] existing resources, the poverty of which had been freely confessed, and it tended to lead to excessive claims later in an attempt to measure up to the task'.[8] Nevertheless the Chiefs' directive has rightly been seen as representing an ideal, outlining a 'best case scenario' for SOE to focus on in the first phase of its existence. It is moreover apparent that the Chiefs' impressive list did not in fact reflect the full extent of SOE's ambitions in the neutrals at the time. Some of the proposals aired in Baker Street for interdicting German-Italian coal traffic, for example, paid little heed to the Chiefs' explicit injunction against endangering Swiss neutrality. Likewise, conspicuous for its absence is any mention of Operation 'Rubble' (later 'Performance'), designed to secure possession of the Norwegian merchant ships that had languished with their cargoes in Swedish harbours since April 1940. Five ships slipped out of Swedish waters, passed Germany's maritime cordon and reached Scotland in January 1941, providing Baker Street with one of its few successes in its early months. The hope of obtaining further ships – the next flotilla arrived in March 1942 – kept Sweden and Swedish neutrality at the forefront of SOE's attention for some time to come.[9] The neutrals were therefore much more central to SOE's strategic outlook than the Chiefs' directive might lead us to presume.

While Britain's strategic objectives varied widely across neutral Europe, SOE's precise role in British strategy towards these countries was remarkably constant. In its essentials it boiled down to three core objectives. The first concerned what might be termed 'exotic' targets: industrial sites, economic facilities or parts of a country's transport or communications infrastructure, whose destruction or seizure promised to significantly enhance Britain's spluttering war effort. In this category can be placed the 'Iron Gates' on the River Danube, the Romanian oil fields at Ploesti and the Soviet oil refineries and facilities at Baku: so too, the Swiss railways used to transport German coal to its partner across the Alps, and perhaps also the dozen Norwegian merchant ships interned in neutral Sweden. SOE's assessments of both the feasibility of attacking these targets and the likely strategic advantages to be gained were marked with a strong dose of wishful thinking. Nevertheless, their existence exercised a powerful hold on the imagination of British planners from the autumn of 1940 and unquestionably helped SOE establish its credentials as a valuable adjunct to Britain's military effort in its early months. According to reports reaching London in late 1940, Italian morale had plummeted so low after the botched invasion of Greece that the prospect of a cold, fuel-less winter might just force Mussolini to take his country out of the war. Bringing Germany to its knees was an altogether more challenging proposition, but intelligence estimates suggested that oil was Hitler's Achilles heel, and any disruption in the flow of Romanian or Soviet oil to the Reich might have serious consequences for the German war economy. While in retrospect such ideas might sound fanciful, it should not be forgotten that over the bleak months of 1940, with southern Britain under constant air attack, Baker Street's talk of landing a few decisive blows against the Axis attracted considerable interest, even enthusiasm, in senior policy-making circles.

The second component of SOE's work in the neutrals was more an exercise in damage limitation. Britain had been caught napping in the summer of 1940. No one had expected the Allied front to collapse in quite such a spectacular fashion, and few had given much thought to the creation of stay-behind groups to operate after the Wehrmacht juggernaut had brushed organized resistance aside. The agent networks belatedly established by SIS in western Europe were nearly all quickly snuffed out by the German Abwehr shortly after German troops arrived. It was SOE's task to ensure that a similar fate did not befall Hitler's next victims. Its stations in neutral Europe were instructed to organize, train and equip forces capable of operating as independent guerrilla bands or undertaking surveillance and sabotage activities at Britain's behest. This entailed establishing safe-houses and dead-letter drops, and laying on re-supply and communications facilities. It also involved gathering information on the countries' transportation and industrial infrastructure so that the key sites and installations could be laid to waste at London's command. Although SOE distinguished between its pre-invasion work, designed to hamper a German advance and prevent important resources falling into their hands, and post-invasion work, which aimed at the creation of agent networks who could survive under a German occupation, the basic objectives were fairly similar. The war could not be won by evacuations, as Churchill pointedly remarked after the 'miracle' of Dunkirk, but Britain's chances of returning to the fray would be immeasurably improved if it could prepare various countries for the return of British forces in the future.

The final area where SOE hoped to make its mark was much more controversial. The establishment of a subversion and sabotage organization in the summer of 1940 did not simply entail the embrace of a new military strategy, it also, at least in the eyes of its most ardent supporters, heralded Britain's willingness to espouse an explicitly political form of warfare. As SOE's first minister, Hugh Dalton, put it in the discussions that led to SOE's creation in July 1940, what Britain needed was a 'democratic international', capable of mixing 'industrial and military sabotage' with 'labour agitation and strikes, continuous propaganda, terrorist acts against traitors and German leaders, boycotts and riots'.[10] Although SOE made full use of trade unionists as agents in neutral countries, the political edge that Dalton gave to SOE's work had an additional dimension in these countries. SOE's contacts amongst socialist and opposition political circles could often be of great value to British diplomacy. In many neutrals, the 'left' was so ostracized from the mainstream of political life that opposition or socialist politicians were largely 'off-limits' to Britain's officially accredited diplomats. This was clearly the case in Spain and Portugal, but was also true to a lesser extent in Turkey and Switzerland. In the early years of the war, socialists in Switzerland were so despised in government and business circles that the British minister, David Kelly, declined meeting socialist politicians in public for fear of compromising his standing with the federal authorities. The advantage of SOE cultivating unofficial, and therefore unattributable, political connections proved its worth in Yugoslavia in early 1941, when SOE was able to keep the British ambassador abreast of opinions within Serbian opposition circles. SOE's involvement in the coup that finally toppled Prince Paul on 28 March has been chronicled elsewhere, and its details should not detain us here.[11] What is important to note, however, is the coup's effect on SOE's standing with the Foreign Office. Overnight, SOE was transformed into an active and distinctive ingredient in Britain's political relations with the neutrals, and from then on SOE made a concerted effort to press its claim over this important area of Britain's wartime diplomacy. Though kept on a fairly tight leash, its staff in neutral countries were given funds and resources to cultivate (or, where necessary, subvert) neutral officials, politicians and businessmen as British diplomatic interests required. Spanish generals and Portuguese police officials were both the recipient of British largesse, channelled through SOE and other covert channels.[12]

The three tasks outlined above appeared to give SOE a firm foothold within British political and military policy towards the neutrals. Whether it concerned striking at 'exotic targets', providing an 'insurance policy' against further German expansion, or merely broadening the spread of Britain's political contacts in unoccupied Europe, SOE could justifiably claim to represent a unique and important component in Britain's relations with the neutrals. Moreover, during the year in which Britain stood alone, the neutrals offered one of the most fruitful regions for Britain's band of irregular warriors to demonstrate the value of their trade. With the benefit of hindsight, however, it is clear that Baker Street's hopes of using the neutrals as a springboard into occupied Europe ultimately proved to be illusory. In a *tour de horizon* of SOE's accomplishments sent to the prime minister in late September 1941, Dalton reluctantly admitted that precious few of the priorities spelt out in the Chiefs' of Staff directive the previous November had been achieved.[13] Though Dalton did his best to strike an optimistic note, the disappointment in failing to make the most of the opportunities for covert action in the neutrals was palpable. Plans to sabotage Switzerland's trans-Alpine railway network had been shelved in early 1941 and alternative arrangements for targeting rolling stock as it left Swiss territory were not in place until early the following year. Little headway had been made to undermine Italian morale – the target which had topped the Chiefs' wish-list – in large part due to the difficulty of recruiting suitable Italians as agents and the problem of creating a base and communications network to coordinate their activities in Switzerland. Only limited progress had been made with the invasion contingency plans for Spain, Portugal or Sweden, and the sudden German descent on south-eastern Europe – pressing 'protection' on Romania and Bulgaria, and invading Yugoslavia and Greece – had confounded SOE's efforts to secure at least some recompense for the loss of these countries to the Axis.

There can be little doubt that SOE's problems in neutral Europe sprung in large part from practical difficulties associated with special operations work and the extraordinarily short time-scale in which this work had to be done. When Jack Beevor arrived to open SOE's station in Lisbon in January 1941, he had 'no funds, no equipment and no organisation' and had to work on the assumption that a German invasion might take place within a matter of months.[14] His counterpart in Berne, John McCaffery, only reached Switzerland in March 1941, while in Stockholm, although a station had been established in 1940, its work was severely hamstrung by its inability to arrange for an adequate quantity of supplies to be shipped over from Britain. In all cases, it is clear that the practical problems of operating in the neutrals were substantially greater than SOE's staff had been led to believe. In comparison with the dangers of working beneath the noses of the Gestapo or *milice*, conditions in the neutrals were, no doubt, luxurious, but throughout 1941 station officers in neutral countries were frequently overawed by the vigilance and pervasiveness of the security and police measures they encountered, and the determination of their hosts to prevent the belligerents playing out their struggle on neutral turf.[15]

Reviewing SOE's record in the neutrals with the hindsight of 60 years, it could well be argued that the success or failure of SOE's various schemes hinged as much on its ability to defend itself against the predatory inclinations of its bureaucratic 'rivals' in London, as it did on the expertise of its officers in the field. SOE's activities in the neutrals were, by their very nature, almost bound to excite the suspicion and concern of other sections of the British government. If in the late summer of 1940, most of Whitehall was ready to agree to SOE salvaging whatever could be saved from Britain's disintegrating position in the neutrals, by the second half of 1941, attitudes had decisively changed. With the Wehrmacht increasingly bogged down in Russia, the future of those few neutrals remaining began to look increasingly secure. Instead of approaching these countries with an eye to 'damage limitation', London could afford the luxury of taking a long-term view, investing political capital in the neutrals in the hope of reaping handsome rewards in the future. The Foreign Office, charged with the protection of Britain's political interests abroad, strongly advocated this approach, and disapproved of, as one ambassador put it, SOE's 'easy philosophy of action for action's sake'.[16] Another critic was SIS, for whom the neutrals provided a vital window into events in enemy and occupied territory. During the autumn of 1940 SIS had rapidly expanded its operations in neutral Europe and was naturally loath to jeopardize their security by letting Baker Street's 'irregulars' off the leash.[17] Over 1941 therefore, the willingness of the Foreign Office and SIS to condone SOE's presence in neutral countries gradually withered. Increasingly tight restrictions were imposed on SOE activities lest their exposure compromise other, more important, British interests in these countries.

So long as the result of Hitler's war in Russia remained in doubt, Baker Street could argue that pre-emptive planning against the possibility of future German aggression against the neutrals was worthwhile. Exotic targets might be beyond SOE's reach for fear of endangering Britain's political interests in the neutrals, but making contingency plans for the worse-case scenario was surely a prudent use of SOE's time and resources. The problem was, however, that the area which SOE claimed for its own, making preparations for action in the event of an invasion and occupation, was increasingly usurped by other agencies. Beginning in early 1941, the War Office began to lure neutral governments into secret discussions over how Britain could best help with the defence of their territory. Although these conversations were highly tentative, and hedged with provisos, by the end of the year progress had been made in assisting the Turks, Portuguese and even the neurotically neutral Swiss strengthen their defences. It was difficult for those sitting in London to know how much faith to place in these talks. Most discussions concerned Britain's provision of military equipment, but in some cases the talks broadened to include assessments of pre-emptive demolition and post-occupational arrangements. The danger of relying on the cooperation of the local military authorities had, however, been graphically revealed in the Balkans in April 1941, when SOE's elaborate sabotage arrangements had collapsed without so much as a whimper. As SOE did not tire of pointing out, in the heat of the moment, local agents or military officials could not be trusted to do the job on their own. Nevertheless, however much SOE derided the War Office's initiative, the fact that it was left out of official talks that bore directly on its area of expertise, was a serious blow for the organization. By the end of 1941, SOE was in serious danger of being marginalized from the very areas of military policy that it had hitherto claimed as its sole preserve.

The slow usurpation of SOE's military functions in the neutrals over the course of 1941 would have been easier to take were it not for the fact that it coincided with a similar erosion of SOE's standing within British diplomacy. Despite expectations to the contrary, SOE never replicated the success it had enjoyed in Belgrade in late March 1941. Far from heralding a new role for SOE, the Belgrade coup proved to be a one-off affair. The reasons for this varied according to the political situation in each neutral country, but on the whole, SOE's problem lay in the fact that as 1941 progressed, the Foreign Office became increasingly confident in being able to bend neutral governments into satisfying Britain's minimum political requirements. True, Franco's fiery denunciation of the Allies and dispatch of the Blue Division to fight in Russia in July 1941 called into question his willingness to accommodate British wishes, but once the crisis had passed and the limits of the *Caudillio's* ambitions became clear, the Foreign Office could rightly claim that Britain had more to gain working with the neutral governments than against them.[18] There was no guarantee that Germany, rather than Britain, would not gain from an outbreak of political instability in the neutrals. Nor was there any certainty that the new governments would be any more susceptible to British wishes than the current incumbents. In fact, SOE's claims notwithstanding, in most neutrals no credible alternative to the current government actually existed. Opposition had either been driven underground, as in Spain, Portugal and Turkey, or had struck a working compromise with the coalition governments that had sprung up when the wartime 'emergency' first broke. To make matters worse, even in those areas where SOE had been given the go-ahead to activate their 'informal' contacts in opposition circles, the results did not always repay their efforts. The pleasure of spiriting the Bulgarian Peasants' Party leader, George Dimitrov, out to the safety of neutral Turkey in March 1941, proved very short-lived. Not only did a bomb go off in his luggage – destroying the lobby of his Istanbul hotel and very nearly wiping out a score of British diplomats in the process – but Ankara took such exception to his presence on Turkish soil, that it immediately insisted that London removed their unwelcome guest without delay. Instead of aiding British diplomacy, SOE's dabbling in neutral politics frequently ended up in complicating their position and aggravating their relations with the Foreign Office and embassy staff.

SOE would have had an easier time convincing the rest of Whitehall of the benefits of its political contacts in the neutrals had its activities been conducted with greater finesse. There can be little doubt that SOE's effort to muscle in on Britain's political relations with the neutrals provoked considerable unease amongst members of the permanent civil service. Part of the fault lay in the prickly personality of SOE's minister, Hugh Dalton. Dalton had been Under-Secretary at the Foreign Office in the late 1920s, and many assumed that this dynamic, self-confident and tenacious politician viewed the post of Foreign Secretary as the natural home for his many and varied talents. His pleasure and amusement at discovering that he was, as he put it, 'a sort of unofficial FO', for 'some British and foreign diplomats' after his appointment as Minister of Economic Warfare, is clear from his diary entries in May 1940.[19] Many old hands in the Foreign Office were alarmed by Dalton's political ambitions at home and his determination to further SOE's political role abroad, particularly as it involved sponsoring a 'democratic international' with the kinds of people – trade-unionists, socialist politicians and so forth – whose political views were so obviously aligned to his own. For British diplomats working in legations and embassies across neutral Europe, Dalton's political ambitions were made all the more objectionable by the fact that it appeared to impinge directly on their own careers. The sudden and frequently unannounced arrival of Dalton's lieutenants, with ill-defined tasks and commanding hidden resources and influence inevitably provoked concern, if not outright resentment, amongst the regular diplomatic staff. For British diplomats, the motley collection of lawyers, insurance brokers, colonial policemen and the like, who staffed SOE's cadres, were simply not cut out for diplomatic work. They lacked those 'rather intangible qualities', as one senior diplomat put it before the war, of 'personality', 'address' and '*savoir faire*' that were essential for anyone wishing to fraternize with the governing classes of another country.[20] A good example of the kind of anxieties that SOE's presence in neutral countries could create is given in an account of SOE's Bickham Sweet-Escott, who visited the Ankara embassy in late 1941. 'One of my friends', Sweet-Escott recalled,

> complained to me at great length of the consequences of giving senior officers of S.O. (2) high ranks in the diplomatic services to enable them to visit neutral countries. Two had even achieved the rank of counsellor, he said and this had made my friend deeply suspicious. What was the object of Mr. Dalton's intrusion into the realms of diplomacy? Was he trying to build up a shadow Foreign Office with which to replace the professionals when the Labour government came to power and he became Foreign Secretary? S.O. (2) already seemed to have a foreign policy of its own which was different from that pursued by our regular diplomatic representatives.[21]

Although SOE's staff were inclined to exaggerate the problem, there are a significant number of documented cases in which SOE's work was unnecessarily hampered by the jealousy and obstructive attitudes of their senior colleagues in the embassies. George Binney, for example, who masterminded SOE's blockade busting exploits out of Sweden admitted in late 1940 to spending 75 per cent of his time 'stopping other people from trying to stop me doing what has to be done ...'.[22]

The second and ultimately more intractable problem which hampered SOE's efforts in building up a political role for itself in the neutrals was articulated most succinctly by Britain's ambassadors. In the eyes of many of these men, SOE's informal political activities were not merely of questionable value to British diplomacy, but also, especially when placed alongside SOE's military work, threatened to upset the embassy's formal relations with the host government and undermine British standing in the country. When Britain's back was against the wall in late 1940 and early 1941, London had little to lose and was, consequently, inclined to ignore the grumbles of their haughty ambassadors. By mid-1941, however, with the war spread into the Soviet Union the Foreign Office, Joint Intelligence Committee and Chiefs of Staff were more prepared to take account of ambassadorial unease. By this stage in the war, especially after America's entry into the war in December, Britain was increasingly in a position to compete for the hearts and minds of neutral Europe and was naturally anxious to avoid any action that might needlessly antagonize relations or give rise to accusations of bad-faith.[23] SOE's most vociferous critic amongst the ambassadorial ranks was Sir Hughe Knatchbull-Hugessen in Ankara. Hugessen flatly refused to allow SOE to establish a station in Ankara (although it did operate out of Istanbul), and pointedly withheld his support whenever any of SOE's agents – such as George Dimitrov – fell foul of the Turkish authorities. Turkey was admittedly a special case: it was Britain's ally since October 1939, possessed sizeable military resources and its influence over political events in the Near East and Eastern Mediterranean was substantial. Nevertheless, Hugessen was by no means alone in voicing his unease at the thought of SOE operating in his bailiwick. 'I am convinced', he wrote in August 1941, in response to Baker Street's latest appeal to open a station in Ankara,

> that the proposed organisation would only destroy [Turkish] confidence and frankness, increase their sensitiveness and have the most disastrous effect on our relations. ... If the proposed organisation were set up it would quite inevitably become known very soon to the Turkish authorities ... I would say seriously and with no desire to exaggerate that in such an event we might as well close down H.M. Embassy altogether.[24]

The mounting opposition towards SOE retaining an offensive capacity in the neutrals increasingly forced Baker Street onto the back foot. Far from extending its operational mandate in these countries, SOE was obliged to expend a considerable amount of time and energy defending what little room for manoeuvre it still enjoyed. Although the threat of a German invasion had not disappeared, SOE's claim to a seat at Britain's policy-making table, as of right, had been challenged and in many cases overturned. Across neutral Europe, SOE was increasingly demoted in British political and military policy. In Turkey, Hugessen's 'deep and ineradicable suspicion of the SO machine', to use the words of Dalton's private secretary, Gladwyn Jebb, remained unchanged, and his opposition to an SOE station in Ankara continued throughout 1941 and 1942. Things were only marginally better south of the Pyrenees. All SOE plans had first to be passed across the desk of Britain's Naval Attaché in Madrid, Alan Hillgarth, who had the authority to veto any operation which might endanger Britain's tenuous relations with the Franco regime. SOE later praised Hillgarth for taking 'the maximum risks' in order to facilitate the work of its small station in Madrid, but in truth, SOE's position in Spain was highly circumscribed. After the war Hillgarth admitted to being 'continually berated by the ambassador and by the F[oreign] O[ffice] whenever I went to London – for allowing anything at all... [while] the D[irector] of N[aval] I[ntelligence] was always fearful that I would slip from controlling into directing and get involved and compromised'.[25] By September 1941, the War Office's secret staff talks had proved so successful that the head of SOE's station in Lisbon felt it necessary to return to London to find out what exactly it was that Baker Street wished him to do with his time. As Dalton's depressing *tour de horizon* for Churchill made clear, the neutrals had singularly failed to live up to their billing. By the winter of 1941, SOE was rapidly becoming surplus to requirements in an area where it had confidently set out to make its mark barely 12 months before.

If SOE had hoped that 1942 would see an upturn in its fortunes in the neutrals, it was to be sadly mistaken. Instead, a series of largely unconnected events conspired to end what little chance SOE had of salvaging some advantage from its beleaguered position in these countries. The setbacks were momentous in themselves, given the neutrals' position in SOE's strategic outlook over these early years, but in retrospect their significance is doubly important since they happened to coincide with one of the many crises that beset SOE's relations in Whitehall. Since the previous autumn criticism of SOE's handling of resistance movements in Europe had been mounting, spawned in part by disputes with the French and Polish governments-in-exile. By early 1942, the Foreign Office looked set to 'crush SOE altogether' and split up its various functions between other departments in Whitehall.[26] While SOE ultimately survived these machinations, the crisis nonetheless resulted in a major reassessment of SOE's place in Britain's strategic and diplomatic policies, and brought to an end its hopes of acting as a major, independent actor in neutral Europe.

Paradoxically, the event that triggered SOE's demise in the neutrals involved an operation which Baker Street rightly considered one of its finest accomplishments to date. On 30 March 1942, after a delay of over a year, SOE arranged for a second flotilla of Norwegian merchant vessels, blockaded in Swedish ports since the spring of 1940, to make its way across the North Sea to a rapturous welcome in Scotland. The two large ships that successfully made the trip, laden with ball bearings and other vital manufactures, were a shot in the arm for the British war economy and provided valuable additional tonnage to the Allied merchant fleet. Baker Street indulged in a rare moment of celebration, but amidst all the back-slapping and self-congratulation few gave much thought to the various 'short-cuts' that had been made in the process of pulling off their coup. En route, while in neutral Swedish waters, the ships had engaged German aircraft using Lewis guns which had been smuggled into Sweden for the purpose. Although the action might, on the face of it, have seemed entirely appropriate, the picture looked very different for the Swedish government whose neutrality had been violated in the process. Nor had SOE done itself any favours in keeping the British ambassador in Stockholm, Victor Mallet, in the dark over these 'technical arrangements'. Mallet's enthusiasm for special operations mirrored that of his colleagues elsewhere in neutral Europe, as his nickname in SOE – 'windy-Vic' – testifies. What little sympathy Mallet had for SOE soon evaporated as his ignorance of the affair came to light under questioning by the Swedish authorities. When the Swedish foreign ministry demanded the expulsion of the officer in charge of the operation, George Binney, Mallet obliged. SOE had obviously overstepped the mark, and only the success of the operation spared SOE from a serious run-in with the Foreign Office over the matter.[27]

SOE's Stockholm staff had had their fingers burnt, but at least had something to show for their endeavours. The same could not be said for their counterparts in Lisbon, whose efforts to establish a functioning network of agents in the event of a German invasion and occupation were exposed to the glare of publicity by Portuguese police investigations over the spring of 1942. Having explicitly warned Baker Street about the dangers of continuing his preparations for post-occupational preparations after the start of the War Office's secret talks with the Portuguese government, SOE's head of station, Jack Beevor, must surely have felt aggrieved when his anxieties were born out and he found himself compromised by the arrest of his agents over the winter of 1941/42. The precise timing of the crack down on Beevor's collaborators had as much to do with internal Portuguese politics and timely tip-offs from the German embassy, as it did to the security of Beevor's networks. Nevertheless, coming as it did, hot on the heels of a serious crisis in Anglo-Portuguese relations, arising out of the unannounced landing of Australian troops on Portuguese Timor in mid-December 1941, Beevor's ambassador, Sir Ronald Campbell, felt that SOE ought to pay the price of failure, and agree to Beevor's return home. SOE did what it could to overturn Campbell's decision, but in the end, it was forced to bow to the Foreign Office's demand and accept Beevor's withdrawal in June.[28]

Beevor always maintained that his expulsion from Portugal was of little significance, either to the work of the Lisbon station or to SOE wider activities. This optimistic assessment fails, however, to stand up to close scrutiny. The exposure of SOE's activities in Portugal, in conjunction with their injudicious treatment of Mallet in Stockholm, prompted the Foreign Office to re-evaluate the functions and operational freedom of SOE stations across neutral Europe. It would be incorrect to assume that the new 'charter' imposed on Baker Street in May 1942 was solely the result of SOE's misdemeanours in the neutrals, but there can be little doubt that SOE's difficulties over the first half of 1942 were affected by these untimely incidents.[29] Lisbon and Stockholm were the worst affected stations. The new sanctions placed on SOE's Stockholm station, and confirmed by the Chiefs of Staff in July 1943, condemned its staff to 'surreptitious economic measures and propaganda'. As a result, as Colin Gubbins, SOE's director-general from September 1943, admitted after the war, 'little effective preparatory action against a German invasion could be taken despite SOE's wishes'.[30] The restrictions on the Lisbon station were equally draconian. Beevor's successors were prevented from undertaking any post-occupational work in Portugal and for almost a year they had to keep themselves busy purchasing various foreign banknotes on the black market: an admittedly useful occupation, but hardly the sort of reward SOE had hoped to reap for its troubles.[31] While Lisbon and Stockholm bore the brunt of the new measures, SOE's staff in Spain, Turkey and Switzerland all felt the heat, and the restrictions that were already in force in these countries were applied with renewed vigour.

The enforced re-assessment of SOE's responsibilities in the spring of 1942 thus had a profound effect on its operational outlook in the neutrals. From being an area of active engagement, the neutrals became something of a sleepy backwater. SOE's neutral stations were kept in business, but they no longer aspired to the same level of importance as they had in the heady days of late 1940, when the hunt for 'exotic' targets captivated Baker Street's imagination. It is perhaps surprising to discover that, for an organization renowned for its ingenuity and vitality, SOE appears to have accepted its demotion with good grace. Its willingness to 'go slow' in the neutrals from mid-1942 was in large measure a result of the sobering influence exercised by Jack Beevor, who returned from Lisbon in June 1942 to take up a position in SOE's planning staff. On a number of occasions Beevor stepped in to temper the enthusiasm of his colleagues and ensure that SOE lived up to its obligations under its new charter with the Foreign Office. In essence, Beevor's arguments were little different from those he had advanced on his return to London in September 1941, and were remarkably similar to the views of his former boss in Lisbon, Ronald Campbell. SOE's primary rationale for working in the neutrals – to stiffen morale, destroy key industrial sites in case of an invasion and train and equip resistance networks for use once the country was occupied – had diminished in importance as the war turned in the Allies' favour, and other less hazardous means were found to fulfil the same objectives. Under Beevor's guidance, Baker Street's staff became increasingly wary of sanctioning potentially hazardous projects in neutral countries. Thus, when a plan was mooted in August 1942 to expand the activities of the Berne station, it was immediately rejected, not least, in the words of one staff officer, because it was 'surely not the best moment to blow another legation'.[32] Baker Street's chastened attitude clearly endeared SOE to its former critics in Whitehall, but the impact on the organization's morale should not be overlooked. Most of the officers dispatched to neutral outposts were driven by the desire to make a direct contribution to Britain's war fortunes. Few could have foreseen the demise of SOE's standing in the neutrals or welcomed the prospect of working within such tight constraints. The files rarely illuminate the personal views of SOE's station staff abroad, but the irritation of one official, long involved in SOE's futile efforts to establish an operational capacity in Turkey, may well reflect the broader pattern. 'At present', he wrote, 'we are wasting money and much hard work begetting and nourishing schemes which are doomed to be stillborn. Personally I do not wish to spend the remainder of the war in such unfruitful work'.[33]

SOE's disgruntled staff had to wait for over a year before their lot improved. Their activities were kept under close supervision by either the ambassador, head of chancery, or, in Spain's case, embassy staff appointed to this function. In London meanwhile, the Foreign Office and SIS were able to scrutinize – and more often than not, veto – all prospective operations in the neutrals during their regular weekly meetings with SOE's planning staff. The onset of this new regime was epitomized by the departure of Hugh Dalton, 'promoted' to the Board of Trade in February 1942, which removed much of the radicalism that had typified the atmosphere in Baker Street during its early, formative, years. His replacement, the Conservative peer, Lord Selborne was cut from very different cloth, and soon came to personify the more temperate outlook in SOE that dates from this time. Little weight was placed on the value of special operations in British policy towards the neutrals, and instead, absolute priority was given to the preservation of Britain's political and intelligence resources in these countries. As the time approached when Allied forces would return to the Continent, gathering accurate information on the enemy and their allies became of mounting importance. In such circumstances,

Baker Street's advocacy of operations which, by their very nature, were likely to upset the tranquillity upon which effective intelligence gathering relied, was always likely to meet with resistance. The importance of all the neutrals to Britain's intelligence agencies and military planners could scarcely be ignored. The success of the Allied landings in North Africa relied in part on the determination of the Spanish and Portuguese governments to resist German demands for transit rights and other facilities. Winning over the Turks meanwhile was considered essential if Britain was to maintain the initiative in the Mediterranean and carry the war into the Balkans. In all these cases, Britain's immediate military and intelligence needs demanded that the neutrals remained benevolently disposed towards the Allied cause. Sweden was a case in point. Any Swedish detection of inappropriate activities on its soil, SOE was warned in March 1943, 'would mean curtailment of the present invaluable SIS activities not only in Sweden, but in Norway, Germany and Denmark and might [also] destroy the link in SIS communication to Holland and Italy'.[34]

It is to its undoubted credit that SOE not only accepted its new status after the summer of 1942, but went on to make the most of the situation thereafter. While the neutral stations entered a period of suspended animation from mid-1942, elsewhere SOE's efforts were at long last bearing fruit. Over 1943, organized resistance against Nazi rule finally begun to gather momentum and offered SOE the chance to prove its worth in precisely those areas where British military interests were best served: in the Balkans, France, and, to a lesser extent, Poland. With agent networks finally up and running in western and south-eastern Europe, SOE found that it had as much reason as the SIS for wishing to placate neutral sensitivities. The neutrals had always been viewed as potential bases for providing supplies, communications facilities and other resources for circuits operating in enemy and enemy-occupied territory. This had been the primary task of the Berne station ever since the spring of 1941, when SOE had given up on the idea of sabotaging Switzerland's Alpine railway lines. Indeed, the choice of an Italian expert, John McCaffrey, to head the Berne station in late 1940 was predicated on the belief that with Italy in turmoil, SOE could most profitably use Switzerland as a base from which to run agent and resistance networks into northern Italy.[35] By 1943 therefore, Baker Street was in a position to take a more philosophical approach to the curtailment of its operational freedoms in neutral Europe. The apparently mundane work of SOE's neutral stations became increasingly important as the activities of their colleagues in adjacent territories intensified. Switzerland was the best suited to lay on these facilities: at one stage the Berne station carried 70 per cent of the communications of the French Section, a similar amount for SOE's various circuits in Italy, while agents in Belgium, Holland, Romania, Yugoslavia, Hungary and Poland all drew on its facilities in some shape or form. SOE's other neutral stations were also valued for their supporting role. So far as Stockholm was concerned, it was, as Beevor commented in June 1943, 'like Lisbon only more so – an invaluable base for working into other countries. Its value as a base far outweighs its importance for purely Swedish work'.[36] The same could be said for Turkey. To illustrate the point, let us draw on the words of the disgruntled official cited earlier. Little over four months had elapsed since he expressed his exasperation working on schemes that seemed destined never to see the light of day. In the meantime, however, the upsurge in SOE activity in the Balkans had given the work of the Turkish Section a new sense of importance. 'When considering SOE policy in Turkey', he wrote,

> it is always necessary to bear in mind the fact that we are using Turkey as a base for operations into the Balkans. Of the five countries into which we work, at least four, Greece, Yugoslavia, Romania and Hungary are each more important than Turkey itself, while the fifth, Bulgaria, is probably equally important. All these countries are actually operational areas: successful work in them has the capacity of doing extensive and immediate damage to the Axis. In Turkey on the other hand, the immediate damage we can do to the Axis is on a very small scale, while the necessity for preparations against its attack and occupation are doubtful.[37]

Nothing had of course changed to turn SOE's neutral stations into 'action lads' but at least those staff connected with SOE's neutral work could see where their work fitted into a recognizable, wider picture.

The need to service SOE's active circuits from secure neutral bases was not the only development to change the work of SOE's outlying stations in the last years of the war. Indeed, for a time, it looked as if the organization might, at this late stage, have found an operational role in the neutrals that had steadfastly eluded it for the past two years. From the middle of 1943, under intense prodding from the Americans, the Ministry of Economic Warfare (MEW) began to pay more attention to reducing the neutrals' economic collaboration with the Axis. Over the autumn and winter of that year, an increasing number of neutral firms were placed on the Allied 'black lists' and all neutral governments were pressurized into cutting their exports to Germany.[38] The campaign reached a climax over the first half of 1944, with the suspension of oil imports to Spain, the slashing of food and fodder quotas through the blockade and the onset of a propaganda offensive against the neutrals which was to continue on and off for the remainder of the war. By the time Allied troops landed in Normandy, thoughts had turned from the immediate question of how to win the war, to the longer-term problem of preventing the Nazis rising from the dust to trouble democracy and freedom in the future. Once again the neutrals held centre-stage in Allied thinking. At the Bretton Woods conference in July 1944, the Allies unveiled their 'Safehaven' programme which was specifically designed to deny Germany and its leaders the benefit of neutral 'safe havens' for either themselves, or their ill-gotten gains in the final months of the war.

SOE's activities had always closely dovetailed with those of MEW. It shared the same minister as MEW, and in their regular strategic directives the Chiefs of Staff always emphasized the valuable role special operations could play in undermining the Axis war economies. The connection with MEW was of particular importance in SOE's early days, when the thought of mobilizing 'secret armies' on the Continent was still a distant pipe-dream. Many of the officers sent out to neutral posts in 1941 and 1942 were either specifically tasked with addressing economic issues, or worked out of the embassies' commercial departments or consular offices and as a result spent a substantial proportion of their time dealing with trade and economic affairs. For many officers stationed in neutral Europe, SOE work had to be juggled alongside their other 'full time jobs'.[39]

Historians have yet to explore the full extent of SOE's involvement in Britain's economic warfare effort. We know of some of SOE's own eccentric commercial activities – such as bribing nationalist Chinese warlords with Swiss watches – but little is known about SOE's role in supporting, or complementing, MEW's activities, or the importance of this work to SOE's standing in Whitehall. A full assessment of this issue will probably show that SOE's ties with MEW and the Treasury were closer than has been appreciated hitherto. At the same time, however, it is reasonable to assume that the crumbling of Britain's imposing blockade after the summer of 1940 reduced the advantages Baker Street hoped to reap from this particular sideline. SOE was not likely to pay its way in wartime Whitehall by playing second fiddle to MEW.

SOE's collaboration with MEW in 1943 was therefore not new. What was new, however, was London's determination to prise the neutral economies out of Germany's clutches before Allied troops hit the Normandy beaches. The gloves were now off, and who better to implement the new bare-knuckle approach than SOE. Over the second half of 1943, Baker Street put forward a series of proposals for integrating special operations into the strategy of economic warfare. The Spanish and French Sections were to mount a coordinated assault against Germany's import-ation of wolfram (tungsten) from Spain and Portugal. As David A. Messenger rightly notes, the wolfram war was 'an extremely important operation on the part of SOE in Spain, [and] their first active operation in Iberia since the start of the war'.[40] In Turkey and Sweden, attention focused on Berlin's chrome, iron ore and ball bearing imports, and various proposals were made with an eye to sabotaging Germany's sea and rail-borne traffic as it left neutral territory. Baker Street also made a concerted effort to stake out a role in the Allied 'Safehaven' programme. As the head of SOE's Spanish Section warned in August 1944, 'I am more than ever convinced [...] that the Germans are going to ground now in neutral countries and that by the time hostilities cease we shall find that many of the birds have flown to well-timed and well-hidden nests'. 'From an S.O.E. point of view', he concluded, the neutrals were 'becoming of increasing significance'.[41]

Sadly, SOE's heightened involvement with MEW in the last years of the war did not prove to be the breadwinner that Baker Street had initially expected. Responsibility lay primarily with the War Cabinet which was ultimately not prepared to match its words with deeds. While MEW initially professed its support for an aggressive sabotage campaign in Spain, it soon baulked at Washington's heavy-handed approach towards Iberian affairs, and scurried back to the path of negotiation. German rail traffic was sabotaged as it passed through southern France, but south of the Pyrenees SOE's staff had to confine themselves to simply gathering intelligence on German smuggling operations. The importance of this information should not be under-estimated, as it provided the ammunition needed to shame Madrid into taking action on its own accord. But such work fell far short of the independent role that SOE had craved for so long in Spain, and inevitably caused friction with SIS, which frowned upon SOE's move into the realms of intelligence gathering.[42]

The story in Turkey was depressingly similar. It was always going to be difficult for Baker Street to overcome Hugessen's objections and secure a free hand to tackle Germany's commercial interests in Turkey. The chaos into which SOE's Cairo station had fallen over the intervening years was, however, hardly likely to make Hugessen any more accommodating to SOE's wishes. Hugessen received a delegation from Baker Street in April 1943, but the results of their discussions were scarcely worth the effort. Since no guarantee could be given that charges laid on German ships would not explode while the vessels were still in Turkish waters, all sabotage operations of this nature were prohibited. The joints and moving parts of German rolling stock could be attacked with abrasive powder but Hugessen rejected the idea of using explosives or, indeed, of targeting Turkey's chrome exports at all, on the specious grounds that the Turkish government had agreed to reduce these deliveries by their own devices. Any hope SOE might have entertained of appealing against Hugessen's decision in London, fell victim to Churchill's desire to woo the Turks into the war and using their chrome deliveries to buy off German pressure until the Allies were ready to come to her aid.[43] Although Britain was prepared to threaten the neutrals with fire and brimstone if their exports to Germany were not reduced, it was not in the end prepared to go the last mile, and turn to the services of its saboteurs. SOE undoubtedly expanded its involvement in economic warfare over the last year of the war, and earned much gratitude in the process, but the opportunities for special operations were never wide enough to make SOE integral to Britain's efforts during this time. Nor was it able to replicate the success of its American counterpart, the Office of Strategic Services, and carve out a niche in the Allied 'Safehaven' programme. Neither the Foreign Office nor SIS was prepared to countenance SOE's involvement in a programme that was likely to dominate Britain's peacetime diplomacy and intelligence effort. The last 12 months of the war, when Britain's 'irregular warfare' strategy finally came of age, thus saw SOE's neutral stations retaining the subsidiary position they had occupied since early 1942. SOE's faith in the efficacy of special operations was more than vindicated in the months before and after D-Day, but its early conviction that the neutrals could play a decisive part in its strategy remained unfulfilled.

What can be said, by way of conclusion, about SOE's work in neutral Europe? One of the most striking features of SOE's treatment of the neutrals was the tendency to view them as a distinct, recognizable group. In any discussion of the neutrals, one must never lose sight of the fact that they comprised of a huge range of different countries, whose place in British strategy varied enormously.

Nevertheless SOE's files give the unmistakable impression that Baker Street approached its work in 'the neutrals' from a remarkably consistent perspective. Only rarely was SOE able to treat events in one neutral in isolation from its activities elsewhere across neutral Europe. This situation was not entirely of SOE's own making, nor did it accord with the neutrals' own interests. It arose rather out of the determination of the Foreign Office and SIS to enforce a blanket set of priorities across neutral Europe which placed the defence of Britain's political interests above SOE's military or strategic objectives. As a consequence, whenever SOE encroached on the Foreign Office's political prerogatives in a neutral, the ramifications were felt far beyond the actual country concerned. Baker Street tried to turn the tables and make the collective approach towards the neutrals work in its favour, but its successes were few and far between.[44] In the end it had more to lose in treating the neutrals as a cohesive unit, than it had to gain.

If Baker Street came to regret the fact that it could not deal with each neutral on its own merits, it is equally true that, collectively, the neutrals occupied a more elevated position in SOE thinking than historians have tended to assume. In the first year of its existence the neutrals were SOE's primary battleground at a time when the opportunities for mounting special operations in occupied territory were minimal. Its failure to take advantage of the relatively propitious circumstances in the neutrals was viewed as a major setback at the time, and must be judged in similar terms now. None of the priorities set out by the Chiefs of Staff in late 1940 had been accomplished by the time Baker Street was forced to scale down the activities of its neutral stations 18 months later. Far from demonstrating the efficacy of its brand of 'irregular warfare' and providing Baker Street with an entrée into the upper echelons of Britain's political and military decision-making, SOE's experience in the neutrals merely aggravated its position in London and cruelly exposed the limitations of its capabilities. It is worth reiterating the point that well before its Portuguese enterprises started to unravel over the winter of 1941/42, SOE's claim to occupy a distinct position within British policy towards the neutrals had been called into question. SOE's difficulties in the neutrals cannot then be brushed aside as some unavoidable, if unpleasant, educational process necessary to prepare it for the decisive engagements later in the war. Neutral Europe was more than just a testing ground for Britain's nascent 'irregular warriors'; it was central to SOE's early strategic outlook and vital to its development as a component in Britain's strategic armoury.

Another notable feature of SOE's work in the neutrals was the extent to which its activities brought it into contact with Britain's political and diplomatic interests. Baker Street's early forays into the murky world of resistance politics soon showed that the occasional spat with the Foreign Office was going to be an occupational hazard. Paying lip service to the Foreign Office's wishes, and pampering the political sensitivities of Britain's numerous small European allies became a staple feature of SOE's activities in occupied Europe. In its neutral work, however, the need to balance SOE's military objectives with the interests of other departments in Whitehall was particularly acute. The room for confusion and conflict was immense, and it is no surprise that this aspect of SOE's work was so greatly affected by the ebb and flow of its standing in Whitehall. Focusing on SOE's neutral work provides historians with valuable insight into some of the many areas which engaged SOE's attention, but which lay outside its principal area of military interest – such as its 'unofficial' political functions in the neutrals, its involvement in Britain's economic warfare campaign and so forth. Baker Street had its finger in many pies: a fact that may have complicated its position in London, but unquestionably added to the complexity of its unique wartime achievement. Historians ignore these aspects at their peril.

Could a different strategy in the neutrals have better served Britain's interests? If we follow MacKenzie's lead and accord SOE a greater role in securing the Allied victory than has hitherto been fashionable, the question over whether the 'no bangs' policy which constrained SOE's work in the neutrals represented, in some respects, a missed opportunity, becomes all the more prescient. There is little doubt that many of SOE's senior staff sincerely believed that Britain threw away important tricks in the neutrals in deference to a set of 'political' interests whose real value, in the circumstances of late 1940 and early 1941, were questionable. If a chilly, fuel-less winter might break Italian morale, if Romanian or Russian oil shipments to the Reich could be interdicted, if Hitler could be denied the benefits of occupying Spain, Portugal, Yugoslavia or Turkey, then surely Britain had the right to act in such a way as to bring this about? While there is much to commend this view, we must be wary of taking SOE's assessments as gospel. Before mid-1942 there was a marked tendency in Baker Street to over-estimate the importance of its work in the neutrals – overstating the size of the political opposition, or exaggerating the danger of a German invasion. To be fair, SOE was not the only agency to get its sums wrong, and it rarely benefited from viewing the latest intelligence estimates. Nonetheless, SOE frequently overlooked the fact that while its services might suit one time and place they could easily become superfluous, if not counter-productive, as circumstances changed. There is more than a suspicion that the tenacity with which Baker Street defended its presence in the neutrals was influenced by the need to deflect its many critics in Whitehall. SOE's officers in the field, faced with the complexity of Britain's relations with these countries on a day-to-day basis, were noticeably more ready to accept their diminishing status in British policy than their desk-bound colleagues in London. While Britain unquestionably lost 'tricks' in the neutrals, it did not in the end require SOE's services to meet its principal political and military objectives in these countries after the spring of 1941.

Finally, what can be said about SOE's influence on Britain's relations with the neutrals more generally? In a paper delivered in 1983, Donald Watt argued that Churchill's decision to take the 'SO genie' out of the bottle represented a notable stage in the development of British attitudes towards the neutrals. Taken together with Britain's efforts to widen the war after the summer of 1940, the creation of SOE represented a radicalization of Britain's war effort and signalled an erosion of the element of restraint and respect for international law upon which all neutrals relied for their security.[45] Churchill's resolute attitude towards the neutrals certainly contrasts with the confused, and frequently contradictory, policies of his predecessor. Any pretence of fighting for the interests of small countries was jettisoned, and replaced by a relentless struggle for survival. And yet, as we have seen here, despite Churchill's rhetoric, SOE soon discovered that 'setting Europe ablaze' did not entail igniting neutral Europe at the same time. Although Britain's effort to expand the war into south-east Europe had a disastrous effect on Balkan neutrality, Britain's conversion to 'total war' was far from whole-hearted and its impact on the neutrals, ambiguous. This was, in fact, entirely in keeping with Britain's historic approach to the issue of abusing neutral rights: as Patrick Salmon observed, 'British policies towards neutral states in the twentieth century, even at their most vehement, were never wholly unrestrained'.[46] If SOE had been allowed to operate in the neutrals with the freedom it desired there is little doubt that its impact on the neutrals would have been profound. But as this chapter has shown, SOE failed to realize its extensive ambitions in these countries. While the neutrals are therefore central to our understanding of SOE, SOE's impact on the development of European neutrality remained slight.

Versions of this chapter were presented to seminars at the Scottish Centre for War Studies, University of Glasgow, and the Graduate Institute for International Affairs, Geneva. The author would like to express his appreciation for the valuable comments he received on these occasions as well as at the IWM conference. His special thanks go to Mr. Ernest van Maurik, Mr. Tony Brooks and the late Gervase Cowell.

Notes

1 M. R. D. Foot's chapter on 'Where and how SOE worked' offers the best coverage of SOE's exploits across the globe: *SOE. The Special Operations Executive 1940–1946*, London: BBC, 1984, 2nd updated edition, 1999, pp. 246–356. William Mackenzie, *The Secret History of SOE: The Special Operations Executive, 1940–1945*, London: St Ermin's, 2000, pp. 12–29, 103–32.

2 Peter Jellinek (SOE Switzerland) to author, 5 Nov. 1994.

3 This chapter will address SOE policy towards the neutrals of continental Europe, and not discuss the Far East, Africa, the Middle East, United States or Ireland. For the latter see Eunan O'Halpin, '"Toys" and "Whispers" in "16-land": SOE and Ireland, 1940-42', *Intelligence & National Security*, 15(4), 2000, pp. 1–18.

4 See especially, David Stafford, *Britain and European Resistance 1940–1945. A Survey of the Special Operations Executive with Documents*, London: Macmillan, 1980, *passim*.

5 Mackenzie, *Secret History*, pp. 3–55.

6 Denis Smyth, *Diplomacy and Strategy of Survival. British policy and Franco's Spain, 1940–1945*, Cambridge: Cambridge University Press, 1986, p. 2.

7 COS Directive 25 Nov. COS (40) 27 (0). TNA CAB 80/56.

8 Mackenzie, *Secret History*, p. 92.

9 'It is perhaps hardly necessary for me to mention here the possibility of bringing off Operation Performance as I am sure you have that in the very forefront of your mind.' Dalton to Churchill, 24 September 1941. Hugh Dalton Papers, LSE, vol. 7/3.

10 Dalton to Halifax 2 July 1940, cited in Foot, *SOE*, p. 18.

11 David Stafford, 'SOE and British Involvement in the Belgrade Coup d'Etat of March 1941', *Slavic Review*, 36(3), 1977, pp. 399–419; Mackenzie, *Secret History*, pp. 103–12. For British

policy towards Yugoslavia at this time, see Elisabeth Barker, *British Policy in South-East Europe in the Second World War*, London: Macmillan, 1976, pp. 78–95.

12 For Spain, see Denis Smyth, 'Les Chevaliers de Saint-George: la Grande-Bretagne et la corruption des généraux espagnols (1940–1942)', *Guerres mondiales et conflits contemporains* 162, 1991, pp. 29–54; and Portugal, Neville Wylie, ' "An amateur learns his job"? Special Operations Executive in Portugal, 1940–1942', *Journal of Contemporary History*, 36(3), 2001, pp. 455–571.

13 Dalton to Churchill, 24 September 1941. Dalton Papers, LSE, 7/3.

14 J. G. Beevor, *SOE Recollections and Reflections 1940–1945*, London: The Bodley Head, 1981, p. 37.

15 For Swedish security see C. G. McKay, *From Intelligence to Intrigue. Studies in Secret Service based on the Swedish Experience*, London: Cass, 1993, pp. 1–40; Swiss, Georg Kreis (ed.), *La protection politique de l'Etat en Suisse. L'evolution de 1935 à 1990*, Berne and Stuttgart: Paul Haupt, 1993, pp. 247–56; and Portuguese, Douglas L. Wheeler, 'In the Service of Order: The Portuguese Political Police and the British, German and Spanish Intelligence, 1932–1945', *Journal of Contemporary History*, 18(1), 1983, pp. 1–25.

16 Cited in Bickham Sweet-Escott, *Baker Street Irregular*, London: Methuen, 1965, p. 60.

17 See for example SIS's burgeoning interest in its Swiss networks, outlined in Neville Wylie, ' "Keeping the Swiss Sweet" Intelligence as a factor in British policy towards Switzerland during the Second World War', *Intelligence & National Security*, 11(3), July 1996, pp. 442–67.

18 See Denis Smyth, 'The Dispatch of the Spanish Blue Division to the Russian Front: 19 Reasons and Repercussions', *European History Quarterly*, 24, 1994, pp. 537–53.

19 Ben Pimlott (ed.), *The Second World War Diary of Hugh Dalton*, London: Jonathan Cape, 1986, p. 18.

20 Knatchbull-Hugessen to Cadogan, 20 January 1939, cited in Peter Hennessy, *Whitehall*, London: Secker and Warburg, 1989, pp. 79–80.

21 Sweet-Escott, *Baker Street Irregular*, p. 81.

22 Cited in Ian Dear, *Sabotage and Subversion, The SOE and OSS at War*, London: Arms & Armour, 1996, p. 75.

23 For a good survey of Britain's propaganda campaign in the neutrals, see Robert Cole, *Britain and the War of Words in Neutral Europe, 1939–1945*, London: Macmillan, 1990.

24 Knatchbull-Hugessen to Foreign Office, 18 August 1941 TNA HS 3/238.

25 A. Hillgarth, 'The naval attaché to Spain and Naval Intelligence: Part II', TNA ADM 223/466. I am grateful to Dr. Anthony Best for bringing this source to my attention. Report by Mjr. L. J. W. Richardson, April 1943. TNA HS 6/957.

26 David Dilks (ed.), *The Diaries of Sir Alexander Cadogan, 1938–1945*, London: Cassell, 1971, p. 448, for 22 April 1942. See diary entries for late February, editor's note on p. 436 and Stafford, *Britain and European Resistance*, pp. 75–8.

27 For Britain's blockade busting out of Sweden, for which SOE partially responsible, see *inter alia* Charles Cruickshank, *SOE in Scandinavia*, Oxford: OUP, 1986, *passim*, and Peter Tennant, *Touchlines of War*, Hull: University of Hull, 1992, pp. 200–28.

28 See Antonio Telo, *Propaganda e guerra secreta em Portugal 1939–1945* (Lisbon: Perspectivas & Realidades, 1990, pp. 104–7. Julia Leitão de Barros, 'O Caso Shell: a rede espionagem anglo-portuguesa (1940–1942)', *História* XIV(147), 1991, pp. 55–83, Wylie, 'An amateur learns his job'?, pp. 455–71.

29 Eden specifically mentioned SOE's activities in Portugal and Turkey as a reason for enhancing the FO's say over SOE operations. Minute by Anthony Eden for Winston Churchill, 7 April 1942. TNA FO 954/24 Folio 125.

30 Major-General Sir Colin Gubbins, 'SOE and Regular and Irregular Warfare', in M. Elliot-Bateman (ed.), *The Fourth Dimension of Warfare*, Manchester: Manchester University Press, 1970. COS directive on SOE operations in Sweden, 9 July 1943. Preliminary comments of the Strategic Planning Section in the draft directive, in consultation with the FO, Dominions Office, Colonial Office, SIS and JIC, 21 April 1943, TNA HS 2/260.

31 The COS strategic directive spelling out SOE's strategic objectives for 1943 kept the restriction in force, upheld Campbell's right of veto and only allowed 'discreet preparations' for post-occupational work if they took place outside the country. COS memo. 'Special Operations Executive Directive for 1943', 20 March 1943, COS 9430 142 (0). CAB 80/68. Printed in Stafford, *Britain and European Resistance*, annex. 7. See also report by Mjr. L. J. W. Richardson, April 1943, TNA HS 6/957.

32 'X' to 'MX', 19 August 1942. TNA HS6/1006. Examples of Beevor's views are cited below, however an early manifestation is found in his response to plans for the 'reopening' of the Lisbon station in late 1942: see memo by 'AD', 8 October 1942 and Beevor's minute in reply, 12 December 1942. TNA HS 6/991.

33 Minute by DH44, 1 December 1943. TNA HS 3/222.

34 Preliminary comments of the Strategic Planning Section on the draft Directive for SOE, in consultation with the Foreign Office, Dominions Office, Colonial Office, Secret Intelligence Service and the Joint Intelligence Committee, 21 March 1943. TNA HS 2/260. For the importance of Spain and Turkey, alluded to above, see *inter alia*, Denis Smyth, 'Screening Torch', *Intelligence & National Security*, 4(2), 1989, pp. 335–56; Robin Denniston, *Churchill's Secret War: Diplomatic Decrypts, the FO and Turkey, 1942–1944*, Stroud: Sutton, 1997, *passim*; H. O. Dovey, 'The intelligence war in Turkey', *Intelligence & National Security*, 9(1), 1994, pp. 59–87; and Richard Cossaboom and Gary Leiser, 'Adana Station 1943–1945: Prelude to the Post-war American Military Presence in Turkey', *Middle Eastern Studies*, 34(1), 1998, pp. 73–86.

35 It was discovered that the networks McCaffrey had erected since the autumn of 1941 had all been infiltrated by Italian military intelligence. See the chapter in this volume by Christopher Woods.

36 Minute by Beevor for Gubbins, 29 June 1943. TNA HS 2/260.

37 'Appreciation of Military Situation in Turkey and of Future SOE policy', by 'DH44', April 1943. TNA HS 3/222.

38 The two sides to this story can best be found in Christian Leitz, *Nazi Germany and Neutral Europe during the Second World War*, Manchester: Manchester University Press, 2001 and W. N. Medlicott, *The Economic Blockade* 2 vols, London: HMSO, 1959, vol. 2, esp. 381ff. For a recent survey of the neutrals see Neville Wylie (ed.), *European Neutrals and Non-Belligerents during the Second World War*, Cambridge: Cambridge University Press, 2001.

39 'History of the Berne post' by John McCaffrey, circulated 6 September 1945. TNA HS 7/199. John Sullivan, for instance, who organized the Berne station's work into France, was also the most senior British commercial official in Switzerland from August 1941 and responsible for managing Britain's enormously complicated commercial and economic interest in the country.

40 David A. Messenger, 'Fighting for Relevance. Economic Intelligence and Special Operations Executive in Spain, 1943–1945', *Intelligence & National Security*, 15(3), 2000, pp. 33–54, (41). Messenger's paper is the first detailed piece of research on this important subject.

41 Memo by Mjr R. G. Head, 21 August 1944. TNA HS 6/929 cited in ibid, p. 45.

42 Ibid, pp. 39–45.

43 For Turkey's chrome exports see Selim Deringil, *Turkish Foreign Policy during the Second World War*, Cambridge: Cambridge University Press, 1989, pp. 168–9. Chrome deliveries to Germany were suspended on 20 April 1944. SOE policy files are in TNA HS 3/222.

44 See, for example, Baker Street's efforts to outflank Hugessen's objections by referring to their amicable relations with Britain's diplomatic staff in over 20 other neutral states in late 1941 – including Spain, Iran, Yugoslavia, Portugal, Switzerland, Sweden, the USA, Nigeria, Russia, China, Afghanistan, the 'Near East', Singapore and Japan. Jebb to Sargent, 14 August 1941. TNA HS 3/222.

45 D. C. Watt, 'Britain and the neutral powers 1939–1945; some general considerations', in L.-E. Roulet (ed.) *Les états neutres durant la deuxième guerre mondiale*, Neuchâtel: La Baconnière, 1984, pp. 245–265.

46 Patrick Salmon, 'British attitudes towards Neutrality in the Twentieth Century', in Jukka Nevakivi (ed.), *The History of Neutrality/La neutralité dans l'histoire*, Helsinki: Finnish Historical Society, 1993, pp. 117–32 (118).

14

SOE IN ALBANIA

'The conspiracy theory reassessed'

Roderick Bailey

One of the most controversial themes to emerge from post-war accounts of the Special Operations Executive has been that of mismanagement at SOE's Cairo and Bari Headquarters. This is the idea that SOE staff officers there, some with left-wing or communist sympathies, had somehow undermined the work of British officers working with groups of Balkan nationalists, and so helped the communist partisans of Yugoslavia and Albania to seize power. It has also been suggested that certain officers had been agents of the Soviet NKVD and that, had Allied policy favoured non-communists instead of being unfairly influenced towards supporting Tito's and Enver Hoxha's Partisans, these countries would never have become communist. First expressed in memoirs, since reprinted elsewhere, and argued with varying degrees of conviction, these claims were only speculation: rumour and anecdotal evidence stood in for hard fact.[1] Partly by relating some of SOE's recently released files to the issue, this chapter constitutes a brief reappraisal of the debate that still surrounds its Albanian operations. These records shed important new light on the precise workings of SOE's Albanian Section in Bari, the port on Italy's Adriatic coast from where SOE's Yugoslav and Albanian operations were directed for much of 1944. Clarifying the Section's role in the development of British policy towards Albania, the files support little of the above conjecture. Before exploring this, however, a short overview of SOE's activities in Albania is necessary to place the 'conspiracy theory', as it has been termed, in its proper context.[2]

   Albania had seen SOE's first attempt at forging some kind of guerilla resistance in the Balkans to occupying Axis forces. In April 1940, Section D and MI(R) – they would merge to become SOE early that summer – began plans to stimulate a revolt in Albania against the Italian forces that had occupied the country since April 1939. Britons with some knowledge of Albania were contacted and recruited; Albanian exiles and émigrés were tapped for their support. In April 1941, a few dozen Albanians crossed from Yugoslavia into Albania intent on beginning a guerilla campaign. Led by Gani Bey Kryeziu, a powerful Albanian chieftain from

Kosovo, they were also accompanied by SOE officer Captain Dayrell Oakley Hill, a former British adviser to the pre-war Albanian gendarmerie. Within days, however, the venture was aborted, when Kryeziu proved unable to secure enough local support and Yugoslavia was heard to have fallen behind them to the Germans. The Albanians scattered; disguised as a peasant, Oakley Hill made it to Belgrade before resolving to give himself up. In late 1943, after 2½ years' imprisonment in Germany, he was repatriated to Britain, whereupon SOE promptly recruited him again to work on Albania in its main Headquarters at Baker Street. By then, both resistance and SOE's presence in Albania had increased substantially.

In April 1943, acting on reports of growing local resistance to the occupying Italians, and anxious to encourage it as a means of speeding Italy's collapse and diverting German resources away from the Eastern Front, SOE had infiltrated a four-man mission into Albania. Code-named 'Concensus' (*sic*), the mission had been instructed to assess the potential of the Albanian resistance and, if they felt it worthwhile, to organize, train and arm it. In late June, the mission contacted Enver Hoxha and his movement of national liberation, the Levicija Nacional Clirimtarë (or LNC). Set up on the initiative of Hoxha's Communist Party of Albania, the LNC at this stage still contained a good number of non-communists. By the end of August 1943, an 800-strong brigade of LNC 'Partisans' had been trained and armed with 20 tons of supplies dropped to the mission by the RAF. By the end of the year the LNC was regularly receiving drops and often in action, and a further 50 SOE personnel had been sent in to assist the resistance and persuade more Albanians to fight the Axis. Unfortunately, SOE's attempts to encourage greater resistance would become increasingly frustrated by the reluctance or refusal of many other Albanians to commit themselves to fighting.

The central problem encountered by SOE in Albania was that, with no government-in-exile, most guerrilla leaders took up arms against the Axis with their eyes fixed to a large degree on securing post-occupation power. But as an Allied victory in the war became more certain and the implications of the communist domination of the LNC more evident, many 'Nationalists' (to use the contemporary SOE term to describe non-LNC Albanians) were simply not prepared to fight the Germans and risk reprisals, or otherwise expend valuable material and energy that could be better spent later against this growing domestic threat. The situation worsened following the Italian surrender and German invasion of Albania in September 1943, when the LNC's communists forced out most of its non-communist members, many of them into the welcoming arms of the Germans. Soon, the LNC was fighting both Germans and Albanians.

Inevitably, British policy-making towards Albania became dominated by a fear that sending arms indiscriminately to both communists and Nationalists merely encouraged civil conflict. At the same time, for many months the resistance picture in Albania was so fluid and confused that few obvious grounds could be discerned for making a declaration of exclusive support for any one movement: it was largely this consideration that, in December 1943, saw Brigadier 'Trotsky' Davies's call for the LNC to be given sole Allied support dismissed by every military and political body that considered it. Until the summer of 1944, SOE thus remained wedded to a Foreign Office-approved directive to give 'financial and material assistance... to all guerrilla bands, irrespective of their political allegiance which are actively resisting the Germans or are genuinely prepared to do so'. No break was to be made with any political or guerrilla movement for fear of alienating a potential source of future resistance and aggravating local tensions. In accordance with this policy, SOE personnel in Albania were ordered to 'maintain contact with all guerrilla bands and individuals actively resisting the Germans, or who may be induced to assist the Allied war effort in any material degree'.[3] In practice, this meant that SOE remained in touch with Nationalist elements and kept working on them to fight the Germans, even though, by the end of 1943, Hoxha's LNC Partisans were the only movement actually doing so and thus qualified to receive supplies.

In the spring of 1944, an attempt was then made by SOE and the Foreign Office to encourage Albanian Nationalists to return to the LNC. This, it was hoped, might make the Partisans more representative of Albanian popular opinion and reduce the intensity of the civil war. In April 1944, Lieutenant-Colonel Billy McLean and Major David Smiley, both members of the first mission sent into the country the previous year, were dropped into central Albania together with Captain Julian Amery. Code-named 'Concensus II', the mission's task was to persuade certain Nationalists to resume cooperation with the Partisans.

In 1948, Amery would publish *Sons of the Eagle*, the first detailed account of SOE's operations in Albania, as seen through the eyes of 'Concensus II'. He described how the mission's efforts had centred on a Nationalist chieftain named Abas Kupi. A gendarmerie officer before the war and one of Oakley Hill's irregulars of 1941, Kupi was a loyal supporter of the exiled King Zog and from the latter's own region of Mati. Though he had never been a leading military or political figure, except within Mati, Kupi's personal reputation had been so enhanced by his resistance to the Italian invasion of 1939 and his association with SOE's efforts in 1941 that he had been appointed one of the few non-communists on the LNC's central council. In late 1943, however, he had ceased fighting, split with Hoxha's movement, and, in the mountains of Mati, established a pro-monarchy group, Legalititi (Legality). He also started talks with the anti-Zogist but fiercely anti-communist Balli Kombëtar (BK) party – the third of the three main Albanian movements (after the LNC Partisans and Kupi's 'Zogists') with whom SOE would deal. To counter the growing communist threat, a good number of Nationalists, including many of the BK, were now slipping into open collaboration with the Germans, who themselves were only too pleased to encourage civil war. But as BK forces fought side-by-side with the Germans against the Partisans, other Nationalists, including Kupi, would choose to remain aloof, maintaining contact with both SOE and collaborators but staying neutral until concrete evidence showed the better option.

Throughout May and June 1944, 'Concensus II' worked hard to persuade Kupi to come off the fence and fight the Germans. Allied policy stated that no arms could be dropped to him beforehand: he had to attack the Germans first and thus commit himself to fighting. This commitment was also demanded of him by Enver Hoxha, who refused to have anything to do with any other movement until it showed evidence of open warfare against the Germans. For a long time Kupi refused to act; then, in June, he relented. On the night of 21–22 June 1944, David Smiley and a party of Kupi's men blew up Albania's third largest bridge at a spot called Gjoles on the main road north from Tirana. 'Concensus II' was content that the operation fulfilled the demands for Kupi to fight, and permitted him to receive weapons from the Allies that he could use to open a wider campaign against the Germans and attract more Nationalists to his side. A few days later, the mission requested SOE in Bari to send enough arms for 2,000 of Kupi's men.

At this point Enver Hoxha trumped Kupi's move. Within 10 days of the Gjoles action, and on the heels of the German withdrawal from south-east Europe, the Partisans launched an offensive against the Nationalist strongholds of northern Albania. The supplies asked for by 'Concensus II', and that Bari had prepared to send, would never be sent. Forced on the defensive, Kupi and other Nationalists mustered their available resources for use against the northward advance of Hoxha's troops. At the end of October 1944, when 'Concensus II' was withdrawn from Albania, Kupi and all other Nationalists found themselves abandoned. By the end of the year, the Germans had also left and the Partisans were in control.

In his account of these events, Amery stressed the dismay he, Smiley, and McLean had felt at British policy towards Albania. On the one hand, they believed sympathy had been lacking for the pressures at work on Kupi and other Nationalists to stay neutral; on the other, they felt the Partisans, whom they considered the instigators of civil war, had been given too much support. After the Partisans launched their attack on Kupi on 30 June 1944, these officers were shocked by the response of their 'Headquarters' in Bari to the crisis and particularly by the decision to resume supplying the Partisans after airdrops were initially suspended. Bari's refusal to evacuate Kupi, when the mission was finally withdrawn, aroused further anger. Indeed, to Amery, the decision to abandon all Nationalist guerrillas seemed not only 'dishonourable' but also reflective of a significant and unwarranted bias in Bari towards supporting the communist Partisans. Amery wrote that 'a genuine enthusiasm' for communism pervaded 'Headquarters' where officers 'revelled with indecent ... glee' at the demise of Nationalist forces.[4]

Amery's sentiments were reaffirmed, with growing passion, in the memoirs of several other SOE officers who had worked in Albania. Some writers suggested that, by arming the communists and enabling them to seize power, British policy had helped condemn Albania to a future of communist rule. Peter Kemp, who had worked closely with Nationalist Albanians, described the country as:

a totally unnecessary sacrifice to Soviet imperialism. It was British initiative, British arms and money that nurtured Albanian resistance in 1943; just as it was British policy in 1944 that surrendered to a hostile power, our influence, our honour and our friends.[5]

Fingers were pointed at SOE's Bari Headquarters as having possibly been at fault, even to blame, while speculation was expressed over the activities of left-wing officers there. David Smiley told of the hostile reaction he was accorded by Bari following his evacuation from Albania in October 1944: in the Headquarters office, to his face, he had even been called a 'fascist' for having worked with Nationalist forces.[6] Attention was drawn to one staff officer in particular, Captain John Eyre, whom Kemp described as 'a serious young communist whose courteous manner could not altogether conceal his disapproval of my Albanian record'.[7] Allegations were made that left-wing or communist officers – perhaps Soviet agents – had manipulated British policy, suppressed important messages sent by 'Concensus II' for onward transmission to the Foreign Secretary, and been the crucial factor in the decision to drop more arms to Hoxha's communists and thus in bringing them to power. 'Loyal' Albanians like Abas Kupi, wrote Alexander Glen, were unnecessarily 'defeated and some ... betrayed. Kim Philby already had his colleagues well enough placed in some of the organisations concerned'.[8]

SOE's Albanian records, declassified in 1997, do suggest that the Section Headquarters in Bari had indeed become increasingly 'pro-Partisan' as 1944 wore on. In early June, even before civil war broke out, Major Elliot Watrous, the Head of SOE's Albanian Section, submitted policy proposals urging for the Partisans to be given full support, casting doubt on Kupi's potential, and then recommending him to be abandoned.[9] His proposals were received with some surprise by SOE in London, where hopes still rested on a Kupi-Partisan alliance being formed and the situation did not yet seem critical.[10] Watrous had been made acting Section Head after the departure of Major Philip Leake for Albania on 10 May 1944, a position that became permanent following Leake's death on 8 June.[11] Throughout May, June and July 1944, in more correspondence with higher authority, the Albanian Section consistently expressed doubts over Kupi's potential strength and whether the Nationalists would ever fight the Germans. Julian Amery's estimate of Kupi's forces at 5,000 poorly armed men, for example, received in Bari at the end of May, was dismissed as illustrating Kupi's weakness, even though Amery felt the numbers could be significant if only weapons could be found to arm them.[12] The significance of the Gjoles bridge action was also played down when it emerged that Kupi, who had been told to commit himself unconditionally, had refused to allow his name to be linked publicly with the operation.[13]

SOE's files also reveal that David Smiley was not the only SOE officer to be called 'fascist' on arriving at SOE's Bari office.[14] Major George Seymour, evacuated in July 1944, had spent almost a year in Albania working with both Partisans and Nationalists. Like 'Concensus II', he sympathized with the pressure acting on Nationalists to stay neutral, and stressed the need for patience when trying to get them to fight. Such was the nature of their society, Seymour and 'Concensus II' argued, that Kupi and others were best suited to a last-minute rising as the Germans withdrew rather than an immediate, large-scale, and sustained campaign which was demanded of them by Allied policy but would bring down on them severe German reprisals. The nature of the Partisan forces, these officers felt, was rather different: being a more mobile force with few fixed bases of support, the demoralizing effect of German retaliation was rather less. It was felt this important distinction was not appreciated in Bari or London, that the Nationalist position was being misunderstood, and that, with more patience and encouragement on the part of the Allies, the Nationalists could yet fight and prove their worth. However, the conclusion to Seymour's debriefing report reads:

> [When] I returned to Base at Bari … I found the entire Albanian section biased to an unbelievable extent on behalf of the Partisans. They were not even prepared to listen to the Nationalist case and views. I attempted to explain this case but when in the office I was called a Fascist I realised that the position was hopeless. I applied to be sent home to state my case there and was informed by Major Watrous, the head of the Albanian section, that I would be sent home but not immediately, because at that time a policy was being decided in London and, if I went home then, it might alter the whole policy. A truly remarkable statement to be confronted with after one had spent eleven months working with and studying both Partisans and Nationalists. That we achieved but little is hardly surprising.[15]

Today, it seems likely that John Eyre, the Section's Political Intelligence officer, later named by Kemp as a communist, was responsible for the 'fascist' remarks.[16] It also seems probable that Eyre would have indeed sympathized with the Partisan cause on ideological grounds: he admits as much in a little known and privately published memoir that seems to have escaped the attention of all previous writers on SOE. Though concentrating mainly on his post-war spiritual development, Eyre briefly mentions his wartime career and writes:

> I came to accept the class basis of society during the war years, when I was working with Special Operations Executive, responsible for economic and political intelligence coming from our missions in occupied Albania … On the staff of the Albanian country section I saw the Marxist-Leninist thesis working out under my very eyes. Julian Amery and [Billy] Maclean [sic], my colleagues in conspiracy, were battling against the winds of change while I and others, in our wisdom or ignorance, helped to stir up the hurricane.[17]

Seymour's obstruction by Watrous also raises the question of whether pro-Nationalist reports transmitted by 'Concensus II' were suppressed inside Bari's headquarters, as has been claimed.[18] In his October 1944 diary, Smiley had recorded that, whilst in the Bari office, he had been told by one of the secretaries there that one of 'Concensus II's' messages had deliberately not been sent to Anthony Eden, the Foreign Secretary, to whom it had been specifically addressed.[19] Now the

'Concensus II' signals log confirms that the mission had sent two messages to Eden. The first, on 23 May 1944, had asked if King Zog, then living in Britain, could send a personal message of encouragement to Kupi.[20] This message arrived in London on time,[21] but the Foreign Office was reluctant to commit to Zog and turned the request down.[22] The second, on 25 October, was a last-minute appeal urging that Kupi should be evacuated.[23] Though Smiley apparently assumed that the latter had been suppressed, records reveal that, in fact, it had been delivered at once to Philip Broad, the FO's man in Bari, and it was not Bari's or Broad's fault that a response was not immediately forthcoming.[24]

However, earlier in June, rather than sending them on to SOE's London Head-quarters immediately and by telegram as they had been specifically instructed to do, SOE's Albanian Section in Bari had chosen instead to send a number of other messages to SOE London by sea.[25] All of these messages had been sent by 'Concensus II' in June and expressed confidence that a Nationalist rising could be achieved in northern Albania. But the significance of this delay in their onward transmission must not be exaggerated. For one thing, it is far from certain that the delay was deliberate (Captain George Cowie, second-in-command of the Section and whom no SOE writer has accused of being left-wing or even mentioned in print, signed off the letters to London that covered these messages) and there is no concrete reason to suggest that the secretary was even referring to the June telegrams. Also later messages, seemingly of greater importance, were sent, received and acted on without a hitch. 'Concensus II's' appeal for enough weapons to arm 2,000 of Kupi's men, for example, was clearly received and went through all the proper channels; and SOE in Bari quickly assembled the plane-loads: it was not their fault that the arms were never dropped.[26] But most importantly of all, had the messages arrived on time, had Amery's 23 May telegram remained uncorrupt, had Seymour even been able to press his views on London in person and at that moment, it is very unlikely they would have had any bearing on policy.

Julian Amery later referred to Bari as 'an instrument of Enver Hodja [sic] in the British camp' and it is possible that some staff officers were keen on the idea of abandoning Kupi and that one was aligned ideologically with Hoxha's cause.[27] It may even be possible that, to some small degree, officers in the Section may have been prepared to suppress information. But SOE's files indicate that the 'conspiracy theory' displays a significant misconception of policy-making, those involved in the process, and the ability of SOE's Albanian Section to influence it. Direct, first-hand experience of Bari's decision-making and command structures was, for most SOE officers returning from northern Albania, relatively fleeting and occurred either long before (Kemp, Glen) or some time after (Amery, Smiley) the key developments in policy: that is, the summer of 1944. Finding both policy and staff at their own headquarters so noticeably pro-Partisan, it was perhaps not surprising that some officers, arriving fresh from working with Albanian Nationalists and angry and confused at the way policy had developed, jumped to conclusions over what factors might have impacted on policy-making. Of all the

SOE officers with the Nationalists, only Seymour arrived in Bari during this period, but it is clear that he, too, assumed too much of London's ability to influence policy, let alone the ability to do so of the 23-year-old Watrous.

That SOE had only a marginal input to policy-making by the summer of 1944, and absolutely no ability at all to dictate it, has become increasingly clear since the release of Foreign and War Office records in the 1970s. These records allowed wartime policy-making to come under much closer scrutiny than had previously been possible. Fresh accounts then pointed out that the key policy decisions had clearly been made far above the heads of SOE and on military grounds, and much of the earlier speculation was rejected.[28] SOE's records do much to confirm this was the case. From late 1943, changes in Allied command arrangements saw SOE – both in Bari and in Baker Street – increasingly subordinated to the regular military and, together with the Foreign Office, sidelined in the decision-making process. By July 1944, the newly created Balkan Air Force, under the command of Air Vice-Marshal William Elliot, was firmly in control of SOE's Albanian activities. Responsible to the Supreme Allied Commander in the Mediterranean, General Sir Henry Maitland Wilson, and based in Bari, Elliot chaired a policy committee that included local representatives of the Foreign Office, the US State Department, Allied Forces Headquarters and SOE.[29]

It was Elliot and this committee, after careful deliberation, that decided each time to halt and then resume supplying the Partisans in July 1944, to refrain from supplying Abas Kupi, to recommend in September the withdrawal of 'Concensus II' and, the following month, to refuse to evacuate Kupi. All military and political decision-making bodies in Italy and London – SOE, the Foreign Office, and the Chiefs of Staff in London, Foreign Office representatives and General Wilson in Italy – were kept informed of these developments. All agreed with the recommend-ations of the Balkan Air Force in deciding who to arm and why. Lieutenant-Colonel the Viscount Harcourt, head of SOE in Bari and, before the war, a managing director at Morgan Grenfell, did sit on the Policy Committee and play an important role in its discussions.[30] SOE's Albanian Section did not: a useful gauge of how junior were both Watrous and Eyre, and how grossly exaggerated has been their ability to have had any direct input to policy-making. Although Eyre was a communist, it is worth noting here that no proof of Soviet infiltration of SOE's Albanian Section has ever been produced. Post-war revelations of Soviet espionage inside British intelligence, and particularly rumours surrounding James Klugman, an officer on the staff of SOE's Yugoslav Section, may do much to explain the vague accusations levelled at Eyre.[31]

No one has accused Harcourt, or, for that matter, Elliot (a career Royal Air Force man) or Philip Broad (a career Foreign Office man and the FO's representative in Bari), of supporting the Partisans on ideological grounds. And it is clear, from the minutes of their discussions, that uppermost in the minds of the Policy Committee was the desire to inflict as much damage on the Germans as possible and as soon as possible, given the fact that the Germans were in retreat. This short-term result was what the Balkan Air Force had been established to deliver;

Elliot's directive instructed him 'to contain and destroy as many enemy forces as possible in the Balkans'.[32] All he now needed were the tools to do so.

That the Partisans were delivering considerable anti-Axis activity was obvious to everyone in Bari, but perhaps less so to SOE officers isolated in northern Albania. Debriefing reports and signals sent from Albania indicated that SOE officers attached to Hoxha's forces were convinced the Partisans were better organized, more united and more hostile to the Germans than any other guerrilla group. Hoping to release the Partisans' full military potential, these officers urged Bari for more weapons with which to arm them. Significantly, however, they also pressed for more exclusive support, since the continued presence of other British officers with the Nationalists, though in accordance with British policy, was hampering their own relations with the Partisans. Major Brian Ensor, for example, who spent over eight months with the Partisans, from February until September 1944, wrote later:

> My briefing before infiltration ... consisted of a statement that on all possible occasions I was to use British material and Partisan manpower to kill Germans ... but I consider the support BLOs [British Liaison Officers] received to help them gain the full co-operation of the Partisans, was criminal ... The Partisans were, and would always be, the most effective fighting machine, provided they were not deprived of weapons and supplies to continue their fight against the Germans to the advantage of any doubtful resistance elements whose only claim to recognition consisted of empty promises and idle boastings ... My signals of April and May prove that I was always a staunch supporter of an immediate change of policy, because it was not possible to carry out my orders properly ... For a long time we were not trusted ... [and] held responsible [by the Partisans] for a policy with which we did not agree and which was inhibiting Partisan resistance to the Germans, and preventing us from carrying out our briefing orders, i.e. harassing the Germans.[33]

This impatience with the inactivity of the Nationalist north was typical of officers who worked with the Partisans in the spring and summer of 1944.[34] What is more, throughout the summer, many of these officers were evacuated from Albania to Bari, where they were able to voice their opinions in person and keep the Albanian Section up to date with Partisan strength.

These officers included Lieutenant-Colonel Alan Palmer, the senior British Liaison Officer with Hoxha's Partisans for most of 1944. Throughout the summer, Palmer dealt frequently, directly, and in person with the key policy-makers in Bari, principally Harcourt, Elliot and the Policy Committee, and it is clear that his views in particular carried considerable weight. It is no coincidence that Bari's growing opposition to persevering with Kupi came at a time when Palmer and other British officers working with Hoxha were urging SOE headquarters for greater help in maximizing Albania's war effort. Though SOE's Albanian Section played an important role in presenting these officers' reports to higher authority, there is no evidence, from comparing surviving signals to the Section's policy suggestions, to suggest that they were exaggerated or tampered with. Nor is it possible to detect, as has been alleged, a significant break in continuity between Major Philip Leake's approach to events and that of Eliot Watrous, his successor as Section Head: signals sent from Albania before his death show Leake to have been convinced by then that the Partisans – estimated then at being 25,000-strong – deserved continuing support.[35] Indeed, the Albanian Section's policy suggestions of this period echo the arguments of Leake, Palmer, Ensor and other officers with the Partisans both openly and consistently.

Hoxha's movement, in stark contrast to Kupi's, had maintained a consistent record of action against the Germans throughout the spring and summer. By early June 1944, the Partisans were at their peak, resisting a major German offensive and battling against what was widely regarded as the finest German unit in southeast Europe, the 1st Mountain Division.[36] And when a Partisan brigade was detached from the battle and launched against Kupi at the end of June, this ongoing, antiAxis performance was enough to win over the Allied decision-makers in Bari. At first, the Balkan Air Force had halted the supply of arms to the Partisans, on the grounds that Hoxha had instigated this wider civil war and in the hope of controlling him. But such was the size and record of Partisan resistance that, by the end of July, the fact that other of Hoxha's forces were in action against the Germans and in trouble and in need of ammunition, saw Elliot and the Policy Committee agree to resume the supply.[37]

Kupi's long record of inaction was similarly obvious. SOE officers with him, including those of 'Concensus II', did not dispute this and no reports ever indicated that the situation was anywhere near as promising as that reported by officers with the Partisans. Until the Gjoles action, Kupi had not moved against the Germans since September 1943 and there had been no compelling reason to think that this would change. In early April 1944, for example, George Seymour informed Bari that Kupi was refusing to take action against the Germans unless the Allies recognized Zog (something the Foreign Office refused to do). Seymour had commented that he felt Kupi's stance was an excuse for not fighting at all: his real aim was to remain militarily inactive and then seize power once the Germans had left. 'Concensus II' found Kupi's attitude had changed little when they joined him at the end of April. In early May, the mission reported that Kupi was now insisting he would only fight if the LNC recognized his Legality movement; a few days later he said he would fight if Zog sent him instructions to do so.[38]

If SOE's attempts to make Kupi fight were meeting with little success, it was also apparent that he was greatly exaggerating the size of his forces. Over the months, reports of numbers varied widely: from 40,000 down to a few hundred.[39] In February 1944, Seymour informed Bari that Kupi was claiming he could raise a force of 25,000 men, though Seymour later commented that 'it was very apparent that his forces were not in the state of preparedness that he would have us believe'.[40] By May, Amery was reporting that he felt Kupi could raise 5,000 poorly armed men from Tirana, Mati and Kruja, his principal regions of support. In July, 'Concensus

II' asked for arms to supply 2,000. To onlookers in Italy this did not look impressive and compared poorly with the 25,000 Partisans under arms in the south.

Added to what, in Bari, was an image of a weak and prevaricating Kupi, was the possibility that he was collaborating. There is no doubt that Kupi associated with Albanians guilty of collaboration and that this association turned into a military alliance at the end of June 1944. The Partisan offensive against the north resulted in a broad-based Nationalist alliance in which Kupi allied himself with Gjon Markogjoni (who had collaborated with the Italians), Mustafa Kruja (who had collaborated with both the Italians and the Germans) and Fikri Dinë (the leading member of the German-backed Council of Regency). However, there remains some debate over how far Kupi went in his dealings with collaborators. Smiley writes: 'the BLOs attached to the Partisans, repeatedly told by them that Kupi was collaborating with the Germans, had absorbed these lies and signalled them to Bari. We ['Concensus II'] all knew that at no time did Kupi collaborate.'[41] That SOE in Bari were more suspicious, however, is clear. Commenting on the fact that the LNC had accused Kupi of direct collaboration with the Germans as early as February 1944, Lieutenant-Colonel Harcourt remarked in December 1944:

It is no more than possible that he personally never conversed with a German, but collectively his organisation, which boasted the inclusion of high-ranking Officers of State, was tending more and more to collaboration. One statement which led to accusations by the [Partisans] was made by a German deserter, Gefr. Forster who claimed to have seen in a German HQ a document purporting to be a pact of non-aggression signed on behalf of both Kupi and the German Commander. This statement was made by Forster on the 13 April and supported a rumour to the same effect which had been reported by Lt Col Seymour on 3 April 1944.[42]

That Kupi, unknown to 'Concensus II', had dealt indirectly with the Germans – that is, through intermediaries – on the matter of securing help against the growing Partisan threat, is now confirmed by 'Ultra' decrypts and captured German documents.[43] That SOE London was privy to this Kupi-related 'Ultra' seems likely, while there is reason to believe that during the summer of 1944 SOE's representatives in Bari also had access to this information.[44]

When Kupi finally fought a handful of actions against the Germans in September 1944, these were dismissed in Italy as last-gasp attempts at insuring with the Allies, unworthy of any attention.[45] Indeed, throughout the summer, the various military decision-makers had been dubious over the wisdom of maintaining a mission with Kupi, doubtful over whether he would fight, and certain that the weight of Allied favour ought to lie with the Partisans. Even in June, around the same time as Watrous was pressing from Bari to abandon Kupi, SOE and the Chiefs of Staff in London and Wilson at Caserta were all recommending that Kupi should not be armed unless some kind of reconciliation could be arranged between him and the Partisans.[46] The Foreign Office, though reluctant to abandon the Kupi option (they had, after all, been behind the plan to send him 'Concensus II'), nevertheless fell into line.[47] Indeed, it was only the support of the Foreign Office, prevaricating to the last over whether it should at least stay in contact with Kupi, that saw 'Concensus II' remain for so long with Kupi. There is no doubt that the longer the mission remained with Kupi, the more irritated became the Partisans, the SOE officers with them and the various policy-makers in Bari.[48] When approval for the mission's evacuation was finally received from the Foreign Office in London, 'Concensus II' was at once ordered out.[49] It is a measure of the frustration felt in Bari with Kupi, and the desire to keep the Partisans on side, that the controversial decision not to evacuate him had been insisted on by Philip Broad, the FO's representative there.[50] It is also a measure of how localized, in 1944, were the viewpoints of the SOE officers who were later so critical of this and other decisions.

Whether giving Hoxha's Partisans exclusive support was the correct line for policy to take has not been discussed here. It is to be noted, however, that what contributed to Allied policy-making was a frustration with Kupi's inaction, and a lack of sympathy for his predicament, that quite possibly were born from a fundamental misunderstanding of the pressures at work on the Nationalist desire to stay neutral or otherwise seek security. But it is clear that the key policy decisions in favour of increased and exclusive support for the Partisans were carefully considered and taken above the heads of SOE's Albanian Section in Bari. Nor is it possible to detect that the Section unduly influenced them in any way, although staff officers may well have wanted to see policy move away from supporting the likes of Abas Kupi and towards all-out support for the Partisans. These were decisions taken on primarily military grounds, reflecting the evidence presented by SOE officers in the field, and at a time when Allied policy-makers were driven overwhelmingly by a determination to inflict substantial and immediate damage on the Germans.

Notes

1 For memoirs, see, for example, Julian Amery, *Sons of the Eagle*, London: Macmillan, 1948; Peter Kemp, *No Colours or Crest*, London: Cassell, 1958; Sir Alexander Glen, *Footholds Against a Whirlwind*, London: Hutchinson, 1975; and David Smiley, *Albanian Assignment*, London: Chatto & Windus, 1984. The claim that one officer of SOE's Albanian Section was a Soviet 'mole' can be found repeated in M. R. D. Foot, *SOE: The Special Operations Executive; 1940–46*, London: Mandarin, 1993, pp. 203–4.
2 Sir Reginald Hibbert, 'The War in Albania and the Conspiracy Theory', *Albania Life*, Issue 57 Spring 1995.
3 GHQ Middle East Directive No. 195, 24 January 1944. TNA HS 5/11.
4 Julian Amery, *Sons of the Eagle*, p. 354.
5 Peter Kemp, *No Colours or Crest*, pp. 231–2.
6 David Smiley, *Albanian Assignment*, p. 152.
7 Peter Kemp, *No Colours or Crest*, pp. 242–3.
8 Sir Alexander Glen, *Footholds Against a Whirlwind*, p. 157.
9 See: paper, 'Recommendation of Policy', Major Elliot Watrous to Lt. Col. Harcourt and Mr. Philip Broad, 1 June 1944 and cipher telegrams, B8 (SOE Albanian Section, Bari) to SOE London, 6 and 7 June 1944, TNA HS 5/11.

10 See: memorandum, 'Comments on Telegram 3094 dated 7.6.44 from Bari', Captain Dayrell Oakley Hill (SOE London) to Major Edward Boxshall (SOE London), 8 June 1944, and letter, Major Edward Boxshall to B8, 9 June 1944, TNA HS 5/68.

11 Report on Albania Military Mission (p. 178), made available by the SOE Adviser to the Foreign & Commonwealth Office.

12 See, for example, letter, Major Elliot Watrous to Major Edward Boxshall, 26 May 1944, TNA HS 5/11 and letter, Major Elliot Watrous to Major Edward Boxshall, 19 June 1944, TNA HS 5/68.

13 Letter (Ref. SF/144/G13/B8 [sic]), Captain George Cowie to Major Edward Boxshall, 1 July 1944, TNA HS 5/69.

14 An incident, it should be noted, that Smiley had recorded in his diary at the time: diary entry, David Smiley, 26 October 1944, IWM Docs ref. A3/63/1/2.

15 Debriefing report, Major George Seymour, TNA HS 5/123.

16 Confirmed in conversations with former SOE officers (both staff and operational).

17 John Eyre, *The God Trip: The Story of a Mid-century Man*, London: Peter Owen, 1976, pp. 23–4.

18 See, for example, David Smiley, *Albanian Assignment*, p. 152 and Xan Fielding, *One Man in His Time: The Life of Lt Col N.L.D. 'Billy' McLean DSO*, London: Macmillan, 1990, p. 51.

19 Diary entry, David Smiley, 29 October 1944, IWM Docs Ref. A3/63/1/2.

20 Wireless Transmitter (W/T) message, CONCENSUS II (BERNARD w/t set 'OUT' log) to B8, 23 May 1944, IWM Docs Ref. A3/63/1/2.

21 Cypher telegram, Philip Broad to Algiers repeated FO London, 26 May 1944, cypher telegram, B8 to SOE London, 26 May 1944, and letter, Major Edward Boxshall to Douglas Howard (FO London), 28 May 1944, TNA HS 5/11.

22 Letter, Armine Dew (FO London) to SOE London, 26 June 1944, TNA HS 5/69.

23 W/T message, CONCENSUS II (BERNARD set) to B8, 25 October 1944, TNA HS 5/72.

24 Cypher telegram, Philip Broad to Caserta, 27 October 1944, TNA HS 5/71.

25 Letter (Ref. SF/143/G13/B8 [sic]), Captain George Cowie to Major Edward Boxshall, 1 July 1944, TNA HS 5/69.

26 W/T message, B8 to CONCENSUS II (BERNARD w/t set 'IN' log), 2 July 1944, IWM Docs Ref. A3/63/1/2.

27 Julian Amery, *Approach March: A Venture into Autobiography*, London: Hutchinson, 1973, p. 405.

28 See, for example, Sir Reginald Hibbert, *Albania's National Liberation Struggle: The Bitter Victory*, London: Pinter, 1991, *passim*; Elisabeth Barker, *British Policy in South East Europe in the Second World War*, London: Macmillan, 1976, p. 181; and David Stafford, *Britain and European Resistance 1940–1945: A Survey of the Special Operations Executive*, London: Macmillan, 1983, pp. 170–2.

29 Reginald Hibbert, *Albania's National Liberation Struggle*, p. 169.

30 Information from Personal File, made available by the SOE Adviser to the FCO.

31 See, for example, Michael Lees, *The Rape of Serbia*, New York: Harcourt, Brace, Jovanovich, 1990, and David Martin, 'James Klugmann [sic], SOE-Cairo, and the Mihailovich Deception' in A. Charters and M. Tugwell (eds) *Deception Operations Studies in the East-West Context*, London: Brasseys, 1990.

32 'History of the Balkan Air Force', TNA AIR 23/1508.

33 Debriefing report, Major Brian Ensor, TNA HS 5/136.

34 See, for example, Debriefing Report, Lt. Col. Norman Wheeler TNA HS 5/127, Debriefing Report, Major Bill Tilman, TNA HS5/128, Debriefing Report, Major Victor Smith, TNA HS 5/129.

35 W/T messages, Major Philip Leake to B8, 14, 15 and 20 May 1944, TNA HS5/68, letter Major Edward Boxshall to Michael Rose (FO London), 26 May 1944, TNA HS 5/90.

36 Report on Albania Military Mission (p. 95), made available by the SOE Adviser to the FCO.

37 Reginald Hibbert, *Albania's National Liberation Struggle*, p. 174 and p. 183.

38 Ibid. p. 159.
39 'Comments on Report by Lt. Col. McLean DSO, Major Smiley MC, and Captain Amery', Lt. Col. Harcourt, undated (c. early December 1944), TNA HS 5/126.
40 Debriefing Report, Major George Seymour, TNA HS 5/123.
41 David Smiley, *Albanian Assignment*, pp. 133–4.
42 'Comments on Report by Lt. Col. McLean DSO, Major Smiley MC, and Captain Amery', Lt. Col. Harcourt, undated (c. early December 1944), TNA HS 5/126.
43 For 'Ultra' decrypts see, for example: untitled note, 7 June 1944, TNA HS 5/119 and letter with 'TOPSEC "U"' enclosure, Air Commodore Archie Boyle to Col. David Keswick, 24 July 1944, TNA HS 5/11. For captured German material see Bernd Fischer, 'Abas Kupi and British Intelligence in Albania 1943–5' in John Monson (ed.) *Europe and the West: Selected Papers from the Fourth World Congress for Soviet and East European Studies*, London: Macmillan, 1992, p. 134, and Bernd Fischer, 'Resistance in Albania during the Second World War: Partisans, Nationalists and the SOE' in *East European Quarterly*, Vol. XXV, No. 1, March 1991, pp. 34 and 36.
44 Letter, Air Commodore Archie Boyle to Col. David Keswick, 24 July 1944, TNA HS 5/11.
45 Minutes BAF Policy Committee Meeting, 14 September 1944, TNA HS 5/72.
46 'Albania: Memorandum by SOE [London]', 7 June 1944; cipher telegram, Chiefs of Staff to AFHQ, 8 June 1944; cipher telegram, General Wilson to Chiefs of Staff, 16 June 1944, TNA HS 5/11.
47 Letter, Lt. Col. David Talbot Rice (SOE London) to Col. David Keswick (SOE London), 24 June 1944, TNA HS 5/68.
48 See, for example, minutes, BAF Policy Committee Meeting, 8 September 1944, TNA HS 5/72.
49 Cypher telegram, FO London to Harold Macmillan (Resident Minister at AFHQ), 2 October 1944, TNA PREM 3/41.
50 Letter, Philip Broad to Lt. Col. Harcourt, 27 October 1944, TNA HS 5/80.

15

SOE AND DENMARK

Knud J. V. Jespersen

The questions

I have been asked in this chapter to discuss in particular the significance of SOE's contribution to Danish Resistance in comparison to other 'home-grown' networks. I have to admit, however, that it is quite impossible here to present anything like a final answer to that problem.

What I can do – based on my research in the archives of the Danish Section of SOE and a certain general insight into the Danish Resistance Movement – is to present a few observations that might perhaps uncover part of the truth. I shall in this chapter try to give answers to the following specific questions:

1   What was SOE's contribution to Danish resistance in terms of men and material?
2   What circles of the Danish resistance were in particular influenced, or even controlled, by SOE?
3   What role did SOE play in the shaping of the politics of the Resistance Movement up to the Liberation?

It is my belief that the answers in combination may paint a rough, overall picture of SOE's military and political role *vis-à-vis* Denmark.[1]

The contribution in men and material

It is rather simple, on the basis of the archives, to summarize the extent of SOE's contribution to the Danish resistance in terms of men and material.

Let us first take a look at the direct human resources thrown into Denmark by SOE in the underground fight against the Germans. In the course of the war SOE sent a total of 57 SOE-trained agents – all Danes by birth – to Denmark. Almost all were dropped by parachute. The chronology in this activity appears from the figures in Table 15.1, derived from the Danish Section's final report of 1945. The subsequent fate of the agents is also shown.

As can be observed from these figures, the dispatch of agents started rather late. The first group was in fact only dispatched at the very end of 1941, even though the Danish Section had been active since late 1940 and the first group of 16 agents had passed through the basic training programme in January 1941. This delay was of course not unconnected with the fact that Denmark was a far away place with open shorelines, making airborne landing the only feasible solution.

The figures tell us moreover that the dropping programme had a slow start, indeed: only from 1943 did the number of those dispatched increase to a level making it reasonable to speak of a permanent SOE presence of any consequence in Denmark.

Obviously, this hesitant start was certainly due to the fact that operations in Denmark ranked low on SOE's priority list in the early part of the war. It must also be explained by the fact that public feeling in the formally, still neutral Denmark was unfavourable to these types of operations, at least until the August Rebellion in 1943 altered the official Danish policy of collaboration. This popular uprising did make an effective end to the official neutrality and brought the Danes in line with other German-occupied nations.

Table 15.2 sums up SOE's physical presence in Denmark, month by month depicting the number of operative SOE agents on Danish soil from the beginning of 1942 and until the end of the war.

This illustrates the very weak presence through the whole of 1942, but demonstrates also the heavy build up of forces during the first half of 1943 as part of the preparation for Operation 'Overlord'. The decrease in the number of agents from August 1943 to August 1944 is partly due to heavy German counter-measures against sabotage after the introduction of 'Norwegian Conditions' in August 1943. It must also be explained by the fact that the main emphasis in the work, during this period, was on building up secret army groups to be activated at an eventual Allied invasion of Denmark – a task for which only few sabotage instructors were needed. The renewed increase in the number of agents from late 1944 is due to the fact that Denmark was then rather close to the main theatres of the war.

The material contribution, in the form of weapons, sabotage material, explosives and other equipment, can in the same way be summarized rather exactly. The drops in Denmark by aircraft and parachute are depicted in Table 15.3 derived from SOE's own calculations at the end of the war.

To this should further be added several thousand pieces of light weapons for the secret army groups, conveyed by sea from 1944 – predominantly in the so-called Operation 'Moonshine'.

The picture on the material side is very similar to that of the agents: until late 1943 the drops were rather few, comprising almost exclusively sabotage material. From the beginning of 1944, however, the volume increased dramatically, and at the same time the emphasis shifted from sabotage material to weaponry for the secret army.

This course reflects with good precision the main stages of SOE's efforts: until the August Rebellion in 1943 the struggle in Denmark was first and foremost a

Table 15.1 Analysis of agents sent to Denmark

Year	No. of Agents	Evacuated	POW	Casualties/ killed	Total
1941	2	1	–	1	2
1942	7	–	3	2	5
1943	20	1	4	2	7
1944	20	7	6	1	14
1945	8	2	–	–	2
Total	57	11	13	6	30

Table 15.2 Number of agents in Denmark

	1942	1943	1944	1945
January	1	2	12	18
February	1	2	10	18
March	1	6	11	19
April	1	9	9	23
May	4	10	11	21
June	4	13	11	
July	4	13	9	
August	7	16	9	
September	7	15	10	
October	4	15	11	
November	5	12	18	
December	5	13	18	

Table 15.3 Air operations to Denmark

Year	Sorties			Delivery		
	Attempted	Successful	A/C missing	Containers	Packages	Tonnage
1941	1	1	–	–	–	–
1942	4	4	–	–	3	–
1943	25	19	1	100	18	12
1944	127	93	4	1642	73	169
1945	257	168	12	4157	468	439
Total	414	285	17	5899	562	620

psychological one, directed mainly against the official Danish policy of collaboration and aimed at calling a popular spirit of resistance into life. For such purposes
sabotage and propaganda were suitable means. With this goal fulfilled by the August
Rebellion the struggle became predominantly a military one, directed exclusively
against the Germans. At this stage the arming of a large number of resistance
groups had a high priority.

SOE's influence with the Danish Resistance

Let me then turn to the next question: with what circles in Danish Resistance did SOE in particular cooperate, and what was the extent of its influence? But allow me first as a background briefly to outline the nature of the Danish Resistance Movement from its first beginnings and up to the Liberation.

During the first years of the German occupation – that is until the spring of 1943 – no civilian resistance of any consequence existed, except for a few scattered sabotage groups. The most important anti-German contribution in those rather peaceful years was delivered by a group of officers in the Intelligence Division of the Danish General Staff. They had, through their man in Stockholm – Ebbe Munck – immediately after the German occupation established a secret contact with England, and they continued during the war to provide London with intelligence on the Germans of such quality and in such quantities that the German forces in Denmark could hardly move a gun without London being informed at once. Because of circumstances, which shall not here be touched upon, the SOE's Danish Section eventually succeeded in establishing itself as the main British contact with those officers from early 1942. And SOE developed on this account close, even if not always confident, operational cooperation with this group – 'the Princes', as they were called in the SOE 'language'. This contact became – not least in the final stages of the war – of crucial importance, because it presented SOE with a direct, informal link to the military part of the Resistance Movement, and through it also to the leading Danish politicians, who even after August 1943 continued to play an important role behind the scenes.

The first sparks of active civilian resistance emanated from the radical right and left-wings of Danish political life. On the right-wing were some members of the party Dansk Samling (Danish Unification Party), an extremist liberal party with certain anti-parliamentarian traits. On the left, were members of the Communist Party, made illegal after the German invasion of the Soviet Union in June 1941. The first category included resistance pioneers like Stig Jensen and Flemming Juncker, both supporters of SOE's activities in Denmark from the very beginning. In the last category was Professor Mogens Fog, who was likewise one of SOE's early and valued Danish supporters.

Some members of the Conservative Party also were early on the go, in particular a small group close to the party leader, Christmas Møller, who in the spring of 1942, with the active assistance of SOE, was smuggled out of the country and over to London. To this group belonged Borch Johansen, SOE's most important contact in Denmark in the early days. Only from the summer of 1943 did people of more moderate observance also join in with active resistance. They were mostly recruited through a moderate, originally educational organization called 'Ringen' (the Ring, or the Network) led by Frode Jakobsen, a more distant SOE contact. Only from this point on did the Danish Resistance achieve the character of a mass movement. SOE succeeded in establishing more or less direct contacts with all those groupings – which of course was not always the same as being in control.

The important thing, however, was that SOE through these contacts did in fact have access to all parts of the Danish resistance.

In terms of numbers the Resistance Movement could boast a rather impressing development: from only a few hundred in 1943 to well above 10,000 in late 1944, increasing further to nearly 50,000 at the end of the war, corresponding in the end roughly to about 1 per cent of the total population.

From September 1943 the efforts of the resistance were coordinated by the self-appointed Freedom Council – an initiative strongly supported by SOE. This Council included representatives from all the important resistance organizations ranging from the communists to Dansk Samling. Also permanently represented in this illegal government was SOE's chief organizer in Denmark – first Flemming Muus and later Ole Lippmann. The SOE representative had a permanent voice in this assembly and was thus able to assert SOE policy with growing weight, following the rapid increase in supplies from England.

The French resistance historian, Henri Michel divided the development of resistance into three typical main stages:

1   *the stage of disobedience* characterized by scattered initiatives without mutual interrelations, without any division of functions, and without a common strategy;
2   *the stage of organization*, in which the initiatives started to converge, and outlines of a common strategy began to appear; and finally
3   *the stage of fighting*, meaning the determined and coordinated military struggle.

If this typology is applied to the Danish Resistance Movement, the stage of disobedience can be said to have come to an end in the spring of 1943 and then passed into the organizational stage, lasting until the late autumn of 1943. The last 1½ years of the war represented the fighting phase.

It will be clear from what I have said so far, that SOE did in fact play important roles in all three stages. The organization established, in the first stage, successful direct contacts with precisely those groups on the wings of political life who were ready to commit civil disobedience, thus creating points of growth for subsequent armed resistance.

The crucial stage of organization corresponded with a heavy build-up of SOE's own forces in Denmark, and with the arrival of a new, charismatic chief organizer, who knew how to utilize the growing quantities of British explosives to achieve maximum psychological effect. This enabled SOE to leave a heavy mark on the organizational phase, perhaps most obviously demonstrated by the creation of the cross-political Freedom Council.

In the final fighting stage SOE's influence was also clear. This is obvious just from the large quantities of weapons and explosives brought into the country by the organization – actually, it is hard to imagine at all an armed resistance of any consequence in Denmark without the British weapons and explosives. But the most outstanding contribution made during this stage was perhaps SOE's successful efforts at dividing Denmark into a number of semi-independent resistance regions.

SOE and the creation of regions

When Flemming Muus, SOE's chief organizer, returned to Denmark in December 1943 after some weeks of consultation in the London HQ, he carried with him orders to divide the country into a number of regions, each with a regional staff of its own, who were to stay in direct radio contact with London. This plan was executed during the following months, in spite of misgivings from some members of the Freedom Council who saw their authority diminished by this decentralization. This initiative had the important effect that all resistance groups formed during the last 1½ years of the war – with the exception of a few independent sabotage groups – were founded by and put under the command of the respective regional organizations, whether those groups were of communist, Dansk Samling, military or whatever, origin.

For SOE HQ this step was certainly intended as a means to flexible direction of the Danish Resistance efforts in close agreement with Allied interests. But it had at the same time the important side effect of counteracting the tendency to create political party armies – a tendency that had been a striking feature in the autumn of 1943. Dansk Samling, the communists and also the dissolved Danish army were at that time actively engaged in such efforts.

One needs only take a glance at the political complications caused by the large political party armies in Belgium and France – not to mention the state of civil war in Yugoslavia and Greece – in order to realize what misfortunes such party-based resistance armies might entail. The Danes have thus good reason to thank SOE for its stubborn insistence on the regional idea, which prevented something similar happening in Denmark, and instead created the preconditions for a peaceful liberation.

This is not to say, however, that SOE's Danish Section was in control of Danish resistance in all its aspects and in all stages of the war. The communists ran their own show on many occasions, and the same was true for other fractions, too, for instance the illegal groups of the disbanded Danish army. Sabotage and other actions were frequently taking place beyond SOE's control, and British explosives were sometimes used for purposes directly contrary to SOE's interests.

The crucial point is, however, that SOE– even in spite of a fumbling and hesitating start – was capable of making its influence felt on the general course of Danish Resistance and moved it in a direction which was desirable from an Allied point of view. By virtue of fortunate personal contacts with key persons from all parts of the Resistance it also proved able to exert its influence with considerable weight in decisive situations. SOE's permanent representation in the Freedom Council and the successful carrying through of the regionalization of Resistance work are outstanding examples. Of particular importance were the trusting relations, which SOE at an early stage succeeded in establishing with the communist leader,

Professor Mogens Fog. He remained through the war SOE's most important link to the extreme left-wing of the Resistance. Without his mediating role this important part of the Movement might as well have turned a deaf ear to SOE's directives and to a much larger extent pursued its own independent goals.

SOE and the liberation

What I have said so far provides much of an answer to the last of my opening questions: what was SOE's role in the shaping of the Resistance Movement's policy in relation to the liberation?

Since Denmark was, at an early stage, pointed out as belonging to the British sphere of influence, British authorities had one prevailing interest in relation to the liberation: that of ending the German occupation of Denmark as smoothly as possible and, first of all, preventing a civil war developing in the ensuing power vacuum.

It was consequently SOE's policy to make the different parts of the Resistance work as closely together as possible and with all its power discourage fractionalizing. This line materialized in SOE's eager support of the Freedom Council and the organization's steady pressure on the Freedom Council as well as on the politicians, for a peaceful solution of the question of a joint liberation government. Those negotiations ended eventually with a fifty-fifty solution – an outcome preferred and supported also by SOE.

SOE's watchfulness regarding fractionalizing tendencies was also clearly demonstrated when, in late 1943, it became clear that the army-in-exile, which the Danish General Staff was building up in Sweden, seemed to have as its most important purpose to fight the communists in the event of a German collapse. These plans were met by SOE HQ with a firm refusal and a clear demand that this army-in-exile – as a condition for British support – was put under Allied command. As a further safeguard against 'White Guard' inclinations, two SOE officers were posted to Stockholm in order to keep an eye on things. Ronald Turnbull, SOE's representative in Stockholm was instructed to watch developments closely. By such precautions this attempt at forming a private army was prevented, and 'Danforce' – which was the name of the exile-army – was only brought over to Denmark after the German capitulation.

SOE – originally created by Churchill to 'set Europe ablaze' – thus ended up as something like a fireguard in Denmark. And it is therefore no exaggeration to claim that one of the most important contributions made by this secret subversive organization in Denmark was to ensure that the flames of war and resistance were extinguished swiftly and effectively as the time for the liberation came.

Epilogue

Danish citizens, who happened to be in England when Denmark was invaded by Germany on 9 April 1940, were regarded by the British authorities as 'enemy aliens' and treated as such. This was the price paid for the Danish government's collaborationist attitude to the Germans. At the end of the war, however, nobody – either in Denmark or abroad – had any doubts that Denmark belonged firmly to the Western Allied camp, even if the country – because of Soviet obstruction – still lacked formal recognition as such.

This radical change in Denmark's position was first and foremost – or rather exclusively – to the credit of the Resistance Movement. And behind the Resistance stood SOE with all its moral and material weight. Until this day it remains an open question whether the outcome would have been different without the determined assistance from this secret organization. I think, for my own part, that SOE, as far as Denmark is concerned, made a difference.

When Major Alistair Garrett in 1945 concluded his final report on the efforts of the Danish Section of SOE during the war years he ended up with this final remark:

> In Denmark it paid to emphasise that Denmark's struggle was a Danish show entirely, for which SOE was providing the tools, liaison officers, communications and directives. Even though this line was sometimes taken with 'tongue in the cheek' it paid never to hint that SOE was in control.

By way of conclusion it might be added that SOE certainly was not always in control: Danish Resistance was – like all other Resistance movements – an unruly quantity, by and large defining its own means and ends. But due to the fact that SOE – at least from 1943 – was able to 'provide the tools, liaison officers, communications and directives' this organization contributed decisively to give the Danish Resistance direction and goal; thus during the last two years of the war turning Denmark from a German vassal into an Allied co-fighter. This was no small achievement.

Note

1 Notes on SOE's Danish Section files are to be found in Louise Atherton, *SOE Operations in Scandinavia – A Guide to the Newly Released Records on the Public Record Office*, London: Public Record Office, 1994 and Knud J. V. Jespersen *No Small Achievement – Special Operations Executive and the Danish Resistance 1940–1945*, Odense: University Press of Southern Denmark, 2002.

16

'HITLER'S IRISH HIDEOUT'

A case study of SOE's black propaganda battles

Eunan O'Halpin

Introduction

This chapter is concerned with aspects of SOE's SO1 (black propaganda and deception) activities between 1940 and 1945. It touches on features of the thinking and bureaucratic processes underpinning British disinformation, as well as its application in respect of Ireland, whether as the subject (for example to press the line in America that Irish neutrality was a mortal threat to British security), the target (for instance to influence Irish opinion against Germany), or simply and perhaps most importantly as a place where the seeds of deception could be sewn. Examples of such operations aimed at German, Italian and Vichy French sources in Dublin are discussed below.[1] The intention in this chapter is to use Irish-related material to cast light on the wider question of British management and use of disinformation. Although Irish affairs were only a minor sideshow for British secret agencies once the likelihood of German invasion of the British Isles had faded in mid-1941, as a neutral state sharing a land border with the United Kingdom, and with an Axis diplomatic presence, Ireland continued to present both considerable security worries and potential disinformation opportunities until after the success of the Normandy invasion.[2] Discussion and implementation of disinformation policy concerning Ireland at various times involved an interesting cast of characters: Gladwyn Jebb and Gerald Templer of SOE, Sir Robert Bruce Lockhart, and at a lower level the Irish historian Nicholas Mansergh of the Ministry of Information and the poet John Betjeman in the British Representative's office in Dublin.[3]

The two agencies which mainly feature in this discussion are SOE, established in July 1940, and the Political Warfare Executive (PWE), set up in August 1941. SOE's initial remit had embraced on the one hand sabotage and irregular warfare (SO2), and on the other subversion, including black propaganda (SO1). From the start the two main elements of SOE had quarrelled about their respective responsibilities, while there was also great friction between the Minister of

Information and the Minister of Economic Warfare, responsible for SOE, about control of overt overseas propaganda. The establishment of PWE, whose *raison d'être* was essentially to study and to find ways of damaging the enemy's sinews of war, including his civilian population, through varieties of psychological warfare, was intended to dispose of most of the ministerial rows. PWE absorbed the SO1 side of SOE, but this perpetuated rather than ended the long-running friction between SO1 and SO2 because the latter controlled the overseas networks of agents through which much SO1 material would be disseminated: PWE was debarred from running their own agents in any country in which SOE operated.[4] SIS also distributed rumours in some countries, again not without some friction because of security concerns.[5] Furthermore, while for strategic purposes SOE was under the ultimate and usually unenthusiastic control of the Chiefs of Staff, reflecting its primarily military purpose, PWE was the direct responsibility of the Minister of Information, reflecting an explicitly political function.

Disinformation is used hereafter as shorthand for a range of techniques used by British agencies between 1939 and 1945. Some of these had been adopted during the First World War, and were partially disclosed in widely read inter-war memoirs such as Sir Campbell Stuart's *Secrets of Crewe House*; some had been refined in experimental work by SIS's Section D in the years leading up to war. Others were newly developed and applied by British agencies in the course of the war both for political ends and for strategic purposes affecting the military operations of those of both the Allied and the Axis powers in the European theatre (including Vichy French North Africa) and in the Far East, particularly once growing Allied mastery of encoded enemy and neutral communications made it possible to keep some track of the progress and impact of disinformation on its target audiences.

Responsibility for the planning and implementation of disinformation operations during the war was shared and sometimes fought over by a kaleidoscope of civilian and military agencies. As the war progressed, a degree of coherence was brought to disinformation activities, but at no point was there all-embracing and effective control of which lines were being pushed in which countries and to what policy ends. This is borne out in the evidence of SOE's limited but contentious Irish activities.

In a war against Nazism, it is not surprising that British disinformation activities were not constrained by ethical quibbles. In addition to covert propaganda work such as the operation of supposed Axis radio stations of various political hues, and the production and distribution of fake publications and documents, even the fabrication of evidence of enemy atrocities was considered fair game. In November 1941 an SOE officer wrote that:

> My section could quite easily provide a regular supply of atrocity pictures, manufactured by us in Canada ... the making of such pictures would require the buying and hiring of costumes, the manufacture of small pieces of scenery and of dummies, the part-time services of a first-class make

up man ... The most obvious for atrocities pictures at the moment is Russia, so that we should get to work while there is still snow in Canada.[6]

This paper, however, will concentrate on the manufacture and circulation of false and misleading rumours – 'sibs' or 'whispers' as they are termed interchangeably in the files.

Directed against an enemy, such unattributable propaganda was, in the words of a PWE document of February 1942, intended to;

> Induce alarm, despondency and bewilderment among the enemies, and hope and confidence among the friends, to whose ears it comes. If a rumour appears likely to cheer our enemies for the time, it is calculated to carry with it the germs of ultimate and grave disappointment for them. Rumours vary immensely in their degree of credibility, the wideness of their diffusion and the type of audience for which they are designed; but they have these factors in common, that they are intended for verbal repetition through all sorts of channels, and that they are expected to induce a certain frame of mind in the general public, not necessarily to deceive the well informed ... Dissemination of those rumours finally approved is the function of SOE. For this purpose whispering organisations have been set up in neutral countries and in un-occupied France.[7]

Because of the potential for overlap and confusion PWE was, inevitably, one of SOE's antagonists. Mark Seaman and others have fairly made the point that to focus unduly on SOE's documented difficulties within Whitehall is to miss the bigger picture of that organization's practical achievements in the field; nevertheless, historians primarily work with documents, and the Whitehall and Cabinet records available, including the papers of Desmond Morton, Churchill's key intelligence aide in the early years of the war, suggest unending friction between SOE and most other British clandestine agencies. Traces of informal cooperation notwithstanding, there is also plenty of evidence of tension and antagonism in the field.[8] This was the case in respect of Ireland as of far more important theatres of activity.

In Britain during the war, all propaganda and disinformation activities from the public dissemination of the unvarnished and painful truth to the covert circulation of the vilest calumny were seen ultimately as an adjunct to strategic objectives. A number of coordinating mechanisms were introduced, intended to reduce conflict between departments and agencies and to impart coherence to covert propaganda work. These became the ultimate source of authority below War Cabinet level. The course of the war saw considerable developments in the harnessing of disinformation for strategic purposes, with the emergence of Colonel John Bevan's London Controlling Section after June 1942 as an effective interface between deception staffs, the intelligence and security services and military planners in the European theatre; the management of political disinformation operations was, however, always far more problematic.[9] In principle, proper coordination was achieved in the latter half of 1941 through the creation of two inter-departmental bodies. These were the Underground Propaganda (UP) Committee of PWE, on which SOE, SIS, and the Ministry of Economic Warfare were represented, and the more narrowly military Inter-Service Security Board (ISSB), where MI5 and the fighting services had a say. The ISSB had been established in February 1940 to advise both on operational security and on misleading the enemy but, to quote the official historian's conclusion, 'was responsible neither for formulating nor for implementing any overall deception "policy". In the early years of the war no such policy existed.'[10] In addition to these filters, the Foreign Office had the right to insist that 'sibs' 'should not conflict with policy'. Furthermore, the Joint Intelligence Committee (JIC) had the authority to block 'whispers' which had cleared all the earlier hurdles.[11] Proposals for rumours were brought weekly to these committees for adjudication. There were frequent arguments, focusing both on the aims of the proposed rumours and on the right of the sponsoring department to propose it – by way of illustration, in October 1942 an SOE officer complained that the Ministry of Economic Warfare sometimes 'get away with sibs which are on the borderline' of strategic matters.[12]

Problems inherent in ascertaining both the dissemination and the impact of disinformation were soon recognized, but effective measurement proved elusive: on 16 April 1941 the SOE War Diary recorded that since the organization:

> Began circulating whispers on 27th November 1940, 387 rumours have been put out there have been 43 'come-backs'. In view of the fact that 'come-backs' are not easy to obtain, and that in the first few months there was little machinery for recording them, this result was claimed as quite satisfactory.[13]

Further surveys by PWE of 'come-backs' were equally inconsequential.[14]

In the realm of political deception, it was impossible at the time, and it remains so today, to find a causal link between a line developed and pushed clandestinely by British agencies and a definite shift in mood or policy in the country, minority or faction at whom the material had been aimed. The problem of measuring the effectiveness of disinformation was compounded by the fact, as the Prime Minister himself was informed as late as 1943, different agencies squabbled continually about the right to manufacture and distribute information, and on occasion may have bypassed the 'whispers' clearance system by one means or another. Furthermore, even where a 'whisper' promoted by one department was duly sanctioned and communicated to an SOE agent in the target country for dissemination, there were obvious problems including accidental or deliberate embroidering or distortion which might vitiate the original aim of the fabrication. Britain's experience in the realm of disinformation intended to serve primarily political ends was, consequently, an activity whose only sure result was infighting between the various agencies with competing property rights on the manufacture or distribution of whispers and other instruments of deception.

It was often difficult to secure an acceptable synthesis between the lines favoured by the varying interests and agencies involved in information and propaganda policy and dissemination. SOE's monopoly on the distribution of 'sibs' was formally uncontested by other secret agencies, but it is safe to assume that each often did as it pleased. Even within agencies, headquarters control over the manufacture and dissemination of disinformation was plainly not always complete. This is reflected in a note prepared by Desmond Morton for the Prime Minister in June 1941 on British propaganda failings during the mismanaged occupation of Syria. These ranged from the obduracy of the BBC, which had 'refused to obey formal instruction given with the consent and in the name of the Foreign Secretary and the Minister of Information' – on this Churchill minuted 'If this is true the personnel sh[oul]d be changed' – to the fact that neither the Ministry of Information nor SO1 (then the propaganda side of SOE) 'knew what line of propaganda was being put out by their local representatives in Jerusalem and Cairo. They were therefore at a loss regarding the line to be taken from this country.'[15]

Two years later, and despite various efforts by ministers to clarify the respective roles of PWE and SOE in the manufacture and distribution of covert propaganda and disinformation, Churchill was again drawn into inter-agency rows about who was entitled to manufacture and spread what rumours and fabrications in the Middle East. Morton told him that:

> there is a dispute in the Middle East between PWE, which does propaganda, and Lord Selborne's[16] secret organisation SOE. Lord Moyne[17] asks the Foreign Secretary to press that all propaganda in the Middle East shall be handed over to PWE and SOE [be] forbidden to do it. Sir Orme Sargent[18] asks you to agree to this, which seems on the surface to be the right solution, but should not Lord Selborne be invited first to explain why he thinks it necessary for his people to do propaganda? Would you like me to see Lord Selborne about this? You can then judge on the merits of the case.[19]

In such circumstances, disinformation from being a useful adjunct to strategy threatened to become a positive liability. SOE and PWE continued to bicker: in March 1944 Selborne and Brendan Bracken, the Minister of Information responsible for both PWE's black propaganda activities and for the overt war reporting of the BBC, asked the Prime Minister to arbitrate on 'the relative priority to be accorded on and around D Day … to secret messages sent out by the BBC in connection with SOE operations', to which Churchill brusquely responded that the two 'should discuss this matter and settle it together'.[20]

This brings the discussion to the question of SOE's involvement in propaganda operations directed against or mounted in independent Ireland. On 2 September 1939 the Irish taoiseach (prime minister) Eamon de Valera reiterated his long-held policy that Ireland would remain neutral in a European war. Yet the state was virtually undefended, with a regular army of less than 7,000 men, with virtually no fighting equipment, whose main function was internal security. It also had an uncontrollable land border with Northern Ireland, whose ports, airfields and dockyards would be crucial for Atlantic operations. Ireland had a potential fifth column in the shape of the irredentist republican movement – in January 1939 the IRA had embarked on a bombing campaign in mainland Britain which was supposed to promote Irish unity, and in July an SIS report from Berlin, accurate in thrust if not in detail, had warned of recent discussions between IRA emissaries and the German Abwehr. Finally, as a neutral, Ireland maintained diplomatic relations with Germany, whose legation in Dublin could be expected to collect intelligence on Britain's war effort.[21]

From the outbreak of war, consequently, Britain had a clear interest in using covert propaganda and disinformation, as well as conventional diplomacy, in Ireland. At the political level, it was important to bring home to the Irish government and people that their country could successfully be defended from German aggression only by active participation in the war; to stress the evil of Nazism and Ireland's likely fate should Hitler attack; to emphasize that Irish survival depended on British shipping and sea routes, and that the defence of the waters around the British Isles was consequently a shared problem which required a shared approach; and to point out that Hitler was highly unlikely to take neutrality as an answer from any small state to which he addressed demands. Abroad, and particularly in the USA, where Ireland hoped to receive some support for her position, it was important for Britain to stress Irish shortsightedness and folly. In addition to the desirability of persuading Ireland to join Britain in the war, furthermore, Dublin was also a place where rumours intended to reach German diplomatic ears could easily be planted.

In the early months of the war accusations began to appear in the British media that Dublin was home to a nest of Axis spies, that well lit Irish towns would act as directional beacons for German submarines and aircraft and, a carry over from the First World War, that U-boats could find succour in remote bays and inlets on Ireland's western and southern coasts. Such charges, understandable though generally without foundation, were also routinely aired in the American press. On balance it seems likely, however, that these widely circulated claims were welcomed rather than created by British secret agencies. The British press knew a shirker when they saw one, and needed no clandestine government encouragement to pillory neutral Ireland. In fact the constant flow of rumours about supposed German activities caused considerable difficulties in Whitehall: the MI5 wartime Irish Section history records that such was the spate of scare stories from Ireland that 'it was difficult, if not impossible, to avoid the fatal and futile search for spies in the "in tray", instead of visualising the situation as a whole', and the Admiralty was also plagued by a stream of Irish U-boat stories even after the newly appointed Naval Attaché reported on the surprising efficiency of the Irish coast watching service.[22]

In the first year of the war, it appears that Britain was the target, rather than the author, of significant deception operations concerning Ireland. Churchill's first cable as Prime Minister to President Roosevelt stated that 'we have many reports of possible German parachute or air borne descents in Ireland', and as conditions in France deteriorated fears of a German attack on Ireland grew in Whitehall: on 27 May Morton informed Churchill that 'a rising in Eire is thought likely now at any time', that 'the IRA is well armed and well organised', and that 'Eire Defence Forces are little short of derisory'. It was also known 'that the Germans have plans to land troops by parachute and aircraft', and escaping Dutch police and army officers had disclosed 'other particulars of a German plan to invade Ireland which came to their knowledge during the period when Holland was neutral'.[23] On 1 June Britain passed on to the Irish government a warning, which they said came from Dutch sources, that a German parachute attack was not simply possible 'but is imminent'.[24] In fact no such operation materialized, and post-war evidence indicated that Germany had given little serious thought to operations against Ireland as an adjunct to an invasion of Britain. From this it might be inferred that the warnings passed by the British were fabrications, intended finally to bring de Valera to his senses and to see that only through joining Britain in the war could Ireland save herself from destruction. Coming just a fortnight after the first arrangements for joint Anglo-Irish military discussions on the defence of the island in the event of a German invasion, the Irish did indeed accept the British warning as genuine. However, they took the view that with Germany apparently on the verge of complete victory it would be madness to enter the war on Britain's side unless the state was directly attacked. The Irish reaction, combined with further disaster in France, caused Britain to embark on a remarkable shift in policy: an offer to the Dublin government to seek to bring about Irish unity after the war in return for Irish participation during it. De Valera declined to be drawn, both because of the likelihood of German victory and because he reasoned that a post-war British government would be unable to coerce Northern Ireland into such a settlement.[25] If these claims about the discovery of definite plans for a parachute assault were false, however, we should note that it was not a British but a German fabrication – it is now known from other sources that German deception operations prepared in anticipation of Operation 'Sealion' included the manufacturing of rumours and stories of plans to attack Ireland as a feint during the build up to an invasion of Southern England.[26]

We have some other evidence of Irish-related disinformation operations. BSC (British Security Coordination, the New York based organization charged both with security liaison and with covert propaganda activities in the USA) claimed some success in SO1 activities aimed at promoting anti-neutrality arguments in Irish-American political circles up to December 1941. This was done partly through supplying material through a third party for the use of the maverick Irish senator Frank McDermott, who was one of the very few Irish politicians who openly favoured abandonment of neutrality in Britain's interests. Irish Army intelligence was justified in judging his 'activities … open to suspicion'. In addition, through a cut-out, SOE controlled the American Irish Defence Association (AIDA), an Irish-American organization established in 1940 to argue for American support for Irish participation in the defence of the Atlantic and of the British Isles. AIDA was supported by prominent Irish-American political, religious, business, labour, literary and academic figures, and amongst its officer board was a descendant of the iconic Irish patriot Robert Emmet, who had been executed for organizing rebellion against British rule in 1803.[27]

Most British efforts to influence Irish opinion, and to influence American opinion on Ireland, were made through more conventional channels. In the Ministry of Information, Nicholas Mansergh, a Tipperary man, was largely concerned with attempting to secure representation of the British view in the Irish print media and discreetly to facilitate sympathetic journalists, while in Dublin the press attaché John Betjeman lobbied as best he could (besides doing some whispering and other clandestine work).[28] Dominions Office records also indicate that the British quietly encouraged the anti-neutrality writings of Donal O'Sullivan, the one-time clerk of the Seanad and virulent critic of de Valera, whose acerbic *The Irish Free State and its Senate* appeared in London in 1940. We should also note in passing that at the apex of British wartime information policy from June 1941 onwards stood another Irishman, Churchill's long time confidant, Brendan Bracken, who used his friendship with the Prime Minister ruthlessly and sometimes vindictively to block propaganda and deception initiatives by SOE and other organizations.[29]

Whatever the possibilities of influencing Irish opinion through unattributable propaganda of one kind or another, British officials were very mindful of Ireland's attractions as a place where rumours could be planted, intended to catch the ears of the Axis powers or of their friends (the Vichy French and Spanish legations in Dublin were regarded almost as German auxiliaries up to 1943). It is hard to say when efforts to plant such stories began: until the creation of SOE such SO1 work was the province of SIS's Section D. But SIS had many more urgent matters on its hands as Hitler swept through the Low Countries and France, and it seems unlikely that it had either the capacity or the will to disseminate rumours in neutral Ireland prior to mid-June 1940, when a Passport Control Officer, Captain Collinson, was appointed to Dublin. Even then, the officer reported to SIS's counter-intelligence Section V, reflecting SIS's priority of detecting and penetrating enemy intelligence activities in Ireland. Irish intelligence penetration of Collinson's networks up to their dissolution in March 1945 also show that SIS's Irish priorities were indeed security and counterintelligence work rather than propaganda and deception.[30] SIS's Irish set up was not the mainspring of British rumour mongering in Ireland aimed at Axis targets.

The available evidence suggests that, for a time, that task went to SOE. In March 1941 SOE had dispatched an agent to Dublin with two main tasks: to begin spreading rumours, and to survey Irish installations for possible sabotage in the event of a German attack.[31] The person chosen was J. R. 'Roddy' Keith, an eternally optimistic advertising man whose indiscretion quickly antagonized SIS, MI5 and the British Military Attaché, who served as his communications link with London. During his three months of activity in Dublin between March and June he was supplied with two sets of 'sibs' for circulation. Of these only two examples have survived. 'S/535' stated that:

the USA has just handed over to Britain, under Lend and Lease, one of three fortified floating islands equipped with electrical defence apparatus, which is to be used as a base for anti-U-boat aeroplanes in the Atlantic. It has already accounted for three submarines in the last ten days.

This presumably was intended to confuse the German naval authorities. 'S/599', also circulated in Ireland in the spring of 1941, is rather more enigmatic: it simply claimed that 'the Pope has excommunicated Hitler but the excommunication has not been made public', a fabrication perhaps intended to discredit the German leader in Irish Catholic eyes.[32]

Very few Irish-related rumours have been traced. 'R/427' stated that 'De Valera is going to allow the Americans to use Irish naval bases'. It is disappointingly pedestrian compared with some of the whispers prepared for other countries. Take, for example, 'R/434', intended for West Africa in early 1942, which posed the enigmatic question 'Did you notice the stars on the First of Ramadan? The Snake and the Scorpion ...', or 'R/438', which disclosed that:

> a ghoul has given birth to a child in the desert north of Timbuctoo. The Archangel Gabriel has explained to the Marabout of Bamako that this signifies great misfortune for the [Vichy] French, who have opened the door of the African Mohammedan world to the Germans.[33]

Nor do Irish 'sibs' have the prurient quality of much of the material prepared for German consumption, with its emphasis on venereal disease amongst servicemen, miscegenation between German women and foreign workers, and sexual deviance. Take 'R/232 ... Baldur von Schirach spent a week at the Ritz in Budapest. In the evening he dressed up as a woman'.

If the Irish public were spared such exotica, one intriguing example has been found of a carefully crafted fabrication prepared for planting in Dublin. This was created by SOE in the aftermath of Rudolf Hess's dramatic arrival in Britain as a self-appointed peace emissary in May 1941. Read in isolation from accompanying papers, this document is a conspiracy theorist's dream:

> Hess has begun to talk. He swears that he is the bearer of a peace offer to Britain, from Hitler himself. He demanded to see Churchill or Eden; this was refused, but HMG went so far as to let Sir Alexander Cadogan[34] visit him.
>
> The offer he makes is typically Hitlerian, broad in concept and very simple. In fact internal evidence makes it seem genuine. It is simply a compromise settlement based on the status quo; Germany to abandon colonial claims, and to recognise British naval supremacy; Britain to recognise Continental Europe as a German sphere of influence. The armament clauses are simply to the effect that the relative strength of the Air Forces and Navies of the combatants are to be maintained in the

proportions existing at the time of the agreement. Land forces have not even been mentioned; this seems genuine, as Hitler knows he has complete superiority in Europe and does not need to codify any agreement about land forces.

Germany proposes permanent Protectorate regimes for Poland, Denmark, Holland, Belgium and Serbia, but agrees to withdraw completely from Romania, Bulgaria and Greece (except Crete) and Norway two days after the conclusion of the peace. As for France, Germany proposes to withdraw from Metropolitan France after imposing complete disarmament including the scuttling of the French Fleet. (The British are certain this bit is genuine, because only Hitler would have thought of it, and only Hitler would be in a position to make the German High Command accept such a clause). German Commissions are to remain in North Africa, however, and the existing German forces in Libya are to be maintained for five years after conclusion of the peace. Crete is to remain in German hands.

Germany proposes to recognise Abyssinia and the shores of the Red Sea as a sphere of British influence.

HMG are rather puzzled. Hess will not say whether this proposal has the consent of the Italians or not. HMG suspect that Hitler characteristically sees clearly that the conclusion of a peace between Britain and Italy would follow automatically, or a compromise along these lines, since there is no other reference to Italy or the Italian Empire. As for Italian naval and air strength, that would seem to be included under the armaments clause about the status quo in relative strengths.

The German campaign to allege Hess's insanity was, Hess declares, arranged beforehand. HMG think it was arranged so that if the proposals are unsuccessful there would be no harm done to German home morale.[35]

This fantastically circumstantial if artful fabrication, prepared for use by 'anyone talking to the Italian contact in Dublin', had been intended to reach Mussolini's ears before a planned meeting with Hitler. In the event, it came too late, and

I am afraid we may have missed an opportunity … In between has come the Brenner meeting [between Hitler and Mussolini]. The fairy tale which I have written tries to take this into account. I have deliberately added circumstantial stuff about Cadogan. I have diverged a lot from … [the original] draft because if we are to convey to Italy that Germany is double-crossing her we must convey the possibility of Hitler having sent Hess.[36]

Because of widespread doubts about his suitability, SOE was obliged to pull Roddy Keith out of Dublin in June 1941. For other policy reasons SOE afterwards found itself disbarred by the prime minister from operating in Ireland. This created considerable difficulties, because SOE claimed the exclusive right to distribute 'whispers' outside the United Kingdom and much resented efforts by other agencies to operate independently or even, as PWE attempted in the USA, to take control of SOE agents involved in 'whispering'. SOE ran into such problems in Ireland in August 1941, when a planned scheme of 'whispers' aimed specifically at the Vichy French Naval Attaché Captain Albertas provoked convulsions within Whitehall's secret world. The interdict against operating in Ireland still stood, as did the ill-will generated by Roddy Keith's brief sojourn in Dublin. The Albertas scheme died a death, but SOE renewed its interest in using Ireland as a 'whispering' gallery a year later after discovering that PWE had prepared and were intending to distribute their own whispers through the agency of John Betjeman. After a certain amount of negotiation, an acceptable compromise was reached: PWE would be deemed to be operating in Dublin on SOE's behalf and would distribute only 'whispers' approved by SOE. This plan in turn collapsed – neither SIS nor British Troops Northern Ireland would give any assistance, and Betjeman pulled out after recruiting a suitable Irish desseminator – and Gladwyn Jebb of SOE headquarters appears to have despaired of further Irish operations.[37] Which, if any, of the other British clandestine agencies took up the challenge of whispering in Ireland is unknown: however, by the autumn of 1943 British intelligence interest in Ireland related almost entirely to issues of security surrounding the preparations for the invasion of France. The thrust of British policy was effectively to isolate Ireland from the outside world in the months running up to D-Day through travel restrictions, censorship, shipping controls, and the delay of and later the prohibition of cables even for diplomatic communications. In these circumstances, although like other neutral capitals Dublin abounded in rumours at the best of times, it was no longer a fruitful place in which to distribute them because neither German diplomats nor their remaining European friends had any reliable and timely means of relaying material, genuine or manufactured, back to their masters.[38]

This brings us to examination of one extraordinary disinformation scheme which SOE put forward for consideration in December 1944. SOE by this time had been assigned one overriding European goal: to target Germany and her people in order to soften her up as the Allied armies advanced, and by that time its Irish vicissitudes can have been no more than a vague memory. SOE's Major-General Gerald Templer, never a man known for circumlocution, baldly attacked a PWE paper on 'Methods of breaking the German will to resist'. This was 'inadequate to meet the urgent requirements of the C-in-C', because:

(a) The time-lag would be too long for the schemes to be effective in the immediate future, as required by C-in-C.
(b) The schemes, while they provide for the subversion of selected and specialised targets (e.g. German industrialists and Nazi leaders) make too little provision for reaching and subverting the mass targets – the German armed forces now facing the Allied Armies plus the civilian population in their immediate rear, whose will to resist at present provides the C-in-C's most pressing problems.

What Templer instead proposed was 'a scheme' which 'is simple', 'can start within a few days', 'will be known to succeed or not within a few weeks', and 'cannot lay HMG open to charges of complicity'. It was:

> submitted that unless HMG agrees to jettison former ideas about the ethics of deceiving friends, and adopts the general principle that 'the end justifies the means' – even to the extent of involving (by unacknowledgeable means) the government of a neutral state – no scheme for breaking the enemy's will to resist can be adopted with the rapidity now necessary; and that rather than a series of ingenious but unintegrated and somewhat long-term plans.

Britain should consequently adopt 'the following "CASEMENT" PLAN' (Roger Casement, a former consular official knighted for his humanitarian work in the Belgian Congo and in Brazil, had been executed for treason in 1916 because of his efforts to secure German help for Irish rebellion). The object of the plan was:

> to reveal to the German Field Army and people that their leaders have made all arrangements, including selection of the D-Day, for escape to safety in EIRE, some by submarine, some by aircraft ... There have already been numerous rumours – some inspired by us – to the effect that Nazis are 'getting away', though EIRE has not been mentioned. On each occasion the enemy Press and Radio have re-acted sharply; newspapers have emphasised the 'impossibility' of such a manoeuvre and have reaffirmed the unity of Leaders and People.[39]

The 'Casement' plan would necessitate '"planted" stories in certain newspapers of neutral countries'; 'rumours circulating along all possible channels, interpreting and exaggerating the published stories'; 'a Parliamentary question, inspired if it does not come naturally', asking if the government has any information about Nazi plans to use Ireland as a bolt hole, and subsequent parliamentary 'criticism of HMG for not demanding a categorical denial from the Eire Government'; 'the substance' of such parliamentary ructions to be 'reported factually by the BBC, all stations, in all languages (white)'; and the use of PWE's clandestine German broadcasting stations:

> Once German home propaganda has been forced into a denial (or even an airy dismissal) of the escape plot, black radio, rumours, cryptic statements by ambassadors and others in official Allied positions, and 'intelligence' sent to the enemy by double agents can have free play. *The German armed forces and people are reached, initially, by the Germans themselves, through their own Propaganda Ministry*. The enemy is forced to act as Allied agents for dissemination and the Allied propaganda (black and white) is in the strong position of using genuine German sources as a peg on which to hang their propaganda.

It may be argued that this proposal should be seen as nothing more than a clumsy idea from a man inexperienced in propaganda work – Templer, 'a martinet in appearance and manner, his displeasure – even his presence – was intimidating', was only killing time in SOE, to whose London headquarters he was attached for six months between September 1944 and March 1945 while recovering from wounds bizarrely inflicted in Italy by a flying piano.[40] But it was considered at a high level in both PWE and the Foreign Office before being rejected on 'political' grounds – it was argued that Ireland was an inappropriate as well as an incredible supposed haven, and that Argentina sounded a far more plausible bolt hole. Undaunted by this rebuff, SOE returned unsuccessfully to the charge. On 18 January Templer played his last card. Since the initial rejection of the plan, circumstances had altered: a question about Irish intentions towards German war criminals had conveniently though coincidentally been asked in the Commons. The Government's reply, to the effect that the Irish government had declined to say how they would treat alleged war criminals seeking asylum, had had the effect of bringing the possibility of Ireland as a Nazi safe haven firmly into the public domain:

> It would seem that policy objections on the part of the Foreign Office to involving Eire can now be waived since any damage on this score has presumably already been done. Under the circumstances, we feel it might be advisable to continue with the next step of the Casement Plan in order to benefit from the flying start which fortuitously we have been given.[41]

Notwithstanding Templer's disclaimer of any role in bringing this happy coincidence about, it is striking that the key question had been tabled by the Ulster Unionist MP Professor Douglas Savory of Queens University, a constant critic of Irish neutrality, who had his own connections with the secret world: he had served in naval intelligence under the legendary 'Blinker' Hall in the First World War.[42] We should also note that Templer was an Ulsterman whose regiment was the Royal Irish Fusiliers.[43] It is at least possible that these loyal Irish links contributed to his championing of a plan which, whatever its likely strategic impact, would have had the incidental effect of embarrassing neutral Ireland and branding it a home fit for Hitler. It may be that Templer, if not his more junior SOE colleagues involved in the drafting of the scheme, was bent on pushing the 'Casement' Plan as essentially the construction of a blood libel against neutral Ireland. This would serve as a punishment for staying out of the war, rather than constitute a genuine disinformation campaign seriously calculated to contribute to the collapse of the German military and civilian will to resist.

In the event, despite SOE arguments that there would be 'no difficulty in convincing the German public of the plausibility of the Eire plan, since criminals are known to hide near the scene of their crimes', and that:

> the German reaction would be much more violent in the case of Eire ...
> He thought the Germans would exploit the idea of a small, powerless

country being brow-beaten by the United Kingdom, and this strong reaction would be much in our favour.

Nevertheless, the views of the Director General of PWE Sir Robert Bruce Lockhart prevailed:

One of the main arguments against Eire was the difficulty of making the idea plausible to the German people; he did not see that the parliamentary question had in any way eased this difficulty. Another important argument against Eire was the political complications involved, which was likewise unaffected by the parliamentary question ... [Furthermore] the idea of the German war criminals' plans for escape had been much used in the past and ... there was danger of the whole thing becoming ridiculous if too many countries were referred to as asylums.

Bruce Lockhart also said that any decision to reinstate Ireland in the 'Casement' Plan would have to be referred to the War Cabinet, who would almost certainly reject it on political grounds. Official endorsement was instead given to Argentina as the more credible and politically less sensitive Nazi bolt hole; the subsequent escape of Adolf Eichmann and others to that country, presumably inspired not by British 'sibs' but by carefully laid plans, suggest that a South American country was indeed a more plausible destination for Hitler's henchmen on a wide variety of grounds, from pre-war German political and commercial links to its rather more agreeable climate.[44] Ireland thus escaped one British calumny, leaving the way clear for the reinvigoration of the Irish-Nazi smear through the autonomous agency of the taoiseach Eamon de Valera when he offered his condolences on Hitler's death to the German minister in Dublin, an act of diplomatic ineptitude beyond the imagination of even the most rabidly anti-Irish 'whisper' monger.[45]

What conclusions can be drawn from this sketch of British rumours and Irish affairs? The evidence of covert propaganda with an Irish angle, while so limited as to make generalization dangerous, suggests that after 1940 Britain was not bent on manipulating Irish opinion into the war, on discrediting the Irish government or on panicking de Valera into public concessions. The SOE material available suggests that Ireland was viewed and used mainly as a convenient entrepôt for material aimed at European targets rather than being the prime object of black propaganda campaigns of one sort or another. The records do suggest, however, that Britain was concerned to discredit Irish policy in the USA by clandestine means through clandestine SO1 activities, both to damage de Valera and to dilute Irish-American hostility to American support for Britain and her eventual entry into the European war – albeit courtesy of Hitler rather than SOE – on 10 December 1941.

More generally, despite – or perhaps because of – the bizarre bureaucratic processes which governed the generation and dissemination of British black propaganda (or at least that produced by the newly created agencies), very little evidence emerged then or since to suggest that political or economic 'whispers' had any serious impact on enemy or neutral states other than perhaps to spur the manufacture and spread of counter-rumours.

Finally, we can speculate about Templer and the 'Casement' Plan. He went on to make his name in Malaya as a commander who not only reorganized and managed combined military and police operations effectively, placing great emphasis on systematic and detailed intelligence gathering, but who also saw the importance of propaganda and disinformation in undermining the enemy's credibility and morale.[46] Was this multi-faceted approach the consequence of his brief exposure to the sowing of confusion and the fomenting of subversion while in SOE, or was it rather that he had learned from his earlier mistakes in confusing personal and national political priorities?

Notes

1 ADA/1 to AD/A, 2 August 1941, TNA, HW 6/307.
2 Eunan O'Halpin, ' "Toys" and "whispers" in "16-land": SOE and Ireland, 1940–42', *Intelligence and National Security*, Vol. 15, No. 4 (Winter), pp. 1–16.
3 Prior to the outbreak of the war Britain had no diplomatic or consular representation in independent Ireland, although Ireland had a high commissioner in London and maintained small missions in a number of European countries, in Canada and in the USA.
4 Charles Cruickshank, *The Fourth Arm: Psychological Warfare 1938–1945*, Oxford: Oxford University Press, 1981, pp. 17–26, 31.
5 Ibid. p. 109.
6 G.106 to A/C, 26 Nov. 1941, TNA HS 1/333.
7 PWE memorandum on 'Rumours', 7 February 1942, TNA, FO 868/69.
8 This writer's most recent encounter with a vehement critic of SOE came in August 2000 when I interviewed a former Indian government security officer, who described Peter Fleming of SOE's Force 136 as devious and untrustworthy.
9 Michael Howard, *British Intelligence in the Second World War volume 5: Strategic Deception*, London: HMSO, 1990, pp. 25–9, 103–22, 167–200.
10 Charles Cruickshank, *Deception in World War II*, Oxford: OUP, 1st edn, 1979; 1981, p. 35.
11 PWE note on 'Rumours', 7 February 1942.
12 D/Q10 to AD/P, 13 Oct. 1942, TNA, HS 6/305.
13 SOE War Diary, 16 Apr. 1941, TNA HS 7/215.
14 See the survey of 'Come-backs 1941–1943' in TNA FO 898/71.
15 Morton to Churchill, 10 June 1941, TNA, PREM 7/4.
16 Minister of Economic Warfare, 1941–1945.
17 Walter Guinness, Minister Resident in Cairo. Assassinated by the Stern Gang in 1944.
18 Sir Orme Sargent (1886–1962), Deputy Under Secretary in the Foreign Office.
19 Morton to Churchill, 16 March 1943, TNA, PREM 7/4.
20 Morton to Churchill, 22 March, and reply, 23 March 1944, TNA, PREM 7/5.
21 'Note on the work of the Irish Section of the Security Service September 1939–1945', p. 33, TNA, KV 9.
22 Ibid, p.43; Eunan O'Halpin, *Defending Ireland*, Oxford: OUP, 1999, pp. 226–7.
23 Churchill to Roosevelt, 15 May 1940, Franklin D. Roosevelt Library, NLR-MR-FDRWSC-1940-3T (document image accessed via the NAIL search engine at http://www.nara.gov); Morton to Churchill, 27 May 1940, TNA, PREM 7/2.
24 Archer (British Representative's Office) to Walshe (External Affairs), 1 June 1940, National Archives of Ireland (NAI), DFA A3.

25 John Bowman, *De Valera and the Ulster Question 1917–1973*, Oxford: OUP, 1982, pp. 218–39.

26 Charles Cruickshank, *Deception in World War II*, pp. 207 and 210.

27 Reports on AIDA, January 1941–January 1942, TNA HS 8/56.

28 Conversation with Professor Mansergh, St John's College Cambridge, 1986, Mansergh to Betjeman, 18 May 1942, TNA, DO 130/30. Professor Mansergh said that neither he nor Betjeman had anything to do with black propaganda or other covert activities, but the SOE files indicate that Betjeman had some involvement in whispering.

29 Cruickshank, *The Fourth Arm*, pp. 132–3.

30 Eunan O'Halpin, 'MI5's Irish memories: Anglo-Irish security cooperation in the Second World War', in B. Girvin and G. Roberts (eds), *Ireland and the Second World War: Politics, Society and Remembrance*, Dublin: Four Courts, 2000, p. 11.

31 AD/A1 to AD/A, 2 Aug. 1941, TNA, HW 6/307.

32 O'Halpin, ' "Toys" and "whispers" ', p. 11.

33 List of approved Sibs, undated, 1942, TNA, FO 868/69.

34 Permanent Under Secretary at the Foreign Office from 1938 to 1945.

35 Undated document, Murray to Leeper, 3 June 1941, TNA, FO 898/30.

36 Murray to Leeper, 3 June 1940.

37 O'Halpin, ' "Toys" and "whispers"', pp. 13–14.

38 Eunan O'Halpin, 'Irish-Allied security relations and the "American Note" crisis: new evidence from British records', *Irish Studies in International Affairs*, Vol. 11 (2000), pp.71–83.

39 Undated SOE document, with Capel Dunn to Bruce Lockhart, 20 December 1944, TNA, FO 898/357.

40 *Dictionary of National Biography 1971–80*, Oxford: Oxford University Press, 1985, p. 836.

41 SOE Council Minutes, 22 December 1944, TNA, HS 8/201; Templer to Bruce Lockhart, 19 January 1945, TNA, FO 898/357.

42 T.s. of memoir 'From the haven into the storm', 1962, Public Record Office of Northern Ireland, D/3015/2/141A.

43 In Public Record Office of Northern Ireland, T2367, are a photograph and one document presented by Templer.

44 Minutes of meeting, 25 January 1945, TNA, FO 898/357. The 'Casement' Plan is briefly discussed in Philip Taylor, *British Propaganda in the Twentieth Century*, Edinburgh, 1999, pp. 209–10.

45 Bowman, *De Valera*, pp. 255–6.

46 Interview with the late Dr Richard Clutterbuck, who served as a senior staff officer under Templer during the Malayan Emergency and who later became a leading commentator on terrorism and counterterrorism, 1983.

17

'OF HISTORICAL INTEREST ONLY'

The origins and vicissitudes of the SOE archive

Duncan Stuart

> This material is in great confusion. Partly through inexperience, partly for reasons of security, SOE began life without a central registry or departmental filing system. Each branch kept its own papers on its own system, from the Minister down to the sub-sections of the Country Sections: if a paper existed in a single copy, it might come to rest finally anywhere in this hierarchy of separate archives. The original confusion was made worse because in 1945, when the end was in sight, SOE made a resolute attempt to impose on the existing chaos a proper system of departmental filing by subject. This was an immense task which was scarcely begun when the department officially came to an end: the registry staff was kept in being for some time, but the work was eventually stopped on grounds of economy when it was about a quarter done. One has therefore to cope with two superimposed systems of filing, both radically imperfect.
>
> W. J. M. Mackenzie

Most serious students of SOE will have read this admirably succinct description of the SOE archive written by William Mackenzie in the Preface to his Official History of SOE for the Cabinet Office, which was completed on 1948 and has been in the PRO since 1996. Still more will be familiar with the more detailed account of the SOE archive in Appendix A, on Sources to *SOE in France* by Michael Foot, written in 1962, which is too long to be quoted here.

Both these historians portrayed the facts, as known to them, as accurately as they could at the time they were writing. But the incompleteness of the information available to them, compounded by the inhibitions imposed upon them in the name of security, inevitably meant that their accounts were less than the full truth. Moreover, since they wrote, a final reorganization of the archive took place in the

217

early 1970s, conducted at last by a professional archivist from the Public Record Office (PRO), Mr. C. B. Townshend. So that the present archive, in the form in which it is being released to the PRO, represents the third superimposed system of filing, which Townshend created only some 25 years ago.

This chapter is an attempt to tell the complete story of the SOE archives, insofar as it can be documented, so that future historians can have a clear idea both of its value and imperfections and of the transformations through which it has passed. Even today, however, it is still necessary for me occasionally to be economical with the truth when dealing with events after 1946. And I do not in any case intend to descend to a level of detail which would make this account unusefully academic and disproportionately long.

From its inception, SOE was a poor record-keeping organization by the standards of normal government departments. This was mainly due to the circumstances of its creation. It inherited the records and operational attitudes of its predecessors, the 'D' organisation and MI(R) and followed their precedents by adopting a hybrid organization, functional in respect of common support services and geographical for operations. Country Sections worked independently of each other and were led by action-orientated individualists with a keen appreciation of the operational needs for close control and restrictive security but little concern for filing systems. There was, initially at least, no substructure of experienced bureaucrats and a constant shortage of support staff. And the bugles were urgently sounding. As Foot puts it, 'security married with haste to beget filing by country sections or even smaller sub-divisions' who 'all kept their papers in separate places, classified on individual plans.' In the judgement of a later archivist, 'some of these [filing systems] were good, some were appallingly bad'.[1]

There was also an institutional bias against more than minimal record keeping. As Sir Douglas Dodds-Parker wrote in his book *Setting Europe Ablaze*, 'From 1940 it had been said "the less the paper, the more the action"; that by the normal rules of a Secret Service, nothing would ever be written by us or about us.'[2] Moreover, SOE's security regulations were quite clear and peremptory on the destruction of records:

> It is absolutely essential that the bulk of the records of this organisation should be kept as small as possible, otherwise in the event of a sudden evacuation, we shall be faced with an enormous problem in first of all sorting out those documents which are to be destroyed and then disposing of them. Only those documents which *must* be kept should be allowed to remain on the files and it is the responsibility of each Section to keep a constant check on their files to obviate the collection of obsolete material.[3]

One can probably accept that those instructions were more or less thoroughly followed in practice, especially overseas, and that they also acted as something of a deterrent to creating inessential records in the first place. To cite Dodds-Parker again writing of 'Massingham': '… by standing orders and sensible self-protection as our base was on a deserted sea-shore, records were minimal and destroyed as soon as they were no longer of immediate use'.[4] Doubtless the enforced destruction of SOE records in the face of the Japanese attack on Singapore and the German advance towards Cairo added persuasive weight to the need to follow this policy elsewhere as well.

Dodds-Parker also recalls the lack of a formal directive when he took over 'Massingham'[5] and it is true that there is a marked absence in the archive of tasking documents of this nature. He also alludes to the drastically restricted knowledge of 'the facilities and equipment entrusted to a Mission Commander for very special operations' but only hints at the nature of such operations as being 'scarcely within the social ambit of an officer and a gentleman'.[6]

It would be interesting to hear more from surviving SOE veterans about the attitude which prevailed in the Service towards keeping records of highly sensitive operations (e.g. assassinations). Again, there is a marked absence in the archive of documents on these. Were they never created? Or were they carefully destroyed? If so, when?

Whatever the imperfections of SOE's record-keeping for most of the war, a change which was at least intended to be for the better began to be set in train in the summer of 1944. This was the period at which SOE began seriously to consider what was going to happen to it at the end of the war and, more particularly, how best to set about the task of preserving the experience gained in the last few years in a form which would be of use in any future war, whether or not SOE itself survived.

In mid-August 1944, D/CD, Gubbins's Deputy and Director of Staff Duties and Administration, Mr M. P. Murray, issued a special instruction to all Directors, Regional Heads, Section Heads and Heads of Country Establishments to conduct a survey of documents 'so as to decide what is to be retained permanently, what can be given a more limited "life", and what can be moved immediately to a Central Archives Section'. This was to include card-indexes, drawings, devices and 'any other exhibits'.[7]

A follow-up circular dated 19 August 1944 described the categories into which documents should fall as follows:

A. Permanent Retention
Documents of permanent historic interest.
Irreplaceable documents likely to be of use in an indefinite future.

B. Long-term Retention
Documents of minor historic interest.
Documents of long-term usefulness e.g. Personal Records, Claims, Charters and Agreements, Accounts, as in A.2 but of shorter duration.

C. Short-term retention
Current Working Files kept by Section.

Dead documents which may revive.

D. Immediate Destruction
Papers of short life and dead papers.
Duplicates.

Each of these categories were to be divided into three further classes:

I Those which can be stored or destroyed immediately.
II Those which must be kept for the time being in the Section.
III Those which can be stored, if recoverable within 48 hours.

The purpose of this exercise was described as 'the gradual elimination of Categories C and D and the eventual inclusion of all documents in a central storage place under Category B'. The circular continued:

> Until SOE is wound up, however, there must be documents in all four categories, and many of them must continue to be in the custody of the sections working on them. The attainment of the objective mentioned above will be a long and tedious occupation for all concerned. It is therefore desired to make a start at once and with the least possible dislocation to current work.

It went on to describe the method to be adopted in carrying out the survey.[8] This untypically bureaucratic initiative is described at some length because it appears to mark the first move towards setting up a Central Archives Section and links it firmly to the twin criteria for retention, historical interest and future utility.

On 29 August 1944, the SOE Council considered a paper by CD/S, Colonel R. H. Barry, which outlined proposals for the preparation of a Handbook of SOE Work, or 'Manual of Subversive Warfare', and a History of SOE. In discussion, Gubbins emphasized that distinctions should be made between the SOE Handbook, the Official History of SOE and 'any history which might be written for public consumption'. The decision was taken that a Handbook should be produced and that Gubbins should discuss with Murray 'the organisation necessary for the assembly of the material for and compilation of the Handbook'. It was also agreed that Gubbins would consult Brigadier Latham of the War Cabinet Offices about the Official History and that he would separately pursue the question of 'a popular and authoritative account of certain aspects of SOE work, e.g., the story of the French Resistance'.[9]

There was further discussion of all these initiatives in subsequent Council meetings and some opposition, led by AD/H, Colonel D. J. Keswick, was expressed to the popular history (which was never in fact written).

The survey of documents continued into the autumn of 1944 and, in parallel, the Sections were winding up and preparing material for the Handbook and for the Section Histories. The requirements of the Sections and of the future Central Archives Section were thus to some extent in conflict: both presupposed use of the same documents. So progress towards the creation of the Central Archives Section was not rapid.[10]

However, on 25 October 1944, Murray, who had been put in charge of both the Handbook project and the creation of the Central Archives Section, was able to outline in a letter to Brigadier Latham the steps which had already been taken and those which were planned in the following terms:

1   He had under review 'the arrangements necessary to centralise our historical records and to ensure that, after use for current operational and security purposes, they are available for research and are then finally housed in proper conditions'.
2   SOE were at present in a preliminary stage in which the operational sections were 'sorting their material and writing up certain portions of it before memories fade; they are also using it for the preliminary draft of a Handbook'.
3   SOE would soon enter a second phase in which 'the records are gradually centralised from the operational and other sections, together with any summaries and monographs which have been prepared'.
4   SOE proposed to 'make up proper indices, etc., against the time, should it come, when an official historian is appointed. Simultaneously we shall be laying down syllabuses for future training purposes and cross-referencing the raw material of the Handbook and the History for the use of future instructors.'
5   He added that SOE's records were not yet in a convenient form for the use of an external historian; that 'we are indeed less conversant with them ourselves than we would like to be. We are also uncertain as to what will be destroyed'; and that 'the ultimate disposal of the records depends to some extent on the future of this organisation.'[11]

Preparatory work continued on all these fronts and minds and responsibilities became clearer as the nature and size of the problems to be faced became more apparent. Lieutenant-Colonel S. H. C. Woolrych, Commandant of the Special Training Schools at Beaulieu, was put in charge of the compilation of an Agents' Training Manual and Lieutenant-Colonel J. W. Munn of the Handbook Project. Squadron Officer J. M. Wollaston, WAAF, who had conducted a preliminary survey of the Country Section records with a view to assessing how they might conveniently be centralized,[12] was being put forward as the prospective head of the Central Archives Section. A draft directive to Country Sections was prepared informing them of their responsibility to hand over their records 'sorted and as far as possible indexed to accord with the scheme outlined below ...' A separate Record of Research and Development was also to be prepared. The subject of the History continued to be discussed with the Office of the War Cabinet.

The Central Archives Section was duly launched in January 1945 with an initial staff of six under Squadron Officer Wollaston as C/A. Its mandate was to create a Central Archive 'for the needs of any future SOE and the official Historians'. It aimed to achieve this by putting all SOE paper thought worth keeping into a central system of filing, indexed and designed to fulfil any call that might be made on it.

The new filing system was designed 'from the top down' and required the physical transfer of papers from their existing files into new ones specified by the system. The papers were carefully studied by readers and then marked to be sorted first to countries, next to one of 40 main subject headings, and finally to specific subjects. (Details of this system, with contemporary instructions, both confusing and contradictory, are contained in a volume entitled 'SOE Bible 1945' in the SOE archive which will be released in due course.) Each paper was marked with a three-figure reference (e.g. 3/210/11 = France/Air Operations, Dropping/ Successful) which established its place in the new filing universe, but provided no indication of its provenance. The bulk of the Directorate files disappeared altogether, as also did most of the specialist sections. There also remained a great number of files containing material for which no subject heading had been allotted.

The method was quite sound, if over-systematic, but demanded a large staff and a fair period of time before results became apparent. In its first nine months, the staff of the Section grew from six to nearly 60. At first, paper came in from the Country Sections rather slowly, since they were finishing their own histories. But, towards the end of 1945, with the end of the war in Europe and the Far East and the consequent disbandment of SOE, the Section began to diminish in numbers (to 30 by the end of December 1945), while the amount of paper handed to it increased greatly in volume.

As the overseas Sections and missions were about to be liquidated, instructions were issued for all surviving papers to be sent home after first being weeded of ephemeral material. Townshend later commented 'it is to be feared that some officers took advantage of the instructions to dispose of material which they thought would prove unduly sensitive should their contents ever be disclosed'.[13] Whatever the truth of this unsupported comment, which is unlikely ever to be verifiable, there were known end-of-war bonfires of virtually all the records of the British Security Coordination organization in New York (at Camp X in Canada) and of the records of the Beaulieu Training Schools. There must have been many others both in the United Kingdom and overseas which we shall never know about.

Thoughts of incendiarism lead naturally to the far-famed fire at Baker Street. It has been difficult to find contemporary documentary evidence for this. Townshend wrote in 1974 that it 'destroyed an unknown quantity of records the subject of which it has been impossible to trace ... some maintain that only finance files were destroyed (and certainly these are conspicuous by their absence) ...' but he added that Colonel H. B. Perkins (ex-Head of the Polish Section) complained after the war that 'a great number of my records have been destroyed by fire'.[13]

One of my predecessors as SOE Adviser maintained that he had been told that the fire started in a waste-paper basket in a room in the Belgian Section. And I can confirm that Michael Foot, while working on his history of SOE in the Low

Countries, has found some Belgian papers charred at the edges. Some records of FANY staff transferred to FANY HQ after the war have been similarly singed. Norman Mott, Head of the SOE Liquidation Section in Baker Street, known as MO1SP, in a letter dated 12 April 1946 on a naturalization case, wrote: 'unfortunately, the greater part of my papers dealing with naturalisation cases were burnt up in a fire which we had in the office here a few weeks ago ...'[14]

Ten years later, Mott recalled that the fire had broken out in February 1946 in his offices on the top floor of Baker Street:

> in a stationery store situated between my own office and the remainder of the wing which was occupied by the FANY Administration Section. The whole floor was practically gutted and a large proportion of the FANY records were destroyed together with the entire contents of my own office where I was holding a considerable number of operational files. Some of the latter related to the activities in the Field of SOE FANY agents. In addition, all the handing-over briefs from the SOE Country Sections were destroyed as well as a good deal of material relating to investigations into blown réseaux.

This seems to be the most detailed and authoritative statement of what occurred and confirms that the fire was every bit as destructive as its mythology suggests.

But there were other losses too. In early and mid-1945, the staff of the Central Archives Section was augmented by postings to it of some officers just returned from the field and awaiting out-posting from SOE. There is anecdotal evidence from two reliable sources who are still alive that these lively young officers did not always approach their duties with appropriate diligence. Two of them, indeed, competed with each other in tossing whole files, unread, into a waste-bin situated between them with happy cries of 'Well, that's a load of nonsense, anyway'. Having later worked with one of them, now alas deceased, I can well believe it of him. By the end of 1945, the twin pressures of reducing staff and the increasing accession of material had slowed progress in reading and re-filing papers. Less than half of the papers held by the Archives Section had been processed. But it was still hoped that the task could be finished by August 1946.

When SOE was formally terminated on 1 January 1946, various relic organs, e.g. the Liquidation Section, continued to carry out their functions for several months. One of these was the renamed SO Archives Section, with Treasury agreement now paid for out of 'C's' budget but further reduced in size to 4 officers and 18 secretaries and clerks. In a review dated 25 April 1946,[16] its head stated that the Section's holdings were as follows:

Steel Filing Cabinets	214
Steel Cupboards	81
Wall Safes	7
No. of files approx.	66,000

Total weight of paper approx.　30 tons
Total incl. containers approx.　50 tons

Of these, as an example, the French files made up 15 cabinets. However, two more tons of paper were expected from the Far East and another seven cabinets from the Liquidation Section.

The Section's work had also begun to change in nature. One of its secondary tasks, to answer enquiries about SOE matters, had begun to assume major importance. There had been an increasing number of requests from various ministries and the intelligence community for information relevant to War Crimes Trials, to security investigations, etc.

This all militated against the Section completing its original task within the timescale envisaged. So it was proposed to change its method of work to a less thorough but more expeditious one: both sorted and unsorted papers were now to be put roughly into the filing system by country without being actually read first. Once this had been done, the papers would be 'looked through with some care, anything unnecessary being destroyed, then indexed and made to function as precisely as possible within the Central Filing System'. This method, it was stated, 'will not be as meticulously accurate as the previous method of working but ... it will suffice and with good indexing be a workable reference library ... it will certainly prove quicker and more expedient in answering the present day to day enquiries.'

The problems of defining the future utility of the material in the archive and of the various handbooks and histories which were still in preparation were reviewed in early 1946 by one of 'C's' officers. It was concluded that Mackenzie's work on the Official History, which he hoped to have in final draft by the autumn of 1947, must clearly continue. Mackenzie himself thought that he would have a continuing requirement for support from the Archives Section until the end of 1948.

It was also proposed that the compilation of the Handbooks, estimated still to require another year's work by one person, should continue. Two further staff should be allocated to it and the work completed within three months.

The work on the War Diary, however, on which one Major, eight other officers and six secretaries were engaged and which was 'exceedingly behindhand', was judged to be without real value. The War Diary was described as 'purely academical past history'. Work on it should cease. There should also be no further work on books compiled by individual officers, such as that on 'Agent Technique' by Colonel Woolrych and 'Special Duties Operations in Europe' by Jean Wollaston. Those already written should be held in the SIS Library.

By mid 1946, plans were being made for the eventual move of the SO Archives Section into an SIS building. (Two moves had already been undergone.) But it was seen as necessary, before this could take place, to achieve further reductions in the amount of paper held. The archivist was therefore instructed to step up the rate of weeding and, in the event, between August 1946 and the end of May 1947, the archive was reduced to a total of 169 steel filing cabinets, 9 steel cupboards and 4 cupboards of card indexes.

Among the papers thus weeded, it is worth noting the following categories and amounts (expressed in filing cabinets or equivalent):

Stores and Supplies	20
Middle East	20
Signals and Telegrams	14
Training	14
Admin and Organisation	11
Far East	9
War Diary	9
French	7
European Countries General	6
Spanish	5
Propaganda	5
Scandinavian	3
Central Europe	2
Italian	2
Belgian	1
Dutch	1

And other smaller categories/amounts

It is not recorded how carefully or systematically the weeding process was conducted, but the Archives Section was working under considerable pressure to meet the move deadline and it appears likely that several categories were jettisoned in bulk.

Mott estimated in late 1949 that 'something like 100 tons of material was destroyed ... more by destruction of categories of material than by removal of redundant material from individual files.'[17] The bald lists on file of the categories destroyed seem to bear this out.

With the winding up of the SOE Liquidation Section in the late 1940s, the files it had kept for its own use passed to the SOE Archives Section. These comprised finance, personnel, security and investigations records. No record appears to remain of the precise volume of papers concerned. But that it was not inconsiderable, even after the fire, can be inferred from some figures which appear in a review of early 1950: '36 4-drawer cabinets of MO1SP material ... 14 4-drawer filing cabinets and 17 cupboards of finance records' and '65 *unopened* crates and tin boxes'.[18]

This review of early 1950 was conducted to determine what of the material remaining in the archive should be kept, and for what purposes, and what should be destroyed or passed to other departments. The introductory paragraphs of the reviewer's report are instructive, containing as they do a good measure of respect for the archive with a barely audible undertone of despair,

So wide was the range of subject covered by SOE, and, in consequence, by the Archives, that it is physically impossible for one person to make a comprehensive list of what should be retained and what should be destroyed. One of the contributory factors is the absence of any complete catalogue of file contents, i.e. although there is a classification system, very few files contain a list of the documents which are in them. This means that *if the job of screening is to be done properly, every file must be read through carefully from cover to cover.*

The Archives represent the only material available on what was in fact a new form of warfare, or, as it was sometimes described, 'The Fourth Arm'. For this reason, if for none other, one is chary of advising wholesale destruction even though it is unlikely that Special Operations in a future War will be waged on similar lines.

Without the availability of something like the S.O.E. Archives, in some manageable and accessible form, much time is liable to be wasted by inexperienced personnel who make mistakes which others made before and from which mistakes those others learnt.

The reviewer listed the main value of the archives under the following headings:

(a) *Historical* The influence here is strong of observations made by Mackenzie, who, it was recorded, had been responsible for marking files and papers in the archive with the now familiar yellow stickers reading 'Historical Document. Permanent Preservation'.
(b) *Planning* 'There are innumerable examples of plans prepared to meet various situations, which in both form and content serve as admirable guides to the preparation of similar plans ...'
(c) *Background material* '... extremely useful and readable reports covering almost every type of SO operations in almost every country in the world where SO was carried out, which provide most useful local colour and give non-SO experienced personnel the "feel" of Special Operations ...'
(d) *Names* '... of people who worked in or for SOE, or with whom SOE had contacts in foreign countries ...'
(e) *Intelligence* Economic, topographical, minorities, populations, DZs, beaches, etc.
(f) *Casework* Relevant to cases for compensation, security investigations, etc.
(g) *Histories* Of individual Sections and Branches.

The reviewer outlined the system of classification of files which had been adopted but commented:

Unfortunately, however, because the re-classification of SOE papers into this system was stopped, the regional files were fitted into these groups as best they could be, and this means:

– that many of the files contain papers which are not strictly applicable to the group in question;

226

- there is considerable duplication ...

There is nothing wrong with the system of classification provided that a proper catalogue is produced showing what papers are in each file.

Furthermore ... there are a large number of crates containing papers from the Middle and Far East which have never been opened.

The reviewer made a number of proposals for continuing the work of the Section both of destroying unnecessary papers and classifying and carding useful ones. His review gave rise to a good deal of internal minuting which, among other things, reveals that the staff of the Section were now down to two. It was recommended that there should be the 'maximum possible destruction and reduction' of material in unwanted categories but that increased effort should be allocated to the creation of an index of SOE agents, of whom 40,000 were estimated to be on record but only about one-tenth of that number sufficiently trained and experienced to be of possible value in a future war.

It has not been possible to locate more than a few scattered and uncoordinated references to policy and practice on the SOE archive during the 20 years between 1950 and 1970. From these, however, it is clear that weeding continued, exacerbated by problems of accommodation. ('The object of weeding is to get rid of unwanted paper and to delete the vast number of "dead wood" names at present carded ... cut away dead wood and clear cellars of unwanted papers'. July 1957.)

During the 1950s, however, pressure grew from former members of SOE and other authors for information from the archive to help with books they wanted to write. This pressure was at first firmly resisted on security grounds. But the determined campaign by Miss (later Dame) Irene Ward, waged both in and out of Parliament, for the release of SOE records, first for her book *F.A.N.Y. Invicta* and later for an official history of SOE, and the publicity generated by other writers, e.g. Elizabeth Nicholas and Jean Overton Fuller, gradually wore down official obduracy.

One result was the appointment as the first SOE Adviser of Lieutenant-Colonel Eddie Boxshall, a former SOE officer, in early 1959 'to advise and assist enquirers on matters connected with the wartime operations of S.O.E. and to deal with questions regarding the release of information on them'. Boxshall's (unpublished) instructions were precise and restrictive in regard to the security limitations placed upon him and it thus seemed to some that his main function was to ensure that as little information as possible was given out.

The other result was the appointment of Michael Foot to write the first public history of SOE's operations in France. Following publication of *SOE in France* in 1966, the trend towards greater openness persisted. More official histories were duly written and successive SOE Advisers were able to be increasingly forthcoming in their assistance to authors, researchers and the media. Eventually, following the Waldegrave Initiative, it was agreed that the archive could be released to the PRO.

But to return to what I said earlier: the SOE archive which is being released is in a form which was the result of five years of admirably industrious and professional work by an archivist seconded from the PRO, Mr C. B. Townshend.

He was appointed with the brief 'to put into the existing files as much order as is still possible' and 'to smooth the path of a tentative historian'. This brief, as he himself put it:

> posed a most perplexing problem which was in no way eased by the knowledge that work on the compilation of a card index to personnel was already well under way. The existence of this vast (albeit uncompleted) index meant that little, if any, alteration could be made to the existing file order. The difficulty therefore lay not in devising a system which could be regarded as reasonably correct but in finding one which would prove the least incorrect.[19]

Townshend's description of the SOE archive he found was that it consisted of :

> the surviving files of a collection of files of which we have documentary evidence that at least 87% were destroyed in London between 1945 and 1950. They are in a confused state as a result of a number of ill-conceived attempts at their reorganisation by, for the most part, inexperienced archival staff with neither the time nor the knowledge to successfully complete the task ... The only list of SOE files available in January 1970 was that contained in the SOE Subject File Index, a list which did no more than describe the files by the late 1945 subject headings.

He further observed during his work, and wherever possible rectified, the following problems and weaknesses,

a   Whereas duplicated material and carbon copies abound, very few original papers have survived. This is remarkable in that most SOE correspondence was internal.

b   A very large proportion of the files were not in chronological order.

c   Enclosures had been removed from covering letters and filed by date. A great number of these enclosures are now untraceable.

d   Files had been added to various series without first ascertaining whether copies already existed elsewhere in a more logical home.

e   Lists had been altered without all interested parties being notified.

f   Papers had been removed from files for reference purposes.

g   Files had been reorganized (some many times) within the same numerical sequence.

h   Papers from other departmental files had been collated within SOE files.

i   A great many papers refer to the activities of secret services other than SOE.

j   Files quoted in the SOE Histories and War Diaries had either been destroyed or dispersed. Most quoted references can no longer be traced.

k   'Historical Document' labels appear to have been used indiscriminately. (On one file a carbon copy had been granted a label while its signed original had been ignored).

l   A number of files have been mutilated by inked marginal notes, annotations and underlinings.

m   Flammable material has been used for the protection of papers in an advanced state of deterioration.

It is not useful to give a detailed description of the way in which Townshend reorganized the archive. From the files which have been released to the PRO anyone who is interested can easily discover the result. The prime categorization is geographical, by region and country; within countries the files are grouped in fairly coherent runs, usually beginning with the more general policy files, working through specific operations and on to personnel lists. In addition, there are various categories of more general files (Headquarters files, Lord Selborne's Papers), some specialist files (Air, Naval, Security, Liquidation) and the Section Histories, War Diaries and Symbols Lists, which have not yet been released but are on their way. And there are some 7,000 Personal Files which it is proposed to release in due course. In total, the archive comprises over 15,000 files.

We owe Mr. Townshend a great debt of gratitude for rationalizing the SOE archive. Any damage done to it occurred well before his time and I believe that what I have outlined in this chapter will enable you to understand just how enormous that damage was over the years. The tale is a sad one for historians. But they should remember that, within the intelligence community, until relatively recently, records have always been regarded primarily as an aid to operations and of little interest from any other point of view. Which is why I took the title of this chapter from a note marked on a file discovered by one of my predecessors: 'Of Historical Interest Only'.

Notes

1   Archivist's report of 25 April 1946 on file HQ 249.
2   Douglas Dodds-Parker, *Setting Europe Ablaze*, Windlesham: Springwood, 1984, p. 123.
3   Instructions of November 1941 on file Security 31.
4   Dodds-Parker, *Setting Europe Ablaze*, p. 163.
5   Ibid., p. 163.
6   Ibid., p. 199.
7   The instruction itself appears not to have survived. It is summarized in ADB/270 of 19 August 1944 on file Security 33.
8   Ibid.
9   Minutes of Council Meeting of 29 August 1944 on file HQ 9.
10   Various papers on HQ 249.
11   Letter by Murray of 25 October 1944 on file HQ 249.
12   D/CD's memo DCD/542 to CD of 14 November 1944 on file HQ 249.
13   C. B. Townshend's report of 17 December 1974 held by SOE Adviser.
14   PF of Miss Gertrude Ornstein.
15   Correspondence dated 5 June 1956 on file HQ 249.
16   On file HQ 249.
17   Minute of 22 December 1949 on file HQ 249.
18   Minute of 21 February 1950 on file HQ 249.
19   Townshend's report of 17 December 1974.

INDEX

'private navies' 42, 44, 45; SIS
operations in Home Waters 34–6, 40,
41
Smatchet knife 28
Smiley, Major David 28, 181, 182, 183,
184, 185, 189
Smith, Bradley 5
Smolenski, Colonel Josef 68
SO Archives Section 223
SO1, Special Operations (Propaganda)
201, 202, 207, 208
SO2, Special Operations (Operational)
201, 202
SOA, Special Operations Australia 25
SOE in France 227
SOE, Special Operations Executive:
activities counter-productive 164, 165;
air supply problems 101–2; airborne
operations 36, 39, 109; Algiers
mission 92, 97; 'Anvil' operation
73–5; Balkans, the 52, 53, 56, 163;
barred from Ireland 210; Belgrade
coup 163; Bhagat Ram 146; Cairo 42,
44, 54, 92, 94, 98, 108, 112, 114, 127,
130, 179; Churchill, relations with 3,
51, 52, 53, 54, 55–7, 58, 59;
collaboration with Soviets 104, 106,
108, 112, 113, 197; conference on 2,
3; core objectives 158–9, 163; creation
of 34, 48, 49, 175; criticism of 47, 58,
155, 165, 166, 173; D-Day 173;
demise of 58, 223; DF Section 36;
difficulties at home 51, 52, 53, 169;
Directorate of Scientific Research 23;
duplication of research 31, 32;
established 17–19, 49; F Section 25,
26; FO relations with 161, 164, 165,
173, 181; focus on sabotage 52;
friction with other departments 4, 7,
49, 162, 163, 174–5, 203; Greece *see*
Stott, Captain D.J.; hostility of
Whitehall 54, 162; Independent
French Section 36; lack of resources
51, 52, 53, 109, 157, 159; legacy of 6,
26, 32; Liquidation Section 223, 225;
loss of status 166, 167, 186;
Madagascar operations 50, 56;
'Maryland' 44; 'Massingham' 43, 44,
97, 98, 218, 219; MEW/SOR 171,
172; Milorg 76–9, 80; Morton,
relations with 49, 50, 51, 55, 57, 58;
Moscow 144; neutral states, early
opportunities wasted 175, 176;

neutrals vital 174; Official History
224; original aims not fulfilled 161;
origins 7, 11; Polish missions 68–70;
Polish Section 64, 65; political 'left'
recruitment 142, 145, 161; political
warfare 160; rationale 33, 47, 49, 65;
recruitment from the Left 161, 164;
recruiting in North America 105, 113,
114, 115; Romania 58; South-East
Asia (Force 136) 3; study of 2;
Supplies Directorate 23; survival
threatened 55, 56, 58, 167;
Switzerland 95, 98, 170; Toronto SOE/
SIS 114; training 25, 28, 29; Yugoslav
Section 186, *see also* conflicts of
interests; seaborne activities, SOE
Sons of the Eagle 181
Sosnowski, General 69
South-East Asia 3, 30, 45
Southgate, Maurice 26
Soviet: collaboration with SOE,
Yugoslavia 103–8, 112–13;
co-operation with SOE, Afghanistan
144–5; Intelligence services 103, 143,
144; oil 159, 160; 'Russian Project'
104, 105, 107, 112; Treaty, NKVD/
SOE 107, 108
Spain/SOE 172, 173
Stafford, David 3
Stalin 106, 107
Starheim, Odd 80
Stärker, Rudi 151, 152, 153, 154
Station IX 23, 24, 25, 26; Section XV 23
Station VI 23
Station XII 23
Station XV 25
Station XVII 25
Steinbeck, John 47
Sten submachine-gun 29, 30, 31
Stephenson, Sir William 105, 108, 113
Stewart, Sir Findlater 55
'Stockbroker' circuit 25
Stockholm/Sweden/SOE 167, 170
Stott, Captain D.J. (Don) 5, 148, 149;
anxiety in London 155; Asopos
operation 148, 149, 156; contacts with
SOE Cairo 150, 151, 153, 154;
German peace offer 150, 151, 152,
153, 154; meeting with German
officials 152–3, 154; unauthorized
meeting in occupied Athens 149,
50–3, 154;
Stuart, Duncan 2